Beating Bureaucracy in Special Educational Needs

Are you overwhelmed by the amount of paperwork that SEN generates in your school?

Would you like to spend more time actually improving the quality of teaching and learning for pupils with SEN or disabilities?

If so, this is an essential book for you.

The government is asking schools to identify fewer children with SEN and place less reliance on Individual Education Plans – but at the same time ensure that children get the help they need. This and the new Ofsted framework challenge schools to find new ways of enabling **all** children to make progress – those with 'true' SEN, and those who may just be lower-achieving or needing help with behaviour problems.

Fully revised and updated, the new edition of this best-selling, practical text contains helpful and achievable strategies to meet these policy challenges. It will provide support for school leaders, SENCOs and anyone undertaking the national SENCO award.

Through school case studies, *Beating Bureaucracy in Special Educational Needs* shows how to increase pupil progress by using existing systems for class and subject teacher target-setting, tracking and planning. It lists the intervention programmes that really work and describes successful partnership with parents. A toolkit of ready-to-use proformas, also available online, includes:

- a model policy to give to Ofsted;
- curriculum planning formats and provision maps;
- strategy sheets for all the main types of SEN;
- proformas to help you plan, monitor and evaluate your provision.

The book shows how to put responsibility for supporting children with most types of additional need firmly back where it belongs – with class and subject teachers. It will help you – in the words of one SENCO – 'get your life back'.

Jean Gross, CBE, is a national expert on special needs, most recently holding the role of England's Communication Champion for children.

nasen
Helping Everyone Achieve

nasen is a professional membership association that supports all those who work with or care for children and young people with special and additional educational needs. Members include teachers, teaching assistants, support workers, other educationalists, students and parents.

nasen supports its members through policy documents, journals, its magazine *Special!*, publications, professional development courses, regional networks and newsletters. Its website contains more current information such as responses to government consultations. **nasen**'s published documents are held in very high regard both in the UK and internationally.

Other titles published in association with the National Association for Special Educational Needs (**nasen**):

Brilliant Ideas for Using ICT in the Inclusive Classroom
Sally McKeown and Angela McGlashon
2011/pb: 978-0-415-67254-2

Language for Learning in the Secondary School: A practical guide for supporting students with speech, language and communication needs
Sue Hayden and Emma Jordan
2012/pb: 978-0-415-61975-2

ADHD: All Your Questions Answered: A complete handbook for SENCOs and teachers
Fintan O'Regan
2012/pb: 978-0-415-59770-8

Assessing Children with Specific Learning Difficulties: A teacher's practical guide
Gavin Reid, Gad Elbeheri and John Everatt
2012/pb: 978-0-415-67027-2

Using Playful Practice to Communicate with Special Children
Margaret Corke
2012/pb: 978-0-415-68767-6

The Equality Act for Educational Professionals: A simple guide to disability and inclusion in schools
Geraldine Hills
2012/pb: 978-0-415-68768-3

More Trouble with Maths: A teacher's complete guide to identifying and diagnosing mathematical difficulties
Steve Chinn
2012/pb: 978-0-415-67013-5

Dyslexia and Inclusion: Classroom approaches for assessment, teaching and learning, second editon
Gavin Reid
2012/pb: 978-0-415-60758-2

Beating Bureaucracy in Special Educational Needs

Helping SENCOs maintain a work/life balance

Second edition

Jean Gross, CBE

Routledge
Taylor & Francis Group

LONDON AND NEW YORK

nasen
Helping Everyone Achieve

Second edition published 2013
by Routledge
2 Park Square, Milton Park, Abingdon, Oxon OX14 4RN

Simultaneously published in the USA and Canada
by Routledge
711 Third Avenue, New York, NY 10017

Routledge is an imprint of the Taylor & Francis Group, an informa business

First edition published by Routledge 2008

British Library Cataloguing in Publication Data
A catalogue record for this book is available from the British Library

Library of Congress Cataloging in Publication Data
Gross, Jean.
Beating bureaucracy in special educational needs : helping sencos maintain a work/life balance / Jean Gross. -- 2nd ed.
   p. cm.
   Includes bibliographical references and index.
   1. Special education--Great Britain. 2. Special education teachers--Job stress-- Great Britain. 3. Classroom management--Great Britain. I. National Association for Special Educational Needs (Great Britain) II. Title.
   LC3986.G7G757 2013   371.90941--dc23
   2012026588

ISBN: 978-0-415-53374-4 (pbk)
ISBN: 978-0-203-11406-3 (ebk)

Typeset in Adobe Garamond Pro
by Bookcraft Ltd, Stroud, Gloucestershire

Printed and bound in Great Britain by the MPG Books Group

For all the dedicated SENCOs who have tried so hard, over the past twenty years, to make the unworkable work.

Contents

Acknowledgements

I am grateful to staff at Ellingham Primary School, Frederick Bird Primary School, Little Ridge Primary School, the former Coombe Boys' School, Hall Mead Secondary School, Stocksbridge High School, Old Ford Primary, Tolworth Infant School, Torriano Junior School, The Trafalgar School, Wallands Primary and Lyons Park Infant School for their help in providing case study material. Also to Sheffield local authority for permission to use their intervention planning outlines and data collection sheet, to Amanda Corcoran for her ideas on monitoring the quality of interventions, to Alex Devlin for his class handover profile, and to the Globetown Action Zone for permission to use examples of their differentiated lesson planning.

A note on terminology

This book is about finding ways to reduce the bureaucracy associated with meeting the needs of children who require something that is 'additional to and different from' what is available to all children, if they are to learn and thrive. Most of this bureaucracy is linked to a statutory framework and associated guidance that uses the term 'SEN'. For this reason the term SEN or disability, or SEN/D, is used in the book, whilst recognising that the systems suggested have a broader application beyond this group.

At the time of writing, the government had not yet legislated to move from Statements of SEN to the single Education, Health and Care Plan and from School Action and School Action Plus to one school-based SEN/D stage. These terms have therefore been retained in this edition of the book. Similarly, categories of SEN/D, such as behavioural, emotional and social difficulties (BESD) were under review at the time of writing, but remain in the text here.

The SEN paperchase

At its peak, the identification of SEN by mainstream primary school teachers ran at one in five (19.9 per cent) of all children. Mainstream secondary schools identified an even higher number (21.7 per cent). This meant a huge and unsustainable workload for Special Educational Needs Coordinators (SENCOs). A SENCO in one large city secondary school, for example, estimated that her department circulated over 6,000 Individual Education Plan (IEP) sheets every term – one in each subject for four hundred pupils, 20 per cent of the school's roll.

This is an extreme example, but it reflects a problem that every teacher who picks up this book will recognise. The problem is the oppressive weight of administration and paperwork generated by the well-intentioned aim that every child with special educational needs or a disability (SEN/D) will have an individual plan describing their needs, and how the needs will be met – each individual plan then generating its own cycle of review dates, discussions and meetings.

The government is now asking schools to identify fewer children with SEN and place less reliance on IEPs – but at the same time to ensure children get the help they need and that all make good progress. Schools will be held to account for the progress made by the lowest-achieving 20 per cent and will not be able to achieve an outstanding Ofsted grade unless their SEN/D practice is good.

This means that they need to find new ways of helping all children to make progress – ways of doing a good job for a smaller number of children with 'true' SEN/D, and ways of maximising the progress of children who may just be lower-achieving or needing help with social, emotional or behavioural difficulties. This is the theme of this book.

It shows how schools can put responsibility for supporting children with most types of additional need firmly back where it belongs – with class and subject teachers. It describes how to use existing systems for class and subject teacher target-setting, recording and planning, rather than time-consuming, bureaucratic separate SEN/D systems, to ensure that all children who find learning difficult make good progress.

The difficulty for SENCOs

Most SENCOs have relatively little non-contact time (one to five hours a week for the majority, according to a 2004 NUT survey). This means that they are carrying a heavy workload and are often unable to maintain any sort of work/life balance. It also means that they have little if any time to do the job they would like to be doing – helping teachers plan their lessons with the needs of children with SEN in mind, supporting the work that teaching assistants (TAs) do with individuals and groups, evaluating practice so as to improve the provision that children receive, or teaching children directly.

A number of researchers have noted that SENCOs feel swamped by the bureaucracy of their task (Lingard, 2001; Wedell, 2002; Cole, 2005). Lingard, for example, surveyed secondary schools and describes responses such as: 'If I update IEPs three times a year, which my school expects, allowing 15 minutes per pupil, and hold one half hour review meeting a year for every pupil, it will involve me in 275 hours' work per annum.' Wedell analysed messages on the SENCO-forum website and noted that:

> SENCOs spend an inordinate proportion of their time keeping up with administration … parents should be regularly consulted about IEPs and there is no way this can be achieved with large numbers of pupils …. Subject teachers are faced with so many individual targets that it becomes impossible to keep track of them.

The problems of excessive bureaucracy are not confined to SENCOs. On average a teacher in Year 5 (the peak year for SEN numbers) might, in a class of 33, be operating IEPs for around eight children. In schools serving areas of high social deprivation, the numbers will be very much higher, sometimes as many as half the class. Each child will have around four targets on their IEP. That makes at least 32 different targets that the teacher is meant to remember. This is clearly an impossibility.

And if the teacher cannot remember what the targets are, how can they possibly use them in any meaningful way to guide their teaching or the child's learning? This is the real emperor's new clothes of the individual-plan system: the fact, rarely commented on, that teachers (like all human beings) have a useful working memory span of no more than seven to eight items, and that if this is exceeded by over-use of IEPs, those IEPs are likely to become static documents with little impact on progress.

Some schools, however, have found a way out of this maze of paperwork. They have found different, less bureaucratic ways of meeting pupils' SEN/D – for example by provision mapping, and helping class and subject teachers to record what they will do to support pupils with SEN/D via their normal curriculum planning.

This book is about sharing the practice of these schools. It represents an attempt to liberate SENCOs and INCOs from an excessive workload, whilst at the same time protecting the rights of children, and their parents and carers, to the best possible inclusive teaching and learning.

Why all this paperwork?

The rewards for schools for producing a high volume of paperwork around SEN/D have until fairly recently been many, enough to outweigh the negative impact on work/life balance and quality of provision. The more children the school logged as having SEN, the more favourably its position in league tables was judged if it appeared to be underachieving in its end of key stage SAT or GCSE outcomes. The former inclusion of numbers of children with SEN in the model that generates contextual value-added (CVA) pupil progress data compounded this problem; if a school identified large numbers of children as having SEN, the pupil progress levels predicted by the model were lower, and the CVA score consequently more favourable.

The IEP, visible indicator of what teachers do to meet SEN, easy to get hold of (in both literal and metaphorical senses) by Ofsted inspectors whose expertise in SEN might be limited, also received heavy emphasis in inspections:

> Some schools had found that inspectors were more interested in the listing, production and number of IEPs than how they related to pupils' achievements and progress … some schools were mechanically producing IEPs for the purposes of inspection, with no planned reviews and no mechanism for their subsequent maintenance.
>
> (Ofsted, 1999)

Until recently, too, funding mechanisms encouraged schools to focus on paperwork. The more and smarter the IEPs compiled by a school, the more additional local authority (LA) funding attracted through audits or Statements. And, once attracted, the only way to keep funding allocated to individuals was to prove, through voluminous records, that the child was still struggling despite being well supported.

The rewards for plentiful, elegantly executed IEPs were thus once great; the SENCO's credibility, and often his or her 'earning power' for the school, could stand or fall on IEP performance.

But things have changed. Now, funding formulae delegate funding for all but the less common or complex (low-incidence, 'high needs') types of SEN/D to schools on the basis of prior attainment. The Pupil Premium provides earmarked money direct to schools to meet the needs of disadvantaged pupils. This means that schools no longer have to submit detailed plans and records for individual children with the more common types of SEN/D, in order to secure or retain funding.

Ofsted, moreover, is more likely these days to be interested in schools' data on the progress of children with SEN or disabilities, and schools' self-evaluation of the impact of their provision on vulnerable groups, than they are in IEPs. What they will look for are the systems in place to quickly identify underachieving pupils, whether the poor behaviour of some pupils may link to unidentified SEN, what actions are taken for pupils who need help, and how the impact of interventions is tracked and evaluated.

Another significant and relevant development in recent years has been the trend towards 'personalisation' – assessing and planning for the unique needs of every child, not just those identified with SEN or a disability. These developments are described in a recent report on effective leadership that promotes the achievements of students with SEN/D (Chapman *et al.*, 2011):

> We take the view that responding to children with special educational needs should be seen as part of a wider set of issues relating to the education of all children who experience difficulties in school … in taking this position we believe that the distinction between 'SEN/D' and 'non-SEN/D' children is now rapidly becoming outmoded, in that it overlooks the considerable developments that have occurred in the ability of the education system to respond to a wide range of difficulties.

Together with Assessment for Learning, personalisation has meant that class and subject teachers are increasingly setting personal targets for groups of children, and sometimes for individuals, and involving children in reviewing how far they have achieved them. This increasingly makes redundant the setting and reviewing of individual targets for some children via IEPs.

Technology, via the opportunities to store and share information about pupils presented by management information systems, has also fundamentally changed the way teachers can build knowledge about individual pupils' needs into their planning. And finally, we have seen the growth of provision mapping. First developed by my colleague Ann Berger in Bristol schools, and later incorporated into materials I wrote for the National Strategies, it provides a simple way of recording the extra interventions that the school provides in each year group. A teacher or SENCO/INCO can highlight on the provision map the interventions that a particular child receives, and use this, together with personal targets set by the class or subject teacher, as an alternative to writing separate individual plans.

What is stopping schools from reducing bureaucracy?

Despite the system changes that ought to be helping schools to reduce bureaucracy, there is as yet little evidence of the widespread changes that might be expected.

Many years ago I wrote an article, 'Paper Promises' (Gross, 2000), that described the overwhelming burden of paperwork that schools were experiencing and suggested ways of achieving the ends of the SEN Code of Practice by different means.

But twelve years later, I still see many SENCOs/INCOs and teachers struggling to manage large numbers of IEPs, meetings and reviews, despite the fact that government after government has clarified that that such systems are not and have never been a statutory requirement.

EXTRACT

From *Effective leadership: Ensuring the progress of pupils with SEN and/or disabilities* (DfES, 2006a)

Where provision mapping is linked to recording outcomes for all pupils or other locally devised systems and personalised learning initiatives are in place, they should gradually replace IEPs for most if not all pupils while still providing the reassurance and accountability to parents/carers that is so important.

EXTRACT

From *Meeting need – minimising bureaucracy* (Implementation Review Unit (IRU), 2007)

Schools do not need to write individual education plans for children with SEN where they have a policy of planning, target setting and recording the progress for all pupils as part of personalised learning that:

- identifies learning targets for individual pupils;
- plans additional or different provision from the differentiated curriculum offered to all pupils;
- reviews provision in the light of individual pupil outcomes.

EXTRACT

From *Support and aspiration: a new approach to special educational needs and disability* (DfE, 2011b)

We know that parents value the use of non-statutory Individual Education Plans (IEPs), which are recommended by the Code of Practice. In the period since 2001, when the Code was last revised and published, we know that many schools have developed new approaches to planning, reviewing and tracking the progress of all pupils that have enabled them to achieve what IEPs aimed to do without many of the associated bureaucratic burdens. These approaches have included new ways of tracking pupil progress, involving pupils in setting their own targets, engaging regularly and effectively with parents, and using individual profiles and provision mapping.

In order to reduce bureaucratic burdens on schools, in reviewing and updating the Code of Practice, we will remove advice on using IEPs and encourage schools to explore the ways in which these and other new approaches can be used to enable pupils with SEN to develop, progress and fulfil their potential.

So what is it that is stopping schools from taking this advice? There seem to be a number of factors:

- pressure from class teachers, who believe that maintaining an IEP for a child will mean that the child gets support, usually in the form of a teaching assistant;
- concerns about parents' reactions if the IEP process or the linked push for Statements are not used;
- a historical belief that the quality and quantity of paperwork is the key to attracting and retaining funding;
- bureaucratic procedures in some local authorities, such as encouraging schools to provide provision maps as well as, rather than instead of, IEPs. Whether or not schools persist with IEPs has been found to be highly dependent on local authority advice, which varies greatly across the country (Ellis *et al.*, 2012);
- a belief that IEPs make a difference to pupil outcomes.

Do IEPs make a difference?

All the paperwork involved in SEN/D would be well worth doing if we knew that it was actually making a real difference to children. But is there any evidence of this?

Schools tend to think there is, because they see children achieving the small-steps targets set for them on IEPs. There is a circularity, however, in school self-evaluation systems claiming proudly that children are achieving the targets set on their IEPs, when the targets are required to be set from the start as specific, measurable, **achievable**, realistic and time-constrained. Achievable targets may not be sufficiently stretching; in their 2010 review, Ofsted noted that:

> the challenge represented by the targets in individual education plans was highly variable … using these targets to judge whether children or young people were making good progress was extremely subjective.

There is an issue too in whether the achievement of a series of these achievable targets actually aggregates, over time, into improved attainment or personal and social skills. National data, as we will see later, suggests that the procedures of the SEN Code have not so far led to these improved outcomes.

Schools have historically embarked on the paperwork involved in SEN for one main reason – the quest for additional resources. And yet those resources, once painfully achieved, may in fact make little difference to the child's progress. Pinney (2004) analysed a wide range of national statistics and found no link between the numbers of Statements maintained by local authorities and the results achieved by their pupils with SEN. A series of key national reports (Ofsted 2004, 2006, 2010) have all made clear that the provision of additional resources to pupils with low or high incidence SEN/D – such as teaching assistant support – does not ensure good-quality intervention or adequate pupil progress. Substantial research from the Institute of Education (Blatchford *et al.*, 2012) even concludes that the more TA support pupils receive, the less progress they make – a finding that holds even after controlling for SEN status, prior attainment and other factors that might explain the relationship.

The lack of any link between current SEN/D systems and improved attainment is most evident for pupils with literacy and numeracy difficulties – the most common type of SEN. Since 1998 the percentage of children with very low attainment at the end of primary school (below Level 3) has hovered round the 6–7 per cent mark in English, and 5–6 per cent in maths, despite ever-increasing numbers identified as having SEN and placed on the SEN Code procedures, and despite any number of IEPs which continue predominantly to focus on literacy and numeracy as their prime source of targets. All those targets, written by thousands of schools on millions of IEPs – 'Will learn to read first 50 high-frequency words', 'Will be able to read cvc words', 'Will know number bonds to ten' – appear to have had little impact. All the training provided to teachers on how to write SMART targets, how to select appropriate strategies to achieve them, and how to measure and document the outcomes, appears to have made no difference at all to the numbers of children failing to learn to read or understand and use the number system.

A similarly static national picture applies to pupils with significant literacy and numeracy difficulties in secondary schools. In Key Stage 3, only around 50 per cent of pupils who have SEN and who attained a Level 4 in science, mathematics or English at the end of Key Stage 2 go on to achieve Level 5 by the end of Key Stage 3.

Nor do the procedures of the SEN Code appear to have had much effect on reducing the frequency of behaviour difficulties. Exclusions have not reduced over the period when more and more children were placed on individual education or behaviour plans because of behavioural, emotional or social difficulties. Being identified as having SEN does not appear to afford particular protection to such pupils; a recent report on school exclusions found that pupils on School Action Plus were twelve times more likely to be permanently excluded, and five times more likely to have a fixed term exclusion, than comparable pupils with no SEN (Office of the Children's Commissioner, 2012).

The only area where it is possible that the SEN Code's procedures have made a difference may be personal and life skills. But here we have no evidence at all either way, since we have as yet no agreed means of assessing and recording children's development in these areas, nor definitions of what would constitute an average, above average or below average rate of progress. What we do know about the well-being of pupils with SEN/D is not encouraging; the Lamb Inquiry (2009) notes that pupils with SEN have double the normal rate of persistent absence, and that the former *TellUs* pupil survey showed that 61 per cent of pupils identifying themselves as having a learning difficulty reported being bullied, compared to 48 per cent of all pupils.

Ofsted (2010) summed up the position by saying:

> Pupils currently identified as having special educational needs are disproportionately from disadvantaged backgrounds, are much more likely to be absent or excluded from school, and achieve less well than their peers, both in terms of attainment at any given age and in terms of their progress over time. Over the last five years, these outcomes have changed very little.

In sum, the evidence that all the work schools have put into implementing the assessment and planning systems of the 2001 SEN Code procedures is justified by the impact is slender, to say the least. And in schools where it has proved possible to bring about significant reductions in the numbers of children failing to achieve basic literacy, numeracy or social, emotional and behavioural skills, this has not been through having more children on the SEN register, or more and better IEPs.

Instead, these gains have been produced by changing the way groups and classes of children have been taught, using the kinds of inclusive classroom teaching strategies and evidence-based additional interventions described later on in this book, in Chapters 5 and 6.

The problem with the individual model

Much SEN/D practice rests on the identification of individual children's difficulties, and the targeting of resources to address their perceived problems. Many writers have commented on the inadequacies of this individual model. Their argument has been that it shifts responsibility away from what schools as institutions might do to better meet the needs of all learners, towards a model which seeks to prop up the child identified as different (and by implication deficient) in accessing an otherwise undifferentiated curriculum through the provision of additional individual adult support.

An example comes from the illuminating story told by David Moore, HMI, who observed a secondary class being taught about the workings of the spinning jenny. The worksheets used were difficult, and the TA who was supporting one young man (herself with a physics degree) had to go and ask the teacher what they meant. 'Don't get worried', the boy said to her, 'I never do'. When HMI asked him why he never got worried, he replied 'Cos she's always here to do the work for me, in't she?'

A model based on the identification of individual children's difficulties thus often prevents teachers from differentiating the curriculum. It may also serve to lower expectations for what children with SEN/D can achieve. Some interesting research (Tymms and Merrell, 2006) compared the progress of children who had been formally identified through screening procedures as having SEN (in this case, ADHD) with those who also had ADHD symptoms but where the child's class teacher was not told of this, nor SEN procedures invoked. The teachers of this second group were simply provided with general information about how to teach inattentive and hyperactive children. The teachers in the first group were provided with both this information and the names of children identified through screening.

Providing information on teaching strategies was helpful; children in the second group had more positive attitudes towards school and reading, and showed improved behaviour, when compared with children in schools not given the teaching information. But formally identifying children as having ADHD was not helpful; the researchers found a significant negative effect on the reading and mathematics attainment of children who had been identified as having ADHD, when compared with children not identified. They suggest that this is because once labelled, teachers focus more on keeping the children happy and calm rather than pushing them to attain. Equally, it might mean that teachers relinquished more of the care of the children to additional adults, rather than working with them directly themselves.

What this research and anecdote suggest is that over-reliance on identifying SEN and invoking the associated procedures can sometimes mean that the teacher who is responsible for the child's learning may do less to adapt his or her curriculum delivery than if the child were not identified. This is a direct consequence of the individual model of SEN, and of the way in which IEP targets for change are located with the child and not with the teacher.

The problem with IEP targets

To understand the problem with IEP targets we need to understand who they belong to. Targets **do** work: we have only to look at the increase in the number of children achieving Level 4s at the end of Key Stage 2 and five good GCSEs, to see this. Most education professionals have by now experienced for themselves the powerful effects of working towards a target for which they felt personally accountable, and which was clear, measurable and time-constrained.

The targets we have all as individuals experienced, however, have one thing in common: for them to work, we needed to know what they were, and to be constantly reminded of them, frequently monitored on them, and recognised if we achieved them. Yet if we undertake the exercise of asking children with SEN/D what their IEP targets are, we consistently find that they have no idea: 'the views of the pupils are rarely sought in the preparation of IEPs or in the review process' (Ofsted, 1999). The targets may have been made up by the SENCO sitting at home with her paperwork, or they may have been spawned by a computer program. Even if the child was involved originally in agreeing targets, the chances are that noone has reminded him or her of them since then.

There are other problems with targets as well as the problem of confused ownership. Individual-child targets also have a habit of replacing meaningful hopes and dreams with what can be readily measured. The drive to get SMART has meant, at worst, a generation of children (and of the adults round them) who believe that staying in their seat for five minutes, not tearing up their work, or packing their bag before school in the morning, will magically make them be able to concentrate, to believe in themselves, or be well organised. We tend to forget that teachers and children still need this broader sense of where they meaningfully want to get to in the end, as well as the tiny achievable tickable targets along the way. Reaching these targets may well mean that deeper objectives are beginning to be achieved, may act as 'success criteria' for the achievement of the objectives, but they cannot and should not substitute for them.

Effective interventions for children with SEN or disabilities, moreover, are often far too complex to reduce to a few SMART targets. The highly effective Reading Recovery literacy intervention provides half an hour of daily one-to-one teaching for a period of 12 to 20 weeks. Each day, the highly-trained Reading Recovery teacher assesses the child's knowledge and skills. Each day, they plan what they will teach on the basis of this assessment. The teaching on any one day might include a new grapheme–phoneme link, a way of breaking a word into chunks, how to use phrasing and expression when reading aloud, a way of forming a letter, how to hold a sentence of increasing length in the mind while writing it, how to write an irregular but common word quickly and fluently. How could all this be expressed in a small number of termly SMART targets?

Consider another effective intervention, this time for children with social, emotional and behavioural difficulties – placement in a nurture group. Such a placement involves around two terms in a small group of around 12 children, working all day every day in a family-like environment to learn the basics of how to relate to others, to share, to concentrate, to listen, to talk. Again, how can all this essential and ever-changing learning be described in a limited number of targets?

And what would be added to either the nurture group provision, or the Reading Recovery teaching, by writing an IEP for the children taking part? In both cases, we have a skilled teacher who is constantly developing, monitoring and reviewing targets for what they want the child to achieve. In both cases, they may well articulate for the child what it is that the child needs to focus on: 'Today, I want to see you … ', 'What I'm looking for when you read this book is that you … ' But they will not waste precious teaching time on writing half-termly or termly paper plans for every child they work with.

The importance of talking

IEPs were never intended to be 'just bits of paper', recording measurable but over-simple and often meaningless targets in the absence of ownership or involvement of the person potentially most willing and able to put in the energy needed to achieve them – the child him- or herself.

Before the paperchase began in earnest, when there were fewer IEPs and those there were had a less bureaucratic purpose, the IEP was just the written record of a much more important human process. This process was about **talking**. It brought together all the people most concerned about the child's progress (parent/carer, teacher and child) at a meeting whose purpose was to share information, clarify the broad objectives for the child's progress, remind everyone of the child's strengths, and arrive collaboratively at some priority targets to which all present could subscribe and all contribute.

Properly done, this kind of meeting – including deciding who will do what to help the child reach the priority targets – takes about an hour. To be effective, it needs to be followed by frequent monitoring of the agreed actions, and frequent monitoring of progress, in a way which keeps the targets alive for the child. There must be a review date set not so far away that participants can forget that they will at that date be held to account for the success or failure of the joint enterprise – more than a term will be too long, and less would be better.

From this it is clear that in schools where high numbers of children are identified as having SEN/D, it will be challenging to implement the talking model of IEP planning successfully. This is why a potentially energising, effective means of joint planning, admirable in its intent, has degenerated into a paper exercise. In these circumstances, it is important to consider whether it is worth doing at all, or whether there might not be other, better ways of planning which will maximise the achievement of pupils with SEN/D.

Schools may decide they need to focus the full, teacher-dependent planning process on only those children who need a fresh, concerted, home–school impetus to move them on, and those with the most complex needs. These schools will adopt simpler systems for meeting additional needs – for the broad range of children with learning or emotional and behavioural difficulties.

In doing so, they will go back to first principles and consider what essential functions the SEN bureaucracy was meant to achieve, so as to decide how those functions might be met in different and less paper-driven ways. In this book, we will take each of these functions in turn, and describe ways of fulfilling them that are manageable, effective and non-bureaucratic.

But first, let us look at some case studies of schools that have made progress in reducing bureaucracy, at the systems they have introduced, and at the impact.

2 | Case studies

1 Ellingham Primary School

Ellingham school is a one-form entry primary serving an area of mixed housing.

When the Inclusion Coordinator (also Deputy Head) took up post some years ago she asked staff what they did with IEPs once they were written. Usually, staff said they just put them in a drawer. When asked whether they looked at them between reviews, they said that they generally didn't. She then investigated whether IEPs were helping to secure parental involvement and found that parents were invited in to sign the IEP or review, but were generally not doing anything to help the children achieve their targets. In discussion with the borough's SEN Adviser, she decided to replace IEPs with a new system for setting targets, monitoring progress and involving families.

The system revolved around five key processes:

• Personal target-setting and review through 'Learning Logs';
• Communicating children's needs through 'Communication Passports';
• Curriculum planning for differentiation;
• The involvement of parents and carers in their child's learning;
• Provision mapping.

Personal target-setting and review through 'Learning Logs'

The school was already in the process of developing a system through which all children would set personal targets for their learning and development. The INCO stresses that reducing SEN bureaucracy would not have been possible without this. The focus is on children owning their own learning – setting targets (with their teacher's help), deciding on what evidence will show that they have met them, gathering the evidence, and discussing the evidence with the teacher. This face-to-face discussion has in many cases eliminated the need for teachers to spend hours marking children's work when the child is not present.

Every child keeps a record of their personal targets, one in each of the core subjects plus one in another area such as personal development or behaviour. Examples would be: 'To get better at roly-polys without balancing on my head', 'To tell back a story', 'To learn my 2 × tables'. Children in the Foundation Stage and Key Stage 1 set one or two targets per half term. Year 3 and Year 4 children set between one and three a week, and Year 5 and Year 6 set one to three targets daily or weekly as appropriate.

All the children, including those with SEN, are very clear what their targets are. Time is allocated on Mondays and Fridays to setting targets and reviewing progress towards them. Children record their self-assessments in a 'Learning Log' (a single book containing all their final pieces of work in all subjects). An example is shown in Figure 2.1.

The school uses Essex Target Tracker (www.targettrackersolutions.org) to track children's overall progress and help children identify what they need to learn next. Numerical targets (National Curriculum levels and sub-levels, including 'P' levels) are broken down to show evidence of achievement at each sub-level. Children use these evidence statements to help them set their own targets and to self-assess. They might, for example, highlight a section in a piece of work in their Learning Log and note that it provides evidence of achievement of a target they have set themselves. Teachers also write notes in the Learning Log to show how and when children have met their learning targets.

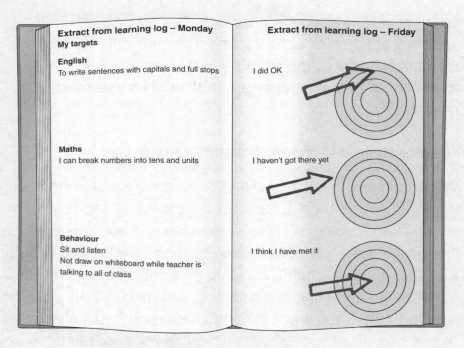

FIGURE 2.1: Extract from Learning Log

Communicating children's needs through 'Communication Passports'

As well as their Learning Log, each child with SEN/D also has a Communication Passport (Table 2.1). These laminated sheets describe the child's strengths, interests, areas of difficulty and the strategies that help them. They are framed in the child's own language, and used to make sure that everyone who works with the child is familiar with their profile and can use it to plan for teaching and learning.

Staff meetings have a slot called 'Children update', where everyone is briefed on issues affecting individual children and on areas they are working on ('This week X is trying to … Please try to notice when he manages it'). The same information is shared at lunchtime supervisors' meetings, so they can also form part of the supportive team around the child.

Curriculum planning

Teaching and learning for the child with SEN/D is shaped through teachers' regular curriculum planning, rather than separate paperwork. Half-termly plans (Table 2.2) have additional columns for staff to note the strategies that will be used to support the learning of those who are gifted and talented, have SEN or a disability, or are English as an Additional Language (EAL) learners.

Regular training for staff helps them to develop skills in differentiation. One focus, for example, was questioning. Staff learned how to use higher-order questions for gifted and talented learners. For children with learning difficulties they practised identifying the most basic question to ask in a hierarchical sequence of question difficulty, and asking other children similar questions before putting a question to a child who would benefit from the models provided by classmates. They shared useful strategies for questioning, such as posing the question then pairing a child with a chat buddy to talk to before answering, and using TV quiz show ideas ('Phone a friend', 'Take someone with you' and so on). Children often work in mixed ability collaborative groups where any one of the group might be asked to answer a question, and rewards (tokens) are given for the success of the group as a whole. This means the group has to make sure that all its members, including those with SEN/D, understand the topic and are able to answer questions.

The involvement of parents and carers in their child's learning

Parental involvement is fundamental to the work of the school. The local authority Social Inclusion Service has been brought in to run parenting workshops covering issues such as behaviour, family relationships, self-esteem and relaxation. The INCO has been much involved in development work in the local cluster of schools, who have run shared workshops for parents, such as the Family Learning 'Keeping up with the children' course. All parents are invited to these courses, but those whose children have difficulties in literacy or mathematics are particularly encouraged to attend. Focus groups of parents in the cluster were surveyed to find out what kinds of support they wanted, and what would make it easier for them to take part in school events. This led to the provision of crèche facilities run by trusted adults from the school, and meetings for parents learning English as an Additional Language (EAL) that were held in the nursery so that their children could play at their feet. Invitations to join events and courses were put on brightly coloured slips of paper; refreshments provided; and certificates used to reward attendance.

The INCO inherited a number of letters and proformas for communication with parents/carers of children with SEN/D, but found it more helpful to do everything by personal contact, either face-to-face or on the telephone.

SEN reviews are held twice a year but incorporated within regular parents' evenings. Where children have SEN, the parents' evening meeting is scheduled to take half an hour rather than ten minutes. The INCO attends these meetings and takes brief notes there and then on a simple review sheet (Table 2.3).

Before the parents' evening, cover is provided for every class teacher to meet the INCO and do a 'class review'. They will discuss every child with additional needs (SEN or disability, Gifted and Talented, EAL). The review takes about an hour per class and is typed up during the meeting. The meeting generates referral lists for outside agencies, and provides the names of children who would benefit from structured buddy support or who can provide such support to younger children. It also forms the basis of the audit of needs that shapes the school's provision map.

Provision mapping

Additional provision for individuals and groups is planned annually with adjustments made mid-year. The provision map is planned by SEN need type and includes:

For communication and interaction: social skills rehearsal groups, social stories, in-class support using visual calendars and timetables, individual speech and language programmes devised by a speech and language therapist.

For cognition and learning: phonics groups, Numbershark with a buddy, '15 minutes a day' literacy programme, reading with an older buddy, memory work with a buddy.

For behavioural, social and emotional needs: nurture/breakfast clubs, daily 'nurture chats' with TA and INCO.

For sensory and physical needs: a fine motor skills intervention called Jump Ahead, individual programmes devised by an occupational therapist

Peer support is extensively used, as well as adult support. The INCO has trained peer buddies to work with a partner on reading, ICT and memory skills.

The provision that each child receives is shown on the overall map and can be used if necessary, together with the Communication Passport, extracts from the Learning Log, examples of teachers' differentiated planning and notes from class reviews and parents' evenings, to provide evidence of what the school has done to meet the child's needs.

Other ways of beating bureaucracy

The INCO's other tips for reducing bureaucracy include making good use of the internet and work in local clusters or networks of schools. She used the internet, for example, to locate audit tools (from the CSIE Index for Inclusion and Birmingham's Inclusion Standard) to help her develop her school's accessibility plan. The net also proved useful in developing school policies, as did examples from other schools in her local cluster. This local extended schools/ECM cluster has proved an excellent source of ideas; the cluster submit shared bids for funding and through this have managed to employ a shared family liaison worker, run social skills groups, and offer shared SEN training to support staff.

Communication Passport

Child's photograph	NAME: A
	D.O.B.
	SEN stage: School Action Plus
	SEN support began: Spring 2010
	Areas of concern: Cognition and learning, social, emotional and behavioural skills

WHAT DO I FIND EASY?
Drawing and painting
Tracing

WHAT DO I LIKE DOING?
Drawing and colouring
Drama
Making up stories
Art club – 'but it's not for very long, you could bring something to eat and we could stay later!'
PE, especially gym
Getting stuff from magazines and making collages

WHAT CAN I DO INDEPENDENTLY?
All art especially drawing and colouring
Sequencing a picture story
Ideas for stories
Some spellings
Setting up games
Making up my own games 'but Morgan doesn't usually want to play'

WHAT DO I FIND HARD?
All maths
Some science
Trying to study when other people are talking
Writing quickly

WHAT DON'T I LIKE DOING?
Everything, except art
'I hate maths.'
Setting my own targets from the board
Sitting with boys
Filing work in folders — 'I just sling it in my desk!'

WHAT DO I NEED SUPPORT WITH?
Maths – 'I like maths games but not all that adding up and stuff.'
Writing – 'Don't give me so much because I get worn out, I would like somebody to write for me.' 'I would like a square pen because I keep forgetting to hold it right and I'm worried about losing my handwriting licence.'
'If a teacher sat on the carpet they could help other people and me.'

Communication Passport – reverse side	
Support received	
Year 2	Small group work with support of TA
	Extra reading sessions 2 to 3 × weekly with TA and parent helpers
	Phonological Awareness Training (PAT) (1 term)
Year 3	Small group work with support of TA
	Increased computer access for writing
	Jump Ahead – 3 × weekly
	OT box of activities
	Extra reading sessions 2 to 3 × weekly with TA and parent helpers
	A peer reading partner to share school reading book
	TA to scribe R's ideas if it involves lots of writing
	Interactive ICT maths games: Numbershark
	Increasing involvement of EP
Year 4	Small group work with support of TA – breaking tasks and concepts down into manageable chunks for R to understand
	Jump Ahead fine motor skills 5 × weekly
	OT box of activities 5 × weekly
	Reading sessions with TA and a parent helper 2 × weekly
	Interactive ICT maths games: Numbershark 3 × weekly
	Social Inclusion Support Service involved (HW)
	Involvement of EP
Year 5	
Year 6	

TABLE 2.1 A Communication Passport

HALF-TERMLY YEAR 2 LITERACY PLANNING

	KEY QUESTIONS AND ACTIVITIES	ICT/RESOURCES/SUPPORT	LEARNING INTENTIONS
WEEK 1	**Can you retell the story of *The Very Hungry Caterpillar?*** As a class read and discuss the story. Children to rewrite the story but using different food. (Focus beginning, middle and end and paragraphs). Children to use dictionary to find different foods. **LINK ICT – (See ICT planning).** **Can you rewrite sentences in correct order adding punctuation?** Work to be done in ICT suite. **Guided reading – numbers – link with maths.** **Spelling – daily – PAT?** **Handwriting – lower case c, a, o, e.**	*The Very Hungry Caterpillar* Dictionary Learning mats Word books	To be aware of the difference between spoken and written language.
		LCP card – Numbers (1)	
G&T & HOTS (Analysis, Synthesis, Evaluation)	<u>Child A and Child B</u> Synthesis – Can you write your own story using a different character and different food?		
SEN	<u>Child C and Child D</u> Writing 3 key sentences from VHC using story frame and word book.		
EAL	<u>Children E, F and G</u> Vocab: caterpillar, cocoon and butterfly and food names.		
WEEK 2	**What happened before and after this picture?** Children given a middle action picture from baby catalogue book. Children use planning sheet to show what happened before and after the picture. From planning sheets children write the story (focus beginning, middle and end) 3 paragraphs. **LINK ICT – (See ICT planning).**	The baby catalogue Planning sheets Order	To understand about beginnings, middles and ends. To understand time and sequential events in stories i.e. what happened when?

TABLE 2.2 An example of a half-termly plan

	Can you rewrite sentences in the correct order adding punctuation? Work to be done in ICT suite. **Guided reading – joining in – link PSHE.** **Spelling – daily – PAT?** **Handwriting – r, n, m, u.**	LCP card – Joining In (16)	To check work through and add adjectives where appropriate.
G&T & HOTS (Analysis, Synthesis, Evaluation)	<u>Child A and Child B</u> Analysis – which words could you add to make your story more interesting?		
SEN	<u>Child C and Child D</u> Sequence pictures in order and oral retelling.		
EAL	<u>Children E, F and G</u> Tell and plan story first in home language. Vocabulary beginning, middle, end.		
WEEK 3	**LINK – ART** **Why did the bears chase Goldilocks?** Children to write about favourite event in Goldilocks. Drama – children to work in small groups to act out the story. Hot-seating characters. Children to rewrite the story with clear beginning, middle and end – focus on adjectives. **LINK ICT – (See ICT planning).** **Can you put words from a word bank into your own sentences?** Work to be done in ICT suite. **Guided reading – 2D or 3D – link maths.** **Spelling – daily – PAT?** **Handwriting – v ,w, x.**	*Goldilocks and the Three Bears* LCP 2,1,3,4 Word books Dictionaries Learning mats LCP card – 2D or 3D (32)	To identify and discuss reasons for events in stories, linked to the plot.

TABLE 2.2 continued

G&T & HOTS (Analysis, Synthesis, Evaluation)	Child A and Child B Evaluation – How would you structure 5 clear paragraphs for *Goldilocks and the Three Bears?*		
SEN	Child C and Child D Use Clicker software to write a sentence for the beginning, middle and end of the story.		
EAL	Children E, F and G Work with TA to act out story with puppets before rewriting.		
WEEK 4	**What happened after Rosie left her hutch?** Read – retell the story of Rosie's walk. Drama – act out the story with children pretending to be different characters. Rewrite the story using own linking words. Going on a word hunt (LCP 2144) – writing sentences using these linking words. **LINK ICT** – (See ICT planning). **Can you replace 'and' and 'then' with better linking words?** Work to be done in ICT suite. **Spelling – daily – PAT?** **Handwriting – l, t, h, b, k.**	*Rosie's Walk* List of linking words (after, meanwhile, then, next and after a while) Going on a word hunt LCP 2, 1, 4, 4 Word books Dictionaries Learning Mats	To use the language to structure a sequence of events.
G&T & HOTS (Analysis, Synthesis, Evaluation)	Child A and Child B Synthesis – Can you rewrite the story as if you were the fox?		
SEN	Child C and Child D Insert linking words into a teacher-provided story	Teacher-provided story.	

TABLE 2.2 continued

			Resources	Objectives
EAL	Children E, F and G			
	Vocab: then, next, after, before, meanwhile.			
WEEK 5	**ASSESSMENT WEEK**		Baby catalogue	To understand about beginnings, middles and ends.
	What happened before and after this picture?		Planning sheets	
	Children given a different middle action picture taken from baby catalogue book.			To understand time and sequential events in stories i.e. what happened when?
	Children use planning sheet to show what happened before and after the picture.			
	From planning sheets children write the story (focus beginning, middle and end) 3 paragraphs.			
	LINK ICT – (See ICT planning).			
	Can you replace 'and' and 'then' with better linking words?			
	Work to be done in ICT suite.			
	Spelling – daily – PAT?			
	Handwriting – j, y, g, p, q.			
	Guided reading – Help! Dial 999 – Link PSHE, history and science.		LCP card – Help! dial 999 (30)	
G&T & HOTS (Analysis, Synthesis, Evaluation)	As assessment – by outcome			
SEN	To retell their story to an adult before writing it.			
EAL	To retell their story to an adult before writing it.			

TABLE **2.2** continued

SEN Review Summer 2011

Issues discussed, including overview of input this year, successes, areas for development and future targets

School needs to monitor occupational therapy position with view to getting X reinstated.

Finds maths really hard but has made progress in her writing – ideas are good, needs help with recording.

Has recently had a 'blip' with behaviour – hasn't enjoyed being out of routine, has 'wandered' out of lessons.

School to involve Dad in appointments – after school, evening.

Needs lots of practice in holding a pencil.

Continue with Numbershark, next stage of Jump Ahead.

Continue to work in small group.

Parent comments

X discharged because Mrs H (OT) is leaving!
Pleased with reading progress.
Still concerned about comments from A – continue to monitor next year.
Has tantrums/indecisiveness at home.
X to continue Mrs D's club.

Statutory Assessment was discussed but Ms L does not want X to go forward at this stage.
V. concerned re experience of her nephew, placement for X and secondary transition.

Date: 11/07/11   Signed:

SEN Review Spring 2012

X continues to be supported in a small group – increasingly needing 1:1 support.
Jump Ahead fine motor skills programme is working well.
School hopes that X will benefit from inclusion in social communication 'Talkabout' group and that through 1:1 nurture chats with Mrs W, self-esteem will be raised.
X v. keen to be involved in setting up of art club – has already chatted to Mrs C about this.
School continues to be concerned re X's academic and social progress.
V pleased that parents supportive of statutory assessment request.

Parent comments

Feel that X would benefit from working with Yr 6 'buddy' on computers at lunch break.

Date: 24/01/12   Signed:

TABLE 2.3 SEN review sheets

2 Little Ridge Community Primary School

Little Ridge is a large primary school in East Sussex, serving a mainly white British area. The proportion of children eligible for free school meals is lower than the national average, but the proportion with SEN is higher than average. The school has a speech and language centre catering for up to ten children with severe speech, language and communication difficulties (SLCN), which has also provided highly valued outreach to nearby schools.

Jane West, the INCO, meets all class teachers at the end of the academic year to identify children who are not making progress. This enables her to plan the interventions that will be needed, to put together a provision map for the coming year, and to prepare 'receiving' class teachers for their new intake.

The school uses a range of interventions which in recent years have included nurturing group provision for children with social and emotional needs, the Numbers Count and 1stclass@number one-to-one programmes for Key Stage 1 children, fine and gross motor programmes, a multisensory intervention for children with dyslexia, and speech and language interventions in both KS1 and KS2. Reception classes use Speechlink and Language Link screening programmes to identify children who need additional help with communication.

TAs delivering interventions all have an identified specialism in one or more of the SEN Code of Practice need areas (communication and interaction, cognition and learning, sensory and physical needs). One TA is studying for a speech and language qualification. She works in the speech and language centre in the mornings, and uses the knowledge gained there to devise group interventions for children in the main school with SLCN.

A highly trained Learning Mentor runs the nurturing groups, which are tailored to the needs of the children – 'moving up' groups, friendship skills groups, and circles of friends. She also provides morning 'meet-and-greet' one-to-one sessions for children who need short-term support because of bereavement or other difficulties in their lives.

Intervention programmes sit against a backdrop of inclusive quality first teaching. Classrooms are dyslexia-friendly; there are visual timetables, resources to help children find high frequency key words for their writing, text on buff rather than white paper, and help for short-term memory problems in the form of Talking Tins used to record and play back instructions, and Task Boards which remind children of the steps in an activity. For children on the autistic spectrum, class teachers routinely use social stories, sandtimers, busy boxes, time out cards and 'calm zones'.

Much emphasis is placed on linking children's work in intervention programmes with their work in class. Every intervention has a feedback sheet for the class teacher, which identifies the targets being worked on, so that the teacher can support them in class. Targets may change weekly or termly, depending on progress. Transfer of learning from intervention to classroom is planned for, with TAs building in one or two sessions when they will work in class to help children to generalise their learning.

Each November, Jane holds an intervention meeting to find out how class teachers feel children are getting on. This follows regular termly pupil progress meetings and parents' evening. The outcomes of the intervention meeting might be additional strategies or resources for the classroom, or for parents to use at home.

Only Statemented children have IEPs. These break down objectives from the Statement into very small steps and are reviewed three times a year.

Partnership with parents is seen as fundamental. Parents are involved in 'keeping up with the children' sessions and are really well informed, for example, on how behaviour is supported and how the four rules are taught in maths. Additional sessions cover how parents can support the Read Write Inc approach to phonics used in the school. The Learning Mentor is a key contact, regularly out in the playground at the beginning and end of the day so that parents can tell her about events at home and be signposted to any help they might need.

CASE STUDY

3 Frederick Bird Primary School

Frederick Bird is a large primary school in Coventry. It serves a diverse population, with around 46 languages spoken by its 675 pupils and a recent growth in numbers of children from Lithuania, the Czech Republic, Romania and Slovakia. Thirty-seven per cent of children are eligible for free school meals.

The school, judged outstanding by Ofsted on its last inspection, stopped using IEPs in 2009. Instead, pupils' progress is monitored via termly attainment and inclusion meetings involving the school's inclusion manager and year leader. These meetings focus on both the attainment and wider well-being outcomes (attendance, self-confidence, friendships and so on) of each individual child with SEN/D, identifying successes and reasons for lack of progress.

The school provides a wide range of intervention programmes. For literacy, the provision map has included Reading Recovery, the National Strategies Early, Additional and Further Literacy Support groups, Read Write Inc and Toe by Toe. The school is involved in Every Child Counts in Key Stage 1 and provides one-to-one tuition in Key Stage 2 for both literacy and maths.

There is a team of five Learning Mentors; two specialist TAs run out-of-class nurturing programmes for children with social and emotional needs. Frederick Bird is also part of a cluster of schools buying in shared support from a counsellor and from a speech and language therapist.

Being part of the national Achievement for All (AfA) programme pilot added impetus to the school's focus on inclusion. All staff took part in an hour a week of CPD on effective strategies to support children with SEN or disabilities, largely provided in-house. Parental engagement was encouraged through the use of the AfA 'structured conversation', described in Chapter 7. Parents of children with SEN/D take part in three such conversations a year with a key teacher, usually the class teacher.

These hour-long conversations help build a picture of the whole child in the context of their family and community; as Catherine Nyman, Deputy Head and AfA leader says, the system 'brings SEN and Every Child Matters together'. The meetings also allow parents and teacher to reach common ground on targets for the child over the next term. Parents are asked, for example, what they think is the single biggest issue standing in the way of their child's progress. The barriers to learning are then systematically tackled.

If, for example, a child is often absent on Mondays, the agreed target will be about improved attendance and the school might plan a Monday after-school activity or club geared to the child's interests. One 'Monday Club' involved 12 Year 1 and Year 2 children. It was staffed by TAs and teachers, and included a choice of activities from bikes to balls to computer skills to card games and creative arts.

Another example was an after-school project involving 120 children in creating a performance. Music and dance are very important to the Roma community, so the project was particularly successful in building confidence and improving attendance for this group of pupils. Parents were simultaneously offered adult education classes, with a crèche; the classes covered English and maths and 'anything else they wanted to learn'. They were invited in to a special Performance Day to watch their children's work.

Another group of children formed a hospitality group, visiting restaurants to learn how to make and serve food at the performance.

In planning its provision, the school came up with the interesting idea of having time-limited out-of-school interventions as well as in-school groups. A group of Year 3 children with challenging behaviour, for example, took part in a six-week intervention themed around dinosaurs and culminating in a 'Dinosnore' sleepover under the enormous dinosaur skeleton in the National History Museum.

On Saturday mornings targeted pupils involved in AfA can take part in a wide range of sporting activities, often involving professional coaches. This type of additional provision has unlocked the potential of many children – such as one Year 4 boy with SLCN who barely spoke intelligibly but by Year 6 was much more confident and able to hold his own in class. This was because staff had identified his passion for cycling and helped him achieve gold level cycling proficiency.

'Whatever it takes' is the school's watchword, and the impact on the progress of children with SEN/D has been profound. Targeted children on average made annual points score gains in line with or greater than children without SEN/D nationally. Expectations have risen; Catherine says she no longer hears staff say 'What do you expect – they've got SEN'. Sarah Douglas, Assistant Head for Inclusion, observes that 'There is a strong can-do culture. Staff within the school have the necessary knowledge and can provide opportunities and challenge pupils in a really positive way.'

CASE STUDY

4 Hall Mead School

Hall Mead School is a secondary Academy with 963 pupils on roll. It serves an urban area that is more socially and economically advantaged than most others, but with some pockets of relative deprivation. The vast majority of pupils are from white British backgrounds. Just over one in ten pupils is identified as having SEN. Numbers of pupils with complex needs are above average; over 40 children have needs at a level that would justify a Statement. They come from the full range of backgrounds, many from professional families with articulate and knowledgeable parents who have chosen Hall Mead even though they live outside the catchment area, because of the high quality of its SEN/D provision.

Elizabeth, the SENCO, has been at the school for 15 years and has always sought to limit bureaucracy by replacing the exchange of pieces of paper with face-to-face contact. She is convinced, for example, that what matters for parents is the chance to talk to her or other staff, and not any resulting paperwork. She cites here her experience of sending home records of Statement reviews with two copies – one for parents to sign and return to the school, and one for them to keep. Invariably, they would send both copies back to the school.

Elizabeth says 'I used to work very hard on IEPs but I was not sure they were helpful to teachers or relevant to the curriculum.' She also found IEPs passed on from primary schools of limited use, as her school could not continue the intervention programmes or support in the same way. What she wanted was information on what worked for a particular child that would help secondary staff use similar strategies.

IEPs are no longer written; instead each child has a single-sheet profile describing their areas of difficulty and the strategies staff can use to meet their needs (see Table 2.4). Feeder primary schools are asked to contribute to this profile for pupils transferring. The profile/strategy sheet is accessible to all staff via SIMS and the school's intranet. When staff register their class online there is a code beside a student's name so they know they should check further. They can click on a box and the profile/strategy sheet will come up.

Staff also receive a paper copy of the profiles at the start of the school year. Updates to the profiles are given at morning staff briefing meetings, and e-mailed to everyone who teaches the student.

Working with subject staff

Targets for pupils with SEN/D are subject-specific and set by subject teachers in the context of target-setting systems for all pupils. A few pupils who need to work on life skills have additional personal plans. Subject teachers have just one sheet in their planners, called the Curriculum Access Plan (now called an Individual Provision Plan to fit in with the local authority's system – see Table 2.5). It contains a list of pupils with SEN/D in the class, and a space for the subject teacher to enter learning targets for the half term, term or for the module they are teaching (they choose the period that is most appropriate), and any strategies they will use to help the pupil achieve the target. They do this only where the pupil needs adjustments made to enable them to access learning in that subject. Some pupils with SEN/D might not need such adjustments in music, PE, or DT, for example.

The Plan is available online and can be e-mailed back to the SENCO once completed, to support reviews. Elizabeth insists on having the Plan returned from the English, Maths and Science faculties at minimum. She also encourages Heads of Faculty to ensure that the forms are transferred at the end of the year from one teacher to the next, and that these are important sources of information within the subject area.

Staff can also add to the list any pupil who is struggling in their subject. A child with spatial awareness difficulties, for example, might be added to the art teacher's list, with a note of strategies to be used to support them.

The principle used is whether or not the teacher has to do *something different* for the child to enable them to succeed in their lessons. The definition of SEN is therefore functional rather than based on labels and need types. The SENCO's message to staff is 'If they don't need anything different, then don't do a plan.'

Another principle used is the need to put time and energy into frequent informal communications rather than into infrequent, formal meetings. With strong support from the headteacher, Elizabeth uses staff briefing time in the mornings for short, sharp case conferences of around fifteen minutes. She brings together all those who teach a particular child, to go through strategies and give out essential information.

These mini-conferences have, she says, 'been one of the best moves I've made'. She continues:

> They are really effective as it is much easier to get a consistent approach across the school. They are too short to become moaning sessions and teachers feel something is being done. I think they feel they have more ownership. Then we have follow up case conferences so there is a sense of working together. Teachers have made very perceptive comments and volunteered strategies they know work. Profile/strategy sheets are handed out or changed as a result of the case conferences but again it is the face to face contact and communication which is making the difference. These have brought about a more positive attitude to our really challenging students.

The school is committed to mixed ability teaching in most subjects and this means staff feel a greater need for advice on how to differentiate their planning and teaching than those with setted classes. Departments prepare schemes of work with different levels of worksheet and buy textbooks at different levels. Learning Support Assistants are encouraged to contribute to the development of departmental resources. Departments play an active part in developing school SEN/D policies and practice, for example developing the initial idea of Curriculum Access Plans. There is now a differentiation working party, and Elizabeth is meeting each Head of Faculty to identify particular issues for their subject. A meeting with the Head of Maths, for example, led to plans to work on assessment tools for lower-attaining pupils. At a meeting with the Head of Design and Technology, Elizabeth explored the need for students to have definitions for key vocabulary; the head of faculty went away and made small laminated vocabulary cards for students, kept on key rings.

Working with parents and carers

Parents/carers are able to talk to the SENCO and her staff in the Learning Support Department when they need to rather than at set times. 'They might ring every day for a week', Elizabeth says, 'but then not at all ... it's all about informality, easy face-to-face and telephone access, and response to need'. She has established a thriving parent support group and her current plan is for the group to be led by the parents themselves.

The SENCO's role

The SENCO puts the majority of her time into these informal communications, and helping staff with their target-setting and planning, rather than into writing or reviewing IEPs. She is also able to contribute to CPD for staff. There is regular INSET on SEN/D, offered in directed time. Recent examples include a session on autism, one on the role of phonics in reading, and one on how to teach spelling across the school.

Elizabeth has no regrets about the move away from IEPs. She hopes the school can achieve further reductions in paperwork in the future, as staff become more confident in setting targets and planning for pupils with SEN/D in their lessons. 'You go through a paper model to get people to think in a certain way', she says, 'and then you can give the paper up when it's no longer needed.'

PROFILE

M has severe visual impairment.

He has good and bad seeing days although will not always say if he cannot see work.

He has a very positive attitude.

He needs specially adapted paper.

M uses a laptop.

Work written on the whiteboard should be in black.

He needs work enlarged to **at least** N18.

Simple enlargement is not always appropriate – see Sally in the learning support department.

Bear in mind that some work may need to be retyped/redrawn/annotated so please allow sufficient time for work to be adapted.

He will need specially adapted exam papers.

M's speech can be hard to understand (although this has improved).

Support needed is physical rather than academic.

STRATEGIES

Encourage M to use his laptop. His writing is hard to read (even for him) and he will need legible notes for revision. This will be good practice for GCSEs in Year 10 and 11.

He should have folders for each subject on his laptop to save his work in.

When speaking please encourage M to slow down and speak up.

Check that he can see the work you have given him.

Suitably enlarged past exam papers are available for M to use for practice. Please liaise with the LSD as these will have to be ordered in. The LSD will be happy to adapt materials for you but please plan work in advance so that M's work is ready and suitably modified for the start of your lesson.

TABLE 2.4 Single-sheet child profile

SPECIAL EDUCATION NEEDS – CURRICULUM ACCESS PLAN

FORM: 10TH Set 2/4	TEACHER: CP	DATE STARTED:	SUBJECT: Half-termly/Termly/Module/Unit/Date expected to achieve by

Name	Learning targets	Strategies/equipment and support details	Final outcomes with supporting comments and evidence
HM	All class targets Algebra skills of expanding, simplifying, solving, factorising to be practised and mastered. Angles on parallel lines (alternate, corresponding, interior . . .).	Ensure that classwork and homework is enlarged in advance of the lesson.	
HK	Angles in polygons to be known!	Monitor H regularly – EACH lesson in case of seizures. Ensure that I read the care plan termly at least. Liaise with Mr H about any intermittent health problems. Maintain regular contact with SEN department if homework proves to be a problem.	

SPECIAL EDUCATION NEEDS – CURRICULUM ACCESS PLAN

FORM: Yr 10	TEACHER: Mr L	DATE STARTED: Autumn term	SUBJECT: Resistant Materials

Name	Learning targets	Strategies/equipment and support details	Final outcomes with supporting comments and evidence
WJ	To keep up to date with GCSE coursework. To meet deadlines.	Positive encouragement. 1-2-1 explanations where possible. Suggest discussing work with a friend to aid understanding.	
KB	As above.	As above. Nag about homework!	
PJ	As above.	Praise where possible. Give choices . . . the option of avoiding sanctions	

TABLE 2.5 Curriculum Access Plans

SPECIAL EDUCATION NEEDS – CURRICULUM ACCESS PLAN

FORM: 8WK/Y	TEACHER: DH	DATE STARTED: October 09	SUBJECT: Religious Studies Half-termly/Termly/ Module/Unit/Date expected to achieve by

Name	Learning targets	Strategies/equipment and support details	Final outcomes with supporting comments and evidence
PJ	Knowledge and understanding of the Church, including beliefs (creed), variety (denomination), Buildings, Leadership, Worship, Ceremonies.	Check knowledge and understanding of key words. Writing frames. Homework noted correctly. Engage him 1–2–1.	
MJ	As above.	Be non-confrontational. Check knowledge and understanding of key words. Writing frames.	
ER	As above.	Check knowledge and understanding of key words.	
CJ	As above.	Writing frames. Engage 1 to 1. As with ER.	
CD	As above.	Keep away from MJ and SB.	

TABLE 2.5 continued

SPECIAL EDUCATION NEEDS – CURRICULUM ACCESS PLAN

FORM: 8WK/Y	TEACHER: HV	DATE STARTED: September 09	SUBJECT: English Half-termly/Termly/ Module/Unit/Date expected to achieve by

Name	Learning targets	Strategies/equipment and support details	Final outcomes with supporting comments and evidence
CD	He contributes regularly to class discussions. He needs to transfer this into his written work.	Encourage him to focus – seat him on his own. Have him use laptop with predictive word processor.	
CJ	To complete a formal letter to an MP using written argument phrases.	Bank of written argument phrases.	
MJ	To complete an agreed amount of work during the lesson.	Listen to his ideas. Give encouragement. Pair him with buddy for joint production of written work.	

TABLE 2.5 continued

SPECIAL EDUCATION NEEDS – CURRICULUM ACCESS PLAN

FORM: 8A/WM	TEACHER: WM	DATE STARTED: September 09	SUBJECT: PSHE Half-termly/Termly/ Module/Unit/Date expected to achieve by

Name	Learning targets	Strategies/equipment and support details	Final outcomes with supporting comments and evidence
BS WD	To ensure he has grasped key concepts. To ensure he is on task and up to date.	See SK. Clear instructions. Move when appropriate. Involve him in discussions.	
SK	To ensure key concepts are understood (democracy, MPs, voting).	Create opportunities for work to be bullet points – simple sentences. Check each lesson that she knows what to do.	
RB	To ensure B remains confident and involved to develop written work.	Give lots of praise. Ensure there are some role-play activities.	

TABLE 2.5 continued

CASE STUDY

5 Coombe Boys' School

Coombe Boys' School in the London Borough of Kingston draws on a diverse community. There is a grammar school nearby that takes the most able pupils, but Coombe itself still has a spread of abilities. There are 500 11–18-year-old pupils on roll, 40 per cent of whom have English as an additional language. A fifth of pupils are eligible for free school meals.

Sam Axbey, the school's INCO until 2007, formerly worked in the school's behaviour base and from that vantage point was able to observe the SEN systems in place, and their impact. 'Teachers were being given piles of IEPs and putting them in a folder never to be seen again', she says. When she became INCO she wanted to design a new system based on what teachers wanted and what they would actually use.

Layers of information

The system is based on layers of information – from the minimum that every teacher needs to know, down to the more detailed information that might only be needed by an outside agency working with a pupil. Information is copied only to those who need it, but is all also kept in a file in the staffroom so that anyone who wants to know more can access information at the more detailed layers if they choose.

The first layer of information (Figure 2.2) is an additional needs register containing, for each year group, the names of EAL learners and the names of pupils with SEN or disabilities together with their areas of need (BESD, cognition and learning and so on) and whether they are at School Action, School Action Plus or have a Statement.

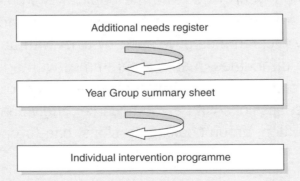

FIGURE 2.2 Layers of information

This register goes to every member of staff. It is updated termly, with changes highlighted in colour. Termly updating is necessary because the school has high levels of pupil mobility.

The next layer aims to provide teachers with more information about pupils with SEN or disabilities, but in a way that will not leave them feeling overwhelmed. It takes the form of a year group summary sheet, on no more than two sides of A4, that lists the names of pupils with SEN/D, the barriers to their learning, and the strategies that will be helpful (Table 2.6). Different colours are used for each year group and the summary sheet is also updated termly. Copies go to teachers and to support staff.

Subject teachers have really valued this information. They highlight the names of pupils they have in their classes, and know, for example 'that one needs to sit at the front ... that one needs to be told what he's going to be doing before he even comes in ... this one needs to be allowed to leave the room and go to the toilet whenever he needs to'. Staff hitherto resistant to SEN ideas have particularly welcomed the new system.

The strategies on these year group summary sheets are written by the INCO and support staff. As a team, they sit down each week and discuss pupils individually, covering year groups one at a time on a rolling basis. TAs are subject-based as well as each acting as key worker for a number of pupils, so the discussions bring in perspectives of how a pupil is doing across the curriculum and the strategies that appear to work best for them. The team meetings serve a dual purpose – both generating the strategy ideas for the year group summary sheets, and providing professional development for the TAs, who are able to learn from each other's strategies and successes.

The next layer of information held on pupils, the 'Individual intervention programme', is aimed at staff who are directly supporting individual pupils, either one-to-one or in a group, at parents/carers and outside agencies. It provides a description of the totality of additional provision a pupil is receiving. Form tutors, year heads and the pupil's key worker also receive a copy. Provisions are varied and are often based on individually tailored packages – literacy programmes developed by a TA with an advanced diploma in specific learning difficulties, maths programmes with a learning support teacher, breakfast clubs to ease troubled pupils into school, residentials, college placements, sessions with a youth worker, individual swimming lessons or music tuition, group cooking sessions, one-to-one counselling and so on.

Identifying needs and working with outside agencies

Any member of staff can make a referral to the INCO, using a simple form with basic information on their concerns that is signed off by the Head of Year or Head of Department. Referrals to outside agencies are managed by talking rather than filling in forms. Every term a whole morning is dedicated to a multi-agency review meeting attended by INCO, pastoral deputy head, heads of year and a range of outside agencies including Connexions, the Youth Offending Team, EP, school nurse and EWO. Before the meeting the INCO puts together a list of pupils to be discussed and circulates it to heads of year for additions. A notice also goes up in the staffroom inviting all staff to make recommendations about students they think should be discussed. The INCO then prepares a spreadsheet, arranged by year group, with pupils' names and a space for her to add actions as they are agreed at the meeting. After the meeting she extracts a separate list of each professional's agreed actions and sends it to them.

Target-setting and monitoring progress

Coombe Boys has a whole-school target-setting system based on an Academic Mentoring day that is held twice a year. On these days each pupil has a one-to-one meeting with their form tutor to discuss their progress and set targets for the next period. For pupils with SEN/D, the key worker (usually a TA) joins the meeting to contribute feedback on progress and to help with target setting. Year heads might also sit in on meetings where there are particular behaviour or pastoral issues.

Pupils' progress is assessed termly by subject staff using NC sub-levels and each pupil receives a 'Position Statement' showing the NC level they were working towards and the level they actually reached. On the back is a graph (Figure 2.3) which totals point scores across subjects and shows progress term-by-term across the key stage. This is sent to parents/carers before the parents' evenings that are held twice a year.

If a referral needs to be made to the local authority for a possible Statement of SEN, or for the local system of 'Enhanced School Action Plus' funding, the INCO is able to submit the detailed pupil progress information held on the Position Statement. Together with a copy of the 'layers' of information held in the staffroom file, this means that strategies, provision and outcomes are clear. None of her requests for funding have been turned down since she began this system

39

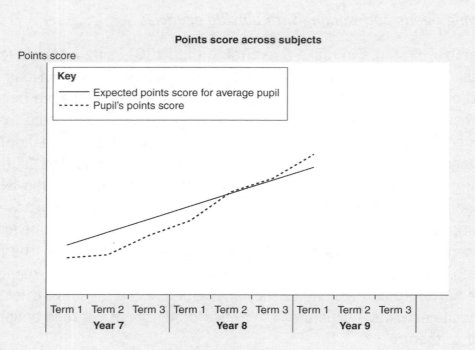

Points score across subjects

Points score

Key
——— Expected points score for average pupil
------ Pupil's points score

| Term 1 | Term 2 | Term 3 | Term 1 | Term 2 | Term 3 | Term 1 | Term 2 | Term 3 |
| Year 7 | | | Year 8 | | | Year 9 | | |

Figure 2.3 Position statement graph

Working with parents

Parents and carers are very closely involved in working with the school
to support the progress of children with SEN or disabilities. Not one, for
example, failed to come into school to meet with staff. Sam puts this down
to strategies like phoning home regularly with good news, being willing to
make home visits, and the messages of respect and valuing she and her staff
give, summed up as 'You know your child best'. Parents provide essential
information to help assess pupils' needs; Sam has devised a set of questions
grouped around the five Every Child Matters outcomes that she uses for these
discussions (Table 2.7).

YEAR 8		
STUDENT	**BARRIERS TO LEARNING**	**STRATEGIES/ACTION POINTS**
K 8GT MATRIX	• Behaviour. • Difficulty staying on task/focusing.	• Seat on his own at the front. • Encourage independent working. • Receives support from MB to consolidate classroom work.
S 8GT MATRIX	• Behaviour. • Low literacy.	• Has some offsite provision and is in school for partial timetable. • Buddy with a better reader in class.
E 8GT SA+	• Possible visual impairment. • Lacks confidence. • General learning difficulties.	• Seat near front.
S 8MS SA+	• Literacy – writing. • Behaviour. • Lack of confidence. • Possible dyspraxia.	• Manageable writing tasks. • Enhanced access to IT. • Emphasise S's achievements.
K 8GT SA+ EAL 1	• General learning difficulties. • Poor peer relationships.	• Responds well to praise and to explicit rewards e.g. merits. • Encourage positive peer relationships through small group work.
L 8GT SA+	• Behaviour.	• Joint placement with PRU. • Recommend speaking to social worker before speaking to mum.
D 8MS SA+	• CP issues. • Volatile behaviour. • Literacy.	• Lunchtime haven. • Focused literacy support with JB. • D to be encouraged to fully participate with other students in lessons. • Receives individual counselling.
N 8GT SA	• Literacy. • Lack of confidence. • Listening skills.	• N needs to complete small tasks in both speaking and writing.
D 8KS SA	• Young carer/home/social issues. • Low literacy levels. • Attention seeking.	• Lunchtime havens. • Acknowledge his concerns, then distract.

TABLE 2.6 Year group summary sheet

Pupil's name ... XXX ... Does the child appear to be ...

Healthy?

Evidence:
Sleeps well, eats well, physically active. Eyesight fine.
Hearing – mild hearing loss in both ears.
No apparent worries but gets angry quite a lot at home.

Safe from harm?

Evidence:
Yes – but did leave the school site on one occasion unsupervised, thereby putting himself at risk.
Says he used to get bullied but not now.

Enjoying and achieving?

Evidence:
No issues with learning, progress or level of attainment. Attends well – seems to like school mostly.
However behaviour is beginning to impact on access to learning opportunities. When XXX is removed
from class he is missing learning time.

Having a positive impact on others?

Evidence:
XXX's behaviour within the classroom can have a negative impact on other children and their access
to learning.
Has been involved in providing reading support to Y7 – really successful.

Heading for a good future?

Needs help in working out what sort of future he wants. Can be a leader. Working in teams is
something he struggles with. Good at taking responsibility and has lots of creative ideas.

TABLE 2.7 Assessment used in discussions with parents/carers

CASE STUDY

6 Stocksbridge High School

Stocksbridge High School is an 840-pupil secondary school near Sheffield. Eleven per cent of pupils are eligible for free school meals. At its last Ofsted, inspectors wrote:

> The support for students with special educational needs and/or disabilities and that provided through the personalised learning base for students who are finding learning challenging for whatever reason is second to none.

Liane, the Inclusion Manager, is highly IT-literate and makes good use of SIMS and the school's virtual learning environment to let staff know about students' special or additional needs. Pupil data held on SIMS shows whether a pupil has SEN or behavioural needs, so by clicking on a student's name on their marksheet staff can access a SEN or behaviour button for more details. Liane has added fields to the basic SIMS SEN categories of provision (targeted groupwork, resourced provision, TA support, access arrangements, therapy); at Stocksbridge staff can also now see, for example, whether a pupil uses a reading pen or digital voice recordings to help them access text, or has received one-to-one tuition.

The system is great for what Liane calls 'Friday afternoon phonecalls' – times when a parent might ring after school to complain that 'Nowt's been done for my kid'. At a glance, whoever picks up the phone (which might be the headteacher) can locate and describe the provision that is in place for that student.

Liane has also set up a 'Positive Participation logging' system to track whether students have taken part in extra-curricular activities such as karate club or after-school art classes, astronomy club, camp and so on. This allows the Inclusion team to look at the profile of students accessing activities and identify any vulnerable groups or individuals not taking part. The system also logs whether students have received awards and rewards, and whether their parents/carers have attended parents' evenings.

The majority of students with SEN/D do not have IEPs. Liane says 'All the students here have academic targets so there seemed no point in having a separate system for students with SEN. I ended up thinking "Who are these IEPs for?" They just sit in a filing cabinet – you need something that's useful.'

What is useful, in her view, is her provision map for each year group (see Table 2.8 for a Year 7 example). The provision map enables Liane to plan, allocate and evaluate provision. She also uses it to record the provision each student has accessed, by simply ticking the relevant items and keeping a dated copy for each year the student is in school.

IEPs and IHPs (Individual Health Plans) are only used in those cases where, in Liane's words 'Staff must know what they have to do to support the pupil – for example a student with ASD where there will be huge problems if the teacher raises their voice, or a boy with a shunt in his head who must not under any circumstances be knocked'.

For these high-profile students, staff will get a brightly coloured sheet in their pigeonhole with a pen portrait of the student, the provision they receive, required teaching and access strategies, and the student's personal targets.

Stocksbridge High was part of the national Achievement for All pilot and this enabled the school to look in depth at the barriers to learning for each individual student with SEN/D, and plan to overcome them. Liane says that 'Every week when we looked at detentions and attendance lists we noted that it was the dyslexic boys appearing over and over again – especially as they got older and moved up the school they just couldn't read the material put in front of them – and all that was happening was that they got told off.' As a result of this analysis she planned a range of curriculum access strategies using technology such as screen readers and reading pens. She also recruited a team of volunteers to make digital recordings of text books, revision guides and teacher revision notes. Students can access these on the school's managed learning environment, or download them onto their own MP3 players at home.

Other strategies developed through Achievement for All aimed to improve students' confidence and engagement with learning. Adult volunteers from Reading Matters charity were already reading one-to-one with students with low reading ages. Liane involved the charity in training Year 9 students with SEN/D to go into a local junior school and read one-to-one with their lower-achieving pupils. Achievement for All also enabled students who were poor attenders and disengaged from learning to take part in outdoor personal development activities, run by another voluntary sector organisation.

Liane introduced the 'praise pod' – a room with video recording facilities on a laptop loaded with special software (www.praisepod.co.uk), where any student who has done something praiseworthy can go and be interviewed on camera by a volunteer who asks them to talk about what they have done that is noteworthy. The pupil sits on a large leather chair – as in *Mastermind* or *Big Brother* – for the interview. They then receive the film on a CD to take home; it is also e-mailed to parents. Photos of the students sent to the praise pod are displayed on a noticeboard in school.

A very important part of the school's provision is the STAR (Support Teaching And Reintegration) learning support unit. STAR supports any pupil who cannot participate fully in lessons. New pupils arriving mid-year start their school experience here; other users include for example students with major health problems, a looked-after child the team are trying to get back into school, a child with ASD who needs a calm space for a while. Pupils attend for anything between a couple of hours a week to full time, on a pre-planned basis, either completing academic work or taking part in social and emotional learning groups geared to their needs – such as a boys' group, or a self-esteem group. STAR works in tandem with the school's off-site Personalised Learning Base for students with more challenging behaviour or attendance issues.

The school's highly personalised provision, combined with staff development, good tracking and use of data has helped the school to go from strength to strength. Last year, GCSE results for pupils with SEN or disabilities were the best ever, with the KS2–KS4 progress made by students at all SEN stages above national averages, particularly so in English for students at School Action. Fifty-eight per cent of the SEN cohort were identified as having some form of specific learning difficulty including dyslexia; almost half of those (46.4 per cent) achieved A*–C in English Language. The same number achieved A*–C in Maths. All gained A–G in English with no lower grade than E.

TABLE 2.8 Year 7 provision map, SEN/D provision

NAME: FORM: 2011–12

SCHOOL ACTION	NEEDS	STAFF COSTS/ OTHER	+ SEN PROVISION / RESOURCES AVAILABLE	SEN PROVISION / RESOURCES AVAILABLE Year-specific	OTHER INCLUSION INTERVENTION Available to all years
Withdrawal (1 period per week) for literacy	RA below 9.5years /standardised score below 85 Spelling 2 years or more below chronological age / standardised score below 85	TEACHER:	☐ Contact – parents/carers ☐ Support in internal tests (TAs) ☐ TA attachments to some depts. offering extra-curricular support, support with resources, data etc ☐ Dolphin Easy Tutor Screen reader installed on all PCs for student use ☐ Targeted students provided with headphones for above ☐ Alphasmart loans: short and long-term negotiated for temporary injury or SPLD needs ☐ Equipment loan: Reading Pen, voice recorder ☐ Lunchtime Club ☐ Homework Club 3.00–4.00 ☐ Lexia ☐ 1:1 programme with Reading Matters volunteers ☐ Individual support as negotiated /appropriate e.g. 1:1 support, specific programmes e.g. Beat Dyslexia * ☐ Outside Agency referral, liaison and intervention * ☐ Support with medication and diet/feeding ☐ Study guides / other equipment loan e.g. coloured overlays, Reading Rulers ☐ Assessments e.g. Dyslexia Screening Test * ☐ Modifications /personalised curriculum * ☐ Close liaison with LAC agencies ☐ Positive Participation tracking	☐ Supported transition ☐ Getting to Know You Day ☐ Flower 125 – Y7 ☐ Y7 Support Manager's groups ☐ Group /1:1 work on allotment with SP ☐ Achievement for All provision * ☐ Other individual /group work as arranged:	☐ Breakfast Club ☐ STAR time – lessons for variety of reasons (see criteria for referral) ☐ STAR – breaks and lunchtimes (safe-haven) ☐ Personalised Learning Base* ☐ School Nurse drop-in ☐ Referrals to other agencies as required and appropriate
In-class support from Teaching Assistants	☐ Dyslexia ☐ Learning difficulties, ☐ SLCN ☐ Behaviour support ☐ Autism ☐ Attention difficulties ☐ Mobility / physical needs ☐ Other:	TA:		* Details:	Review/Impact:

ADDITIONAL NOTES OVERLEAF

Be healthy
Stay safe
Enjoy and achieve
Make a positive contribution
Achieve economic well-being

3 Doing SEN differently

The case studies: common features

What can we learn from the schools, described in the previous chapter, who have chosen to 'do SEN differently' and less bureaucratically? First, the schools avoid over-identifying pupils as having SEN. Numbers identified in the schools with lower levels of deprivation are around 10–12 per cent of the school roll, rather than the higher figures we have seen across the country in recent years – up to 70 per cent in some schools, according to Ofsted (Ofsted, 2011).

The reasons for identifying children as having SEN are interesting. Can it really be, for example, that nearly one in three nine-year-old boys have SEN? This is what their teachers think, according to official figures (DfE, 2011a). We know why this happens. Pressure to achieve ever higher standards encourages teachers to attribute the lack of success of some children to within-child deficits; children can have extra time in their end of key stage tests if they have SEN; schools are concerned about pupils not coping when they transfer to secondary school, and so on.

But as the Lamb Inquiry (2009) reminded schools, 'Being behind your peers in learning does not of itself mean that a pupil has SEN'. Ofsted (2010) also notes that it is important to avoid over-identification of SEN occurring because 'the standard offer of education or care is insufficiently adapted for frequently found needs', or because 'such identification is the only way in which parents and schools can gain access to support from a range of in-house or external providers'.

It is important to remember that there is a distinction to be made between pupils who have 'a learning need, but not necessarily a special educational need' (DfE, 2012b). Schools can ensure that pupils who have learning needs and have fallen behind can access 'catch-up' intervention programmes at Wave 2 of the well-known 'three-Wave' model of provision for children. They do not have to identify them as having SEN to do so.

It is a sensible idea, therefore, to restrict the identification of SEN to children requiring the more individualised and specialist Wave 3 provision, and so reduce the numbers identified as having SEN to a relatively low percentage of your roll. Having done this, you may also want to learn from the case study schools described in Chapter 2 and as far as possible use **the ordinary systems used for all pupils** to establish targets for pupils with SEN/D, to track their progress and to communicate progress to parents and carers. This is the feature that characterises all the case study schools, who were able to make use of existing paper- and IT-based systems (pupil Learning Logs, teacher mark books, medium- and short-term planning documents) rather than set up separate paper trails for pupils with SEN.

This has benefits beyond reducing bureaucracy. It locates much of the responsibility with the class or subject teachers – those who are in greatest contact with the pupil and therefore have the greatest influence on their learning – rather than with the SENCO or learning support department. It means that teachers keep pupils' targets and the strategies required to meet them in their minds, because they are embedded in planning tools and records that are in daily use. It makes a reality of the well-known statement that 'every teacher is a teacher of SEN'.

It is not, however, what a literal adherence to the 2001 SEN Code of Practice has led us to. For many years, such adherence has placed a whole group of children outside of schools' regular systems for setting expectations, monitoring progress and reviewing and adapting curriculum, organisation and teaching methods. Pupils with SEN/D were felt to require **different** systems from the systems used to secure the welfare and progress of all pupils.

This has rarely been helpful. Ofsted, for example, noted that:

> Defining achievement in terms of the number of targets on an individual education plan achieved across a given time rarely ensured rigorous evaluation of provision or pupils' progress. What made the difference to higher outcomes was effective target-setting within the curriculum or personalised programme as part of a whole-school policy on assessment.
>
> Ofsted (2006)

The major Ofsted 2010 SEN review (Ofsted, 2010) further noted that 'the keys to good outcomes were good teaching and learning, close tracking, rigorous monitoring of progress with intervention quickly put in place, and a thorough examination of the impact of additional provision.'

Abandoning separate SEN systems, however, also carries distinct risks. At the extreme, it could mean that the particular needs of pupils with SEN or disabilities get lost – that teachers are unaware of their needs, that no special efforts are made to teach them in the ways they learn best, that additional provision is not made for them and that parents are left in the dark about what the school is doing to help their child.

The aim of this book is to show how these pitfalls can be avoided. It will describe how we can 'do SEN differently', whilst never losing track of the essential purposes of SEN/D legislation and guidance – protecting the rights of a minority group of children to have their needs identified and met.

The role of the SENCO

Many SENCOs feel concerned that their expertise and knowledge will not be used if children who are finding learning difficult are not formally identified as having SEN. This need not be the case.

What is suggested in this book, and already in place in many schools, is a **universal** system for identifying individual needs and acting on them. In this system we can envisage SEN practice as simply bringing to bear on these universal systems a particular expertise in SEN and disability, provided by the SENCO/INCO and outside agencies. This represents an intensification of existing systems rather than using separate ones, and locates action within everyday classroom teaching and learning rather than a parallel universe of separate SEN record-keeping and review.

This idea of progressive intensification was expressed by the House of Commons Education and Skills Select Committee in its 2006 report on SEN:

> To achieve real progress in terms of early intervention the Government needs to change the premise on which SEN is provided to one in which literally every child matters. This would mean a radically new approach to SEN provision where a system of assessment of learning and intervention takes place for every child on a spectrum of provision that can be geared up for children that require high levels of support.

It is in this 'gearing up' that the SENCO/INCO has a vital role, applying their particular knowledge of SEN and disabilities so as to scale up existing systems in place for all children.

Let us look at one example to see how that might work in practice. The example chosen relates to the interaction between routine whole-school processes for identifying children who may need a boost to their learning, and the identification and assessment of needs element of the SEN procedures.

There will always be children who come to school with needs that have already been identified – children with developmental disorders or impairments evident before they started school, or children who move from an early years setting to school, or from primary to secondary school, with an existing history of receiving SEN/D provision.

For many children, however, special educational needs are identified in the course of a key stage, usually as a result of expressions of concern by teachers or parents/carers. Recent developments in whole-school assessment and tracking, however, offer a more systematic route to identifying children who may require extra help in one form or another. In these systems class or subject teachers track all pupils' progress using ongoing assessment supplemented by discrete assessment tasks and tests, and review each child's progress regularly.

These reviews, held two to three times a year, consider data on prior and current attainment, attendance and behaviour, and effectively identify any pupil who is not on track to make the levels of progress expected over a key stage. In a primary school, this review might be the trigger for the class teacher to discuss what extra steps could be taken to accelerate the child's progress with the INCO, SENCO, Ethnic Minority Achievement (EMA) coordinator, Gifted and Talented coordinator or the person who leads on behaviour. In the secondary school, the information on pupils who are struggling is expected to be fed to the year leader, whose role is to identify pupils causing concern in a number of subjects because of effort/behaviour, academic progress or attendance. The year leader in turn works with other middle managers to determine what interventions might be needed to support the pupil – some of which might come under the aegis of the SENCO/INCO.

Much guidance is available to support class and subject teachers in how to track and assess pupil attainment levels, so as to identify pupils who are experiencing difficulties. The SENCO's or INCO's role can usefully be to 'coach' subject teachers and class teachers in upper Key Stage 2, so that they are able to assess against National Curriculum levels and sublevels at which pupils with SEN or disabilities may be working. Teachers will need help in recognising, for example, the key indicators of progress from level 1 to level 2, and level 2 to level 3, not just those from level 3 upwards. Subject teachers and primary teachers are also now expected to develop skills in assessing against the P levels, with the help of the SENCO.

SENCOs/INCOs can also support colleagues' assessment skills by providing training, modelling and coaching on child–adult conferences, aimed at obtaining 'a window into the child's mind' and acquiring a deeper and shared understanding of what it is that holds the pupil back and what can help them as a learner.

Children with the more enduring learning difficulties and with the behaviour difficulties we might class as 'true' SEN, however, will need more in-depth assessment. SENCOs/INCOs have a crucial role in contributing specialist expertise to assessment that seeks to establish not only that a given pupil is not trying hard, behaving well or making progress, but also *why*. Such an assessment might involve one or more of classroom observation, use of questionnaires, standardised tests, analysis of children's work, analysis of underlying perceptual, motor or memory skills, or gathering information from parents/carers. A range of tools a SENCO/INCO can use are suggested in *Special Educational Needs in the Primary School* (Gross, 2002). An hour spent on this kind of assessment and feeding the outcomes into the kinds of child profiles we met in Chapter 2 will make more difference than many hours spent on organising IEPs.

The importance of this kind of assessment is to identify the child's strengths, so that they can be helped to draw on them, and barriers to learning, so that plans can be made to overcome them. It is a moot point whether assessment also needs to attach a diagnostic label to the child or not. In some cases, formally identifying individuals and making special plans for them appears to hinder their progress rather than help. For example, in Chapter 1 we saw how pupils identified as having ADHD made less progress than similar pupils whose teachers were simply given information sheets about general strategies for inattentive and overactive pupils. Similarly, research by Freeman (2010) has shown that children labelled as gifted were far more likely to experience emotional and social difficulties at school and in later life than were those with equally high IQs who were not labelled. On the other hand, there is evidence that some labels, such as dyslexia and Asperger's syndrome (Gross, 1994; Papps and Dyson, 2004) are actively helpful because they help adults to respond in more effective ways to behaviours they would otherwise construe as evidence of 'laziness', 'bad behaviour' and so on.

There is also the risk of failure to make appropriate adaptations to learning and teaching if particular impairments or disabilities are missed because the school does not have effective procedures for identification. Tales of pupils subsequently discovered to have serious hearing loss or visual impairment after years of failure are not apocryphal. For this reason, effective SENCOs/INCOs build periodic screening into the school's tracking systems, using staff meeting time for staff to use quick checklists to pick up pupils with minor hearing loss or visual impairment, language difficulties, motor difficulties and poor emotional health and well-being issues (Gross, 2002).

In these ways the SENCO's or INCO's expertise can be used to enhance the systems used in the school for identifying pupils who need additional support. The principle, however, is of building on the whole-school systems used for all pupils, rather than replacing them with a separate system for SEN/D.

Functions that SEN procedures were meant to fulfil

To ensure that in moving towards universal systems we still protect the rights of children with special needs or disabilities, and their parents, we need first to reflect on the objectives that effective SEN/D processes should seek to meet.

These include:

- Identification – ensuring that children's needs are identified as a result of expressions of concern by teachers or parent/carers.
- Assessment – ensuring that some assessment takes place, to better understand the barriers to learning and how they might be overcome.
- Communication – making sure that all relevant staff and outside agencies know what the child's needs are and what should be done or has been done to support them.
- Identifying priorities and setting targets for learning or behaviour.
- Identifying strategies, in the classroom and elsewhere, to help the child achieve targets.
- Reviewing progress and celebrating success.
- Engaging parents and carers – agreeing priorities and targets with them, making sure they have a say in and know what is being done to help their child and to what effect, suggesting ways in which they can support their child's progress.
- Coordinating the actions to be taken by the school and outside agencies
- Informing decisions about the allocation of resources – extra adult time and/or physical resources.
- Supporting transition – making sure that information about the child's needs is passed on as they move from one class or setting to another.

Other less intrinsically useful but necessary functions of the SEN/D systems are those of accountability and referral:

- proving to parents, Tribunals, Ofsted and the local authority that the school is meeting pupils' needs effectively;
- demonstrating a need for additional resources (the involvement of outside agencies, extra funding) by showing that the school has done all it reasonably can before seeking outside help.

Let us now take each of these functions in turn, and consider ways of fulfilling them that are manageable, effective and non-bureaucratic, using our case studies from Chapter 2 as the starting point.

 ## Identification and assessment

All the schools in our case studies used sophisticated **pupil tracking** (moderated by sensible teacher and parent judgement) to identify children causing concern. They all then kept some sort of register of pupils flagged up in this way.

Ideally, their pupil tracking systems could be supplemented by routine screening to identify children who may on the face of it be making adequate progress yet are not fulfilling their potential or are not secure in their well-being. These will be children who have special needs of a more subtle, less obvious kind. The SENCO/ INCO might, for example, ask year group teams once a year to look through checklists of indicators of dyslexia, autistic spectrum disorder, dyspraxia and minor sensory impairment, and consider whether any of the children in their care show evidence of these potential special needs. The school might, like Little Ridge, use the computerised Language Link screening system to identify children with SLCN; versions are now available for Key Stage 2 and secondary schools as well as Key Stage 1.

Equally, SENCOs/INCOs might in addition want to spend some of the time freed up from paperwork working with individual pupils, using tools suggested by outside agencies, so as to develop a more in-depth picture of the child's cognitive, physical or social/emotional profile that can guide curriculum planning.

 ## Communicating needs

One of the prime functions that IEPs were meant to fulfil was that of communication, for example:

- making sure that staff teaching a child were aware of their needs, targets and the strategies to be used;
- making sure that parents/carers were involved and were updated regularly on the child's progress;
- making sure that if the child failed to make progress, information on what had been done to help them would be available for outside agencies and the local authority;
- making sure that if the child moved, information would follow them to a new placement.

In practice, the volume of IEPs that many schools maintain has made it impossible to use them as an effective communication tool. As we saw in Chapter 2, they often languish in the drawers of the primary class teacher, or in the drawers of the learning support department in secondary schools, brought out only when accountability – in the shape of Ofsted or IEP review dates – looms. Parental involvement in many schools is reduced to token status, with the class teacher or SENCO pursuing a parent in the playground to ask them to sign an IEP in which they have had no part, simply so that it can be forwarded to the local authority to prove the case for additional resources. Paperwork is passed on to other schools if the pupil moves, but does not always tell them what they need to know and know quickly – what are this child's strengths and difficulties, what works for them in the classroom, and what additional provision they require.

There are, however, simple and more effective ways in which the IEP communication function can be met, that do not require volumes of paper. The case studies in Chapter 2 exemplify good, non-bureaucratic practice in communicating with staff, parents/carers and the outside world. At Ellingham, a child-held Communication Passport is used to summarise needs and the strategies required to meet them. At Hall Mead and Coombe, subject teachers receive customised lists of pupils they teach who have SEN or disabilities, in the form of a set of individual profiles, or a year group summary sheet.

Other schools provide a profile of pupil need in each class a subject teacher will work with by creating pupil profiles that are short enough to fit into one cell of a spreadsheet (Table 3.1). They then sort the profiles into class sets electronically.

And why stick to paper? Some schools support pupils in making Communication Passports in the form of PowerPoint presentations. There is an excellent example (Matthew's Passport) in the government's Inclusion Development Programme autism material, available on the web at https://schools.educationbradford.com/schools/CMSPage.aspx?mid=1891#Transition and helpful blank templates at www.communicationpassports.org.uk/Resources/Creating-Passports/Templates/.

Morris, Joanne. Excellent at art. Plays for school netball team. Learning difficulties. Reads at level of an 8 yr old. Numeracy similar. Needs a buddy reader, short instructions, writing frames, learning linked to everyday real experiences. Can get very upset/difficult when falls out with friends – show understanding and ask her if it would help to go and talk to Miss Perry.

TABLE 3.1 A cell from a spreadsheet

Then there is film. A secondary SENCO in Bristol took a video camera out and interviewed Year 6 pupils with SEN or disabilities who were due to come to his school. He asked them what helped them learn and what got in the way of their learning. A hearing-impaired child with good lip reading skills described how 'I can't manage when two people talk at once', and 'It's really bad when the teacher talks when they are writing on the board 'cos I can't see what they are saying'. Shown to all subject staff who were to teach the incoming Year 7, these short films were far more powerful in changing teacher behaviour than any number of written communications.

There is no logical reason, either, why communication systems that let staff know about children's special needs or disabilities should not extend to wider 'additional needs'. One primary school uses 21 'special categories of need' which include 'children who do not shine in anything' and 'children who receive minimal support at home to achieve basic skills'. Children are evaluated against these categories and efforts then made to tailor provision to the need. Other schools use a 'risk and resilience' system. They keep a list of 'at risk' pupils that might include a range of factors – being a summer-born boy, living in a home where there is domestic violence, parental separation, poverty, and so on. They alert staff to pupils on this register and suggest a range of strategies they can use to promote the pupils' resilience – for example, all members of staff having the names of two pupils they will make a point of chatting to in the corridors and around the school each week, offering residential opportunities and before- and after-school clubs, or linking the pupil with a member of staff who shares an interest they have.

At Lyng Hall secondary in Coventry, there is a register that can embrace **all** the pupils in the school, their need, and the provision in place for them at any point in time. Some students might only be on the register for a week or so, perhaps because of an event at home that means they need extra support for a short period; others will be on the register throughout their time in school. Headteacher Paul Green calls this 'mapping all our provision for all our kids' and describes how it has enabled the school to sort attainment and progress and wider outcomes data by a range of pupil characteristics, so as to analyse the impact of all its provision.

 ## Identifying priorities and setting targets

As the case study schools in Chapter 2 illustrate, setting individual targets is now commonplace, whether they are recorded on Learning Logs (as at Ellingham), teachers' planning (as at Hall Mead), or wall displays like those in schools which display 'Learning ladders' to which children affix their names to the next step they need to reach in a sequence of steps.

Systems like these can meet the purposes of effective SEN/D systems and remove the need for separate IEPs, as long as progress against targets is systematically recorded and parents are kept informed.

Where more effort may be needed for children with SEN/D is in making sure that the right priorities have been established for the child's learning, even before targets are set. These priorities may not always be in the core academic subjects. Underpinning areas such as language development or social and emotional learning may be more important. This though is not just an SEN/D issue – teachers have to judge priorities carefully for many children, including those going through a difficult time at home, those learning English as an additional language, and so on. Schools will be good at setting the right priorities to the extent that they have robust systems for gathering information on all their pupils, listening to parents/carers and listening to children and young people themselves.

 ## Planning strategies to meet needs and reach targets

The SENCOs/INCOs in our case study schools all spend considerable time on staff development, so that teachers have a good sense of how to make their everyday teaching as inclusive as they can. On top of this, they provide class and subject teachers with suggested strategies for individual pupils. At Ellingham these strategies can be found on the laminated Communication Passport, framed in the child's own language. In other schools, they can be found on classroom walls (Figure 3.1). At the secondary schools they are on year group summary sheets or in a folder of individual profiles for each class. Essentially, the role of the SENCO/INCO and their team in these schools has switched from paper manager to acting as a consultant to colleagues on what works for lower-attaining pupils or those with behavioural, emotional and social difficulties.

To encourage positive behaviour in this class we try to:
• Repeat instructions three times
• Use children's names
• Say 'I feel sad when …'

Strategies to support TB
• Ignore as much low level attention seeking as possible
• Attend to him doing the right thing using descriptive praise
• Two areas of focus:
  ▪ Doing what an adult says
  ▪ Kind hands and feet (no hurting)
Rewards:

FIGURE 3.1 Posters to remind staff of inclusive strategies

The second way in which the case study schools record the strategies used to help pupils meet targets is through provision maps. These set out the additional provision made in each year group under the broad areas of literacy, mathematics, language, motor skills and social/emotional development. A map highlighted with the provision a particular pupil receives, together with guidance for staff on strategies to use in everyday class teaching, fulfils the 'planning strategies' function of an effective SEN/D system effectively in a time-saving way, obviating the need to keep writing the same descriptions of provision over and over again on separate IEPs.

 ## Reviewing progress and celebrating success

Once strategies have been planned, monitoring progress is readily achieved through the excellent tracking systems in place in our case study schools. These schools also have a means of *evaluating* progress that was never available under the IEP system. Provision mapping enables schools to use simple baseline measures before an intervention is put in, and repeat these at the end of the intervention. These may be measures of reading or spelling age, standardised scores on a language or maths test, measures of social and emotional competence or simply teacher-assessed NC sub-levels. The measures allow not only for the progress of individuals to be evaluated (and shared with parents), but also for evaluation of the overall impact of the intervention on a number of pupils.

Children who experience barriers to their learning often need more effort put into the celebration of success than do their peers. IEP review meetings sometimes provided for this. To make sure this celebration function is not lost, schools can flag up some children for extra 'noticing'. In secondary schools, this may be by asking staff to send good news home – to make a note in a pupil's planner or send a pre-printed card home when the pupil has met a target, however small. It may be more frequent meetings between a pupil and a tutor or mentor, to review what has been achieved. Home-school diaries and good news postcards can also be used, along with praise assemblies, 'praise pod' films like those used at Stocksbridge High, class plenaries and so on.

 ## Engaging parents and carers

A prime function of any effective SEN/D system must be to provide parents and carers with guaranteed involvement in the school's efforts to meet their child's needs, and a way of challenging the school if these efforts are insubstantial. In practice, this function has been poorly fulfilled by bureaucratic systems.

In contrast, the relatively paper-free systems at our case study schools are partnered by conspicuous efforts to engage parents and carers. This is achieved in different ways at each school. What characterises them all is informality and ease of access. Extra time is given at parents' evenings where children have additional needs (as at Ellingham), meetings are more frequent and follow the very helpful Achievement for All structured conversation format (as at Frederick Bird Primary), or the school has drop-in sessions and identifies a key link person for parents to speak to whenever they need to. The additional provision that can be made for their child is made clear to parents through a provision map that describes different interventions and provision, and what entry levels entitle a child to access that provision.

IEPs and reviews were also meant to enlist the help of parents in supporting their child's learning at home, and provide them with guidance on how best to go about this. Again, as we will see in Chapter 7, they have rarely achieved this. What does seem to be both successful and time-efficient, however, is practice like that at Ellingham and Little Ridge, where parents are involved in curriculum workshops and support groups that are explicitly aimed at empowering them to provide the best possible home learning environment.

 ## Coordinating the actions to be taken by the school and outside agencies

Where a number of agencies are involved with a pupil there is a need for a system that coordinates and records their work. Some schools may wish to continue using IEPs where several different agencies are involved with a pupil. Equally effective, however, in recording who is going to do what (and when) can be a simple note of actions agreed in multi-agency meetings. This is the system at Coombe Boys' School in our case studies. And to keep an overall perspective of which agencies and personnel have been involved over time, the SENCO/INCO can add a column labelled 'external agency involvement' to the school's provision map and write in the agencies involved when pulling off a copy and highlighting provision that an individual pupil receives. Alternatively the agency involvement can be recorded on a chart like the one in Table 3.2, or the cumulative overview/record of progress which will be described in Chapter 4.

 ## Informing decisions about the allocation of resources

The 2001 SEN Code was intended to make sure schools allocate resources according to pupil need, basing decisions on staged procedures in which

Child: xxxxxxxxxx DOB: 21.02.99 Class: 3R

Updated: March 2007

Foundation Stage intervention group – numeracy	Foundation Stage intervention group – literacy	Hearing Impairment team support	Visual Impairment team support	TA supported Literacy 1:1
TA supported Numeracy 1:1	Handwriting Programme	Speech and Language Therapy	Language group	RML
Specialist Literacy support	Learning Support Unit	Learning Mentor	CAMHS	Educational Psychologist
EMAG Support	1st Language Assessment	Lang. & Communication Team	Behaviour support	Child Development Team
Stephen Hawking Special School Outreach team advice	Liaison with Phoenix Special School	Statement provision	Physical Disability Team	IEP
IBP	Occupational therapy	Daily Physiotherapy	PSP	Medical intervention
CT supported writing group	1:1 maths with TA			

Past provision	Present provision

TABLE 3.2 Record of provision and multi-agency involvement, Old Ford Primary School

progressively more resources were allocated as pupils moved from School Action to Action Plus or a Statement. The theory was that if the resources deployed at one stage were not successful in helping the pupil progress, more resources were needed. In practice, the staged system often served only to distort efficient management of time and money. It drove much of the excess paperwork schools undertook, as they sought to document in detail what had been done at each stage so as to make a case for a move to the next. It assumed that if resource allocation was unsuccessful then the *child* must have needs greater than those resources could support. It did not prompt schools to consider whether they had deployed resources effectively in the first place. Nor did it lead to equity. Several pieces of research have now shown (Gross, 1996; Pinney, 2004) that resources tend to be skewed towards those children whose parents are most able to articulate the case for extra help.

The schools in our case studies tend to use more effective ways of allocating resources. These are based on data analysis that identifies the level and type of need in each year group. On the basis of this analysis provision is planned pro-actively, at the start of the year, then regularly adjusted through pupil tracking systems that quickly identify pupils who are not making the expected progress.

 ## Supporting transition

Another purpose of good SEN/D systems is to secure the effective exchange of information at times of transition for pupils – moving from one class to another, or from one school to another. Our case study schools have not found that the transfer of copies of individual paper plans is useful. Instead, they allocate time for primary and secondary staff to meet, or explicitly ask for information on the strategies that worked in the primary school, as at Hall Mead. Another useful idea for primary schools is an end of year staff meeting, where staff team up in pairs (Year R with Year 1 etc.) and go through class lists, discussing particular children's needs, what has worked for them in the past, what triggers to avoid, and any other useful information. The pair record a profile for each child discussed and photocopy it there and then for the SENCO/INCO and the teacher whose class the child will be joining.

 ## Proving that the school is meeting pupils' needs effectively or demonstrating a need for additional resources

This is the big worry for many schools. How, without drawers full of IEPs and fat pupil files containing dusty records of what is often years of SEN/D support, can a school show Ofsted that their practice is good, convince a SEN Tribunal that they have acted appropriately, request the involvement of outside agencies, or compile evidence so as to request a Statement of SEN or an Education, Health and Care Plan?

Let us look first at Ofsted. In a recent inspection, the SENCO was asked to select a number of children and show their progress over the key stage, and what had been done to support them. At another, the SENCO was asked for records of meetings with parents and the IEPs that went with them. At another, the focus was on how the SENCO could show the overall impact of the school's SEN provision on pupil progress.

On the face of it, some of these inspectors could be seen to be asking for paperwork. But they asked for it not so as to tick a 'paperwork-in-order box', but so as to explore particular issue and hypotheses. The issues and hypotheses will have emerged from the school's data profile, from any self-evaluation the school may have done, and from first-hand evidence during the inspection.

In the school where the SENCO was asked to show the progress of individuals over time and what had been done to support them, there might have been an indication in the school's data that pupils with SEN or disabilities as a group were not making good progress.

In the school where documentation of meetings with parents was the apparent focus, the inspectors may have picked from parents' questionnaires broader issues about parental involvement and satisfaction, and decided to explore whether these issues extended to parents of pupils with SEN or disabilities.

In the school where the SENCO was asked how she could show the impact of the school's provision, the inspectors might have been testing a hypothesis about leadership and management, having noted an absence of any data analysis relating to the progress of lower-attaining pupils, and any evaluation of the impact of the school's interventions for pupils with additional needs.

In all cases, Ofsted were not interested in compliance with procedures. Their interest was in outcomes – pupils' academic and personal development, and in what the school was or was not doing to help pupils achieve these outcomes. In some cases they did look for evidence in the paper systems that are generally used; they did go to the familiar (to IEPs and reviews) because that is where they would expect to find evidence.

But they can equally be directed to other forms of evidence. It is up to the school to point them in the right direction. The SENCO/INCO can do this by writing a single sheet, part of their SEN or Inclusion Policy, that describes how the needs of children with SEN/D are met – the systems for identification, assessment, setting targets, identifying strategies, working with parents/carers, involving pupils and so on. The sheet will make clear for which children the school uses IEPs (for example, those with the most complex needs) and for whom it uses alternative means of planning. It will give the rationale for the systems that are in use, so that the reader understands the benefits that result from reduced bureaucracy and increased class/subject teacher involvement.

An example of such a policy statement is provided in the toolkit section of this book. Suitably adapted, this information sheet can be given to inspectors so that they will know where they need to look in order to test out the effectiveness of the school's work with pupils who have SEN/D. In the examples above, they could be pointed to these sources of information:

Progress of individuals over time	→	Class tracking sheets and cumulative overviews/records of progress
Parental involvement and satisfaction	→	Notes of meetings with parents Results of a survey undertaken by the SENCO as part of SEN self-evaluation
The impact of the school's provision	→	Data analysis showing the number of NC level jumps made by all the pupils with SEN over a key stage Evaluations of interventions on provision map

All of these would provide fruitful ground for testing of inspectorial hypotheses, whilst at the same time demonstrating that this is a school that has thought carefully about how to develop truly effective systems for supporting pupils with additional needs.

Another big fear for schools, which often drives unnecessary bureaucracy, is the fear of being called to account by parents through Tribunals or the courts. As the Implementation Review Group of headteachers put it, 'Too often we are driven by what appears to be the overriding concern of protection from litigation' (IRU, 2006). But, just as for Ofsted, similar 'evidence' (this time solely at the individual pupil level) can easily be pulled together from existing sources to demonstrate what has been done to support a pupil. At Tribunals, the focus is likely to be on the provision map and evidence of strategies used by class or subject teachers (like the Curriculum Access Plans in the case studies) as the questions will usually be about what provision the school can make available, and whether this is sufficient. Similar issues will be of interest in any court procedures.

Finally, in relation to outside agencies, it is not difficult to provide succinct information about the child's needs and what has been done so far to meet them, through:

- Personal Profiles or Communication Passports;
- pupil tracking records showing progress in NC levels and sublevels and in personal development;
- highlighted provision maps.

If further 'proof' is needed, for example when requesting a statutory assessment, then photocopies of records of class-based target-setting and review, and of differentiated classroom planning, can also be appended. Again, you may need to include your information sheet on how you manage SEN/D in your school, so that the agency or local authority administrators will understand that you haven't just forgotten to enclose 'copies of the last three IEPs' or whatever else their own bureaucracy asks for, but are providing the same information in a different way.

Beating bureaucracy: the essential kit

A simple set of systems will allow you both to provide information to others who ask for it, and at the same time manage SEN/D effectively internally. We can call this the essential bureaucracy-busting kit. It is illustrated in the toolkit section of this book and should include:

- a note in your SEN/D policy on how you fulfil essential SEN/D functions without over-reliance on IEPs, as described in the previous section;
- a register of pupils with SEN/D;
- a provision map to show what additional provision you are making for pupils;
- a pupil-led way of communicating needs to all who work with the pupil, such as a Personal Profile or Communication Passport;
- strategy sheets for the main types of SEN, to highlight and give to staff;
- a way of differentiating curriculum planning;
- a way of tracking pupil progress and reporting regularly to parents/carers.

The **register** is needed so that you can complete your pupil census (PLASC), identify the percentage of your roll with SEN/D, and make links to the range of data the school holds on each pupil. Without a register you cannot define the group whose progress you will want, as SENCO/INCO, to evaluate and compare with that of pupils not on the SEN register. The simplest way of keeping a register is to use an existing information management system, such as SIMS or RAISEonline, recording a 'Yes' in School Action, School Action Plus or Statement columns and the type of SEN in another column. You can then print your register, if you need to, using the filtering function.

The **provision map,** described in Chapter 6, is fundamentally a planning tool for you but also, when copied, dated and highlighted to show the provision received by an individual child, serves as a record of what the school has done to provide support.

The **Personal Profile** or **Communication Passport** is the way that staff know about individual pupils' strengths and barriers to learning, and what helps them best.

Strategy sheets give handy hints on strategies for specific types of SEN/D (dyslexia, autistic spectrum disorder, speech and language difficulties, ADHD and so on). They can be copied, highlighted as appropriate for the individual pupil, and given to staff who work with the child.

A **system for differentiating curriculum planning** is the way that staff translate information from personal profiles and strategy sheets into learning and teaching in the classroom.

Reporting to parents can be through written reports and through meetings. For children with SEN/D, there will need to be additional agenda items, over and above those used in standard parents' meetings, plus a brief record of the key points of discussion at meetings, and any actions agreed.

Summary

In this chapter we have considered systems that can be used to fulfil the purposes of current SEN procedures, and the essential toolkit to support these less bureaucratic ways of working. We have explored the purposes of current procedures, and the alternative ways of fulfilling them. In subsequent chapters we will return to these headings and consider some of them in more detail.

Setting targets and monitoring progress

Setting targets for pupils with SEN has always been a non-negotiable. The 2001 SEN Code of Practice, for example, said that schools must:

- identify learning targets for individual pupils with SEN;
- plan provision that is additional to or different from the differentiated curriculum offered to all pupils;
- review provision in the light of individual pupil outcomes.

Chapter 6 of this book will examine ways of planning and reviewing additional provision, other than through IEPs. In this chapter we will look at how target-setting (and even more important, target-getting) can be embedded within whole-school systems rather than make extra work for SENCOs/INCOs and teachers.

The national and Ofsted focus on pupil attainment and progress means that most schools have and continue to use such whole-school systems. The process starts with setting individual progress targets that say what P level, NC level or sub-level the pupil is aiming to achieve at the end of the key stage and – working backwards from that – the end of each year. These are *numerical* targets. They are not the same as the kinds of targets we see on IEPs, but they fulfil a function that is missing in an IEP-driven system. In such a system small-steps targets are set for what the pupil will know, understand and be able to do at the end of each term or six-month review period. But no longer-term goals are set, and it is possible for the pupil to achieve all the IEP targets but not make the 'level jumps' in attainment that are possible and achieved by other pupils with similar learning needs.

The point about numerical targets is that they are based on data. Using RAISEonline or similar local systems, they benchmark the pupil against others with similar starting points and predict what they ought to be able to achieve. The comparisons with national progress rates – for example, an expectation that Year 7 pupils should achieve 2 sub-levels' progress in the year – inject challenge into a SEN/D system that can easily become cosy and complacent. Ofsted now rely on them when inspecting schools, rather than on progress against targets in IEPs. They note in their guidance for inspectors:

> Unless IEP targets are effectively linked to moderated expectations outlined in RAISEonline, it is very difficult to evaluate the degree of challenge they provide. These targets are, therefore unlikely to contribute strongly towards the judgement on pupils' achievement unless there is very secure external moderation.
>
> (Ofsted, 2012)

The systems for making comparisons with national progress rates are not yet perfect. We know what the chances are of a pupil at a given starting point achieving a particular end of key stage level, but not yet what the chances are of a pupil at a given starting point who also has special needs in communication and interaction achieving a particular end of key stage level, or a pupil with BESD, or difficulties in cognition and learning, or a physical impairment, or any combination of these. The national data have not yet been refined to take in SEN need types. They do now, however, include information to help schools set numerical targets for pupils functioning at P scales levels. All this information provides a good starting point, that can be moderated using teacher professional knowledge about the child and what is available within the school or setting (including intervention programmes) to accelerate progress and 'add value' to the predicted levels of attainment.

Numerical targets for pupils with SEN or a disability are, moreover, very motivating for the individual. To know what level you are at and what level you are aiming for is immensely helpful, if combined with knowledge of what it is you need to do in order to reach that level. And that is the essential next step – turning the numerical target into *curricular* targets.

An example comes from Frederick Bird primary school, one of the case study schools we met in Chapter 2 of this book. At Frederick Bird, wall displays include 'learning ladders' showing the steps children need to take on the way to achieving at or above the expected NC level for their age. Children attach their names to the step they are on; arrows show them the next step. In one class, for example, a display backed with paper to look like a brick wall had the following steps:

Step 1 To use connectives to improve my sentences.

Step 2 To use connectives and pronouns to improve my sentences.

Step 3 To use a range of interesting connectives to join ideas together and to start new paragraphs.

Step 4 To vary sentence length and word order, to keep the reader interested.

Step 5 To use a variety of sentence openings in my writing, e.g. verbs, adjectives, connectives.

Curricular targets, phrased in 'I can …' terms, describe what it is the pupil has to learn in order to make the necessary learning jumps that will keep them on track to reach their numerical targets. The process of arriving at them is described in a number of publications, such as the Planning unit in the former National Strategies *Excellence and Enjoyment: learning and teaching in the primary years* (DfES, 2004b) and the *Assessment for Learning* secondary materials (DfES, 2004a).

The *Tracking for success* materials (DfES, 2005g) provide a helpful definition: 'Curricular targets are the link between pupils' long term numerical targets and the next steps in their learning, described in lesson learning objectives.' They define *key* pieces of learning that children will work on over about half a term; they are broader than lesson objectives, which are often specific to the particular content of a given lesson. They often stem from a whole-school target.

For example (Figure 4.1), a secondary school might analyse its pupils' results and decide that a priority is to improve enquiry skills in science. This whole-school curricular target is then 'layered' into age-related targets so that each year group has its own curricular targets. In Year 7 the target might be 'Pupils can plan their own investigation'. This is then layered further into medium-term curricular targets for each half term or unit of work. *Tracking for success* gives the example 'In an investigation pupils are able to identify the key variables that they can and cannot control'. In pupil-speak, this becomes a group or pupil target 'I will focus on

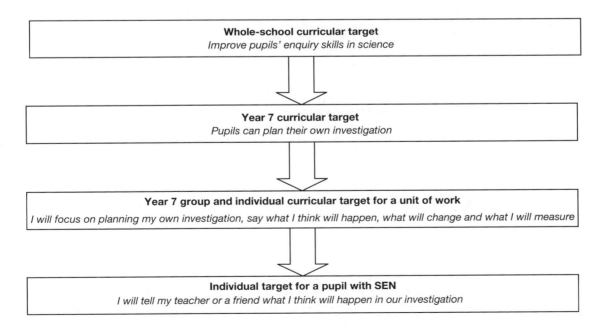

FIGURE 4.1 Layered curricular target for science

planning my own investigation, say what I think will happen, what will change and what I will measure'.

How might this be relevant to a pupil with SEN or a disability? If the pupil has difficulties in cognition and learning, the target might be differentiated so as to focus on the skill of prediction (a useful, cross-curricular learning-to-learn skill that the teacher knows will be relevant to the pupil's progress in a wide range of social and learning situations). Over a series of lessons the pupil's target might then be 'I will tell my teacher or a friend what I think will happen in our investigation'.

In English (Figure 4.2), a Key Stage 3 target to ensure that pupils use paragraphs appropriately might 'layer' back to a Year 8 target 'When writing, pupils use topic sentences to begin paragraphs', and a group target 'I can write a paragraph using a topic sentence, and group points so that they are clear and support the topic sentence'. For a pupil with learning difficulties, the *individual* target might be 'I can plan clear sections for my writing', something expected of the average Year 2 pupil under the former National Strategies' guidance.

Common practice in the primary school is often three levels of differentiated curricular targets in any given class – targets for pupils performing above age-related expectations, targets for pupils performing at age-related expectations, and targets for pupils performing below age-related expectations. It is important to recognise, however, that for some children there will be a need for a further level of personalisation, with individual targets set where appropriate.

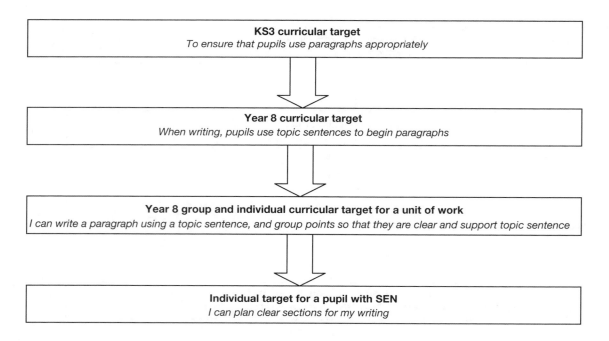

FIGURE 4.2 Layered curricular target for English

As an example (Figure 4.3), when working on measurement for length the overall curricular target for a Year 2 class might be 'To estimate, measure and compare lengths using standard units'. For an average group, the differentiated target might be 'I can estimate the lengths of different objects, compare their size and measure them and compare their length', for the more able 'I can measure a length in centimetres, find half and double the length in centimetres and millimetres', for a lower-attaining group 'I can measure and compare the length of different objects using ruler lengths'. For a child with SEN/D the personalised target might be 'I can compare the lengths of two ribbons or necklaces'.

Good sources of curricular targets in core subjects are the core learning in literacy and mathematics by strand in the former National Strategies Primary Frameworks, and the maths planning track back documents that form part of *Mathematics planning guidance for pupils working below age related expectations* (on www. teachfind.com). For secondary the Progression Maps (still available on a number of local authority websites, such as the one-to-one tuition area of Leicestershire County Council's site) allow teachers to identify descriptors that fit particular groups of pupils or individuals, and then suggest relevant next-step core targets. For example, in English the progression maps for Reading suggest the characteristics of the 'developing reader' (below level 3), the 'secure developing reader' (level 3), the 'competent reader' (level 4), the 'active reader' (level 5), the 'reflective reader' (level 6) and the 'versatile reader' (above level 6). Examples of pupil work are given for each of these. If the teacher thinks that the description 'sounds like my pupils' they

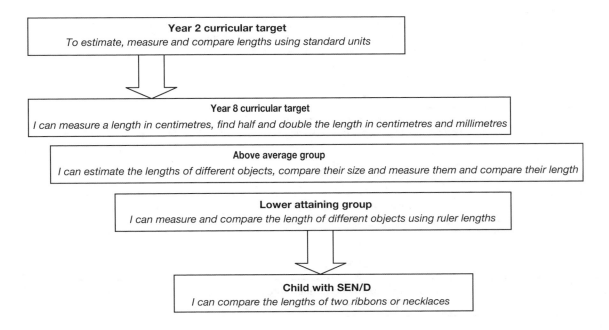

FIGURE 4.3 Layered curricular target for measurement

can then click on a menu for a list of relevant next-step curricular targets, and ideas on how to help a pupil achieve them.

In the Progression Maps for mathematics, each strand of learning is broken down into curricular targets appropriate at different ability levels. Handling data, for example, shows the progression from Step 1 (NC level 2) 'Solve a given problem by organising and interpreting numerical data in simple lists, tables and graphs' through to Step 10 'Identify possible sources of bias and plan how to minimise it' (Year 9).

Curricular targets need not be confined to the core subjects. They can also embrace social and emotional learning. For example (Figure 4.4), a school might decide on a whole-school target that children will work well together in groups. Using the Social and Emotional Aspects of Learning (SEAL) materials (DfES, 2005a) they might then set layered targets for each year group. In Year 6 the target might be 'When working in a group I can tell others if I agree/don't agree with them and why, and listen to others' views, thinking about what they have said'. But some children might not yet have secured earlier learning and have a personal target taken from Year R, 'I can take turns in a group'.

Using differentiated curricular targets for pupils with additional needs has the great advantage of keeping the targets within the realm of the class or subject teacher. The

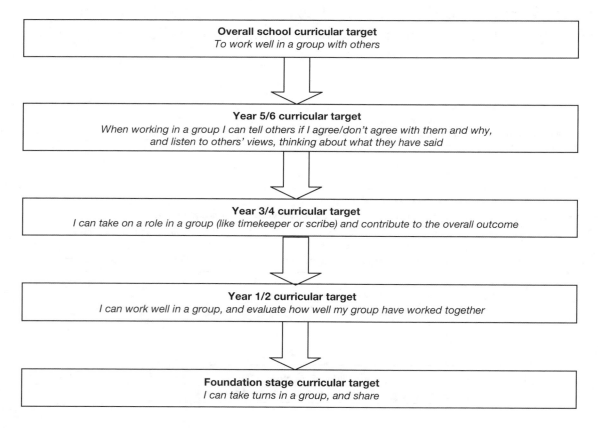

FIGURE 4.4 Layered curricular target for social and emotional learning

targets are linked closely to the work of the class as a whole and will be addressed through the teacher's regular differentiated classroom planning. They have a much better chance, therefore, of guiding teaching and learning than the computer-generated, filing-cabinet targets that characterise too many IEPs.

The SEAL progression in both primary and secondary materials, the facility in the primary literacy and mathematics frameworks for teachers to track back to find linked but earlier core learning objectives, and the exceptionally useful secondary Progression Maps tool all also mean that class and subject teachers *should* (subject to any conclusions the 2012 National Curriculum review may come to on this) reasonably be expected to set differentiated curricular targets for all their pupils, including those who are performing well below age-related expectations. This is the key to a reduction in the SENCO's /INCO's workload. It is also the key to better progress for children who experience barriers to their learning.

Differentiated curricular targets set by the class or subject teacher also have disadvantages, however. While they may be highly relevant to the direction the whole school, class or group is taking, they may not be particularly relevant to the unique and pressing needs of the pupil with SEN or a disability. IEP targets, when arrived at through a shared, group process of prioritising problems (as described in Chapter 1), do help everyone to focus on what really matters. And what really matters is likely to be:

- a problem which the child feels is important and on which they want to work – that is, one which ties in with their main life concerns at the time (like 'learn to do joined-up writing' when the child is really bothered by the difference they have just begun to notice between their written work and that of their peers);
- a problem which underpins others – such as poor concentration, personal organisation or willingness to tackle something new.

Such priorities are often cross-curricular, may relate to outcomes that are wider than just attainment, and will not be addressed solely by curricular targets set by subject teachers, or literacy and mathematics targets set by primary teachers.

An example of the need for targets that go beyond attainment is a story told by Janet Thompson, HMI. Janet describes a Year 10 pupil with a visual impairment who she tracked in school. When Janet observed in class she saw lots of opportunities for paired and small group work – but her tracked pupil always worked with her TA at these times rather than with other students. The girl said 'It has to be like that because she understands my disability. I don't go to after-school clubs because my taxi comes at quarter past four. I don't go to lunch time clubs because that's when I do my Braille'. This girl lived in a small rural village and saw few people other than her mother and sister. Her academic attainment was good, but what life chances would she have in the future? For her, some targets around working and socialising with other students would have been helpful.

Cross-curricular, highly personal targets are not unique to children with SEN or disabilities, however. All children have particular things they want and need to improve on or achieve that are about themselves as individuals rather than as subject-fodder. And as we saw in Chapter 2, some schools do expect all children to set themselves a personal target of high relevance to their immediate concerns. The role of the SENCO/INCO may be to ensure that whole-school target-setting systems do include this element. SENCOs/INCOs are likely to have considerable expertise in devising such targets, and in making them 'SMART'. They might use this expertise to provide pupils, form tutors and class teachers with banks of example targets on which they can draw, covering behaviour, study, organisational, 'learning to learn' and life skills. This would be a very good use for the IEP software that many schools have bought, which often has excellent target banks.

The Achievement for All structured conversation between class teacher/form tutor and parents and pupils (described in Chapter 7) provides another way of arriving at targets. Each structured conversation generates just two to three targets – at least one academic curricular target, and at least one target for what the programme calls 'wider outcomes' of behaviour, attendance, confidence and engagement. For many children, the key target is this 'wider outcome' target, and it often comes from the parent's or pupil's answer to the question 'What is the one thing that is most getting in the way of the child's progress?'

At Torriano Junior school in Camden, for example, the agreed targets for one Year 6 pupil involved in Achievement for All were 'to improve attendance to school target of over 95 per cent', 'to understand personal boundaries and avoid invading the personal space of others', and 'to edit my work including correct use of full stops and capital letters'.

Targets need to be highly visible to children and teachers. That means not kept in filing cabinets, but put on Post-its on the child's desk, in their books, on the wall, on cards hung above their heads, or written in their planners. The more visual they are, the better – a photograph of the child doing what the target requires, for example. Some schools, like Perry Beeches Infants in Birmingham, have developed a range of 'I can' target sheets from which children chose – castles, trains, rockets. Their chosen sheet is then laminated and blu-tacked to the wall, or kept in a basket on the table where they work. Every time children work towards their target they place a coloured spot on their chart. Once they have achieved the target a star is placed on the chart. Three stars mean the target has been consistently achieved.

Class xx

Literacy targets To proofread my work (Morgan) To plan clear sections for my writing (Sayeed, John)	Speech, language and communication targets To say if I haven't understood and ask my teacher to say again/explain (Marius)
Behaviour targets To get to class on time (Morgan) To sit a long way away from people who wind me up like Jack (Paul)	Other targets

TABLE 4.1 Achievement for All targets: Class map

Some secondary schools involved in Achievement for All put the structured conversation targets on the school's intranet, with ideas on how subject teachers can help students achieve them. Others have compiled the targets for pupils into class-by-class composite target maps (Table 4.1).

Whole-school systems for setting and reviewing personal targets, as distinct from simply subject targets, are evident in an increasing number of schools. Here, form tutors, learning mentors or class teachers meet regularly with pupils to discuss their overall learning needs, and consider progress not only in subject learning but also in so-called soft or non-cognitive skills such as communication, the ability to work as part of a team, reliability, punctuality and perseverance, knowing how to work independently without close supervision, and being resilient in the face of difficulties.

If whole-school systems for setting personal targets that transcend subject boundaries are not in place, however, a system for pupils with SEN or disabilities might be the one used at Coombe Boys in the case study in Chapter 2. Here, teaching assistants joined in the Academic Mentoring days and contributed suggestions for appropriate personal, cross-curricular targets to the meeting between form tutor and pupil. Another model is used at King Solomon High in Redbridge, where TAs act as key workers for students with SEN/D and meet with them to jointly set and monitor weekly targets.

Tracking progress

Tracking overall curricular progress

As with target-setting, systems for tracking the progress of *all* pupils on the curricular and numerical targets set with and for them are now expected of all schools. Ofsted (2011), for example, noted that in the most effective schools, teachers 'carefully assessed and tracked pupils, responding quickly with targeted interventions if there was any indication of underachievement'.

The most effective tracking systems for pupils with SEN/D will be embedded within the systems used for the class or group. This ensures that class or subject teachers are monitoring their pupils' progress throughout the year and have ownership and responsibility for taking action where any pupil's progress is causing concern. The SENCO's/INCO's role will be to develop and refine whole-school tracking systems so that they are fully inclusive and so that all pupils' progress is systematically monitored and reviewed, with the findings acted on.

An example of the kinds of whole-school tracking systems now used in many effective schools comes from the Trafalgar School in Wiltshire. The school uses a 'Tick/Star/Cross' target-setting system where each student is given a good GCSE grade and an aspirational GCSE grade in each subject from the start of Year 7. These targets are based on all available data on entry. Each year group receives six reports a year. If they are working at their good grade they achieve a tick, if at their aspirational grade they receive a star. If they are not achieving either good or aspirational grades, they get a cross. If a student is achieving their aspirational grade three times in a row, then that grade will be upped to maintain the challenge. The students also have their own personal 'flight path' – as a visual representation of their achievement – which they complete after every round of Tick/Star/Cross. Rachael Faulkner, Deputy Head, notes the advantages of the system for pupils with SEN/D. Whereas IEPs 'helped to make our SEN students look different, which is certainly not what we wanted', the Tick/Star/Cross system enables the Learning Support team to work effectively:

> Our department has a very high status role in the whole school process and we work across the whole school with all teaching staff to ensure that our students receive the strategies they need. If it does not work then we change it more quickly than previously, as we have these reports six times a year.

Tables 4.2 and 4.3 show examples of tracking systems typically used in primary schools, developed in the Intensifying Support Programme (DfES, 2006f) and adapted here to include pupils with learning difficulties. Children's names are entered each term against the NC level they have reached. The shaded areas show the NC levels that correspond to nationally expected attainment. The tracking sheet shows at a glance those pupils who are not moving at the rate they should be over the course of the year.

74

	Summer Year 1	Autumn Year 2	Spring Year 2	Summer Year 2
Upper L3/3a				Simrun
Secure L3/3b		Simrun	Simrun	Mehnaz Marion
Lower L3/3c	Simrun			Mahfuza
Upper L2/2a		Mehnaz Marion	Mahfuza Sofia Mehnaz Marion	Anass Ruby Chloe Charlotte Sofia
Secure L2/2b	Mehnaz Marion	Anass Mahfuza	Anass Ruby Chloe Charlotte	Sumayyah Shaylayne Michal Jennifer Rhiannon Georgia Ioana Anthony Jem Mikaeel
Lower L2/2c	Mahfuza	Ruby Chloe Charlotte Sofia	Joshua Sumayyah Shaylayne Michal Jennifer Rhiannon Georgia Ioana Anthony Jem Mikaeel	Joshua Erin Jacob Caitlin
Upper L1/1a	Ruby Chloe Charlotte Sofia	Sumayyah Shaylayne Michal Jennifer Rhiannon Georgia Ioana Anthony Jem Mikaeel	Erin Jacob Caitlin	Finlay Lemin Joseph
Secure L1/1b	Erin Sumayyah Shaylayne Michal Jennifer Rhiannon Georgia Ioana Anthony Jem Mikaeel	Joshua Erin Jacob Caitlin	Finlay Lemin Joseph	Tia Aiisha Meia
Lower L1/1c	Lemin Joshua Jacob Caitlin	Shivan Tia Aiisha Meia Finlay Lemin Joseph	Shivan Tia Aiisha Meia	Shivan Kitty
W/1c	Kitty Shivan Tia Aiisha Meia Finlay Joseph	Kitty	Nermien Kitty	Nermien
P4/5/6	Nermien	Nermien		
	Summer Year 1	Autumn Year 2	Spring Year 2	Summer Year 2

TABLE 4.2 Tracking progress: Year 2 reading

	Summer Year 2	Autumn Year 3	Spring Year 3	Summer Year 3
Upper L4/4a				
Secure L4/4b				
Lower L4/4c				Mary Ann
Upper L3/3a		Mary Ann	Mary Ann	Zakiriya
Secure L3/3b	Mary Ann		Ronan Zakiriya Marsha	Ronan Marsha Grace Aysa
Lower L3/3c		Ronan	Grace Aysa	Jasmine Destiney Lily Eren Samir Joshua
Upper L2/2a	Ronan Zakiriya	Zakiriya Marsha Grace Joshua Aysa	Jasmine Destiney Lily Eren Samir Joshua	Julia Dea Rocco Helen Suruti Jordis Gulse
Secure L2/2b	Marsha Grace Aysa	Jasmine Lily Eren Samir	Julia Dea Rocco Helen Suruti Jordis Gulse	Jumana Yasir Pia Siddita Holly
Lower L2/2c	Jasmine Destiney Lily Eren Samir Joshua	Julia Destiney Dea Rocco Helen Suruti Jordis	Jumana Yasir Pia Siddita Holly	Daniel Josphine
Upper L1/1a	Julia Dea Rocco Helen Suruti Jordis Gulse	Yasir Pia Siddita Holly Gulse	Daniel Josphine	
Secure L1/1b	Jumana Yasir Pia Siddita Holly	Jumana Daniel Josphine	Patrick Melissa	Patrick Katie Melissa
Lower L1/1c	Daniel Josphine	Melissa	Katie	
W/1c	Patrick Katie Melissa	Patrick Katie		Alfie
P4/5/6	Alfie	Alfie	Alfie	

TABLE 4.3 Tracking progress: Year 3 mathematics

Table 4.4 shows another type of tracking system, used in a language unit at Wallands primary school in East Sussex. Children's names are entered in an appropriate cell according to the progress they have made over a school year; colour coding shows at a glance which children have stood still or gone backwards, which have made satisfactory progress (a 3 points score gain), which have made good progress (4 points), and so on.

Tracking systems like these are helpful in setting high expectations, enabling class teachers to identify all pupils not on track to achieve nationally expected levels. They can then seek advice from the SENCO or other inclusion specialists (such as EMA coordinator or intervention manager) on appropriate interventions to enable these children to catch up.

They do, however, run the risk of leaving out that very small group of pupils for whom achieving national benchmark levels is not an appropriate expectation. For this reason, a more inclusive tracking system will gather termly information on whether each child is on track to meet their own individual numerical targets. At Kentish Town Primary School in London, for example, each class teacher receives a termly print-out showing which children have exceeded, which have met and which have fallen short of their termly NC sublevel targets. A simple traffic light system (green for progress ahead of expected progress towards end of year targets, amber for on target and red for below expected progress) is also used in some schools. The SENCO's/INCO's role is then to monitor the proportion of pupils with SEN or disabilities (or if they are inclusion coordinator, pupils from other vulnerable groups such as EAL learners or gifted and talented pupils) who are on amber or green.

In the secondary phase, the system used at Coombe Boys' School in Kingston fulfils a similar purpose. Each pupil's end-of-term 'Position statement' tells them whether they are on track to achieve their numerical targets.

Effective schools will also keep track of pupils' year-on-year progress. An example can be found in the toolkit at the end of this book, in the form of a class handover profile. If this is not part of whole-school systems, the SENCO/INCO can keep such individual records for pupils with SEN/D, adding information on additional provision that was in place in a given year or term (Tables 4.5 and 4.6). Nothing will impress an Ofsted inspector more than this kind of overview.

Tracking like this needs to be informed by a secure knowledge of what constitutes satisfactory progress – approximately three NC level 'points' over a school year in Key Stages 2, 3 and 4, using the points system shown in Table 4.7.

	P	1c	1b	1a	2c	2b	2a	3c	3b	3a	4c	4b	4a	5c	5b	5a
P																
1c																
1b																
1a																
2c																
2b																
2a																
3c																
3b																
3a																
4c																
4b																
4a																
5c																
5b																
5a																

Children who have stood still or gone backwards
Children who have made 2 points progress
Children who have made 4 points progress
Children who have made 6 points progress
Children who have made more than 6 points progress

TABLE 4.4 Wallands CP School: progress tracker for maths

Child X   d.o.b. 03.04.05

	MATHS	SPEAKING AND LISTENING	READING	WRITING
November 2010 Support: Social skills: 2 x 20 min per week	P5	P5	P5	P5
March 2011 LSA 1:1 in class 10 mins/day Sp&lang group of 2, 3 x 20 mins/week Lit group every day Reading group 2 x week	P6	P5	P4	P6
November 2011 *Place to be* provision Plus the above support continued	P8	P7	P8	P6

Update January 2012: CAMHS referral made. All support continues. Most ability levels have remained the same.

TABLE 4.5 Overview of support and progress

Information on what constitutes satisfactory progress for pupils working at the level of the P scales is available from the DfE in progression matrices and via RAISEonline.

Progress over the course of an intervention

A second element of tracking that is specific to pupils with additional needs is tracking progress over the course of an intervention, using 'before' and 'after' measures. A small-group intervention to improve pupils' social, emotional and behavioural skills might for example have a before and after assessment using GL Assessment's emotional literacy measures, or the Goodman Strengths and Difficulties Questionnaire. Children in a nurture group would be assessed at the beginning and end of their placement using the Boxall Profile. Children taking part in a literacy intervention might have their reading or spelling age assessed using one of a number of standardised tests. A useful proforma for collecting pre- and post-intervention data can be found in the toolkit section of this book.

NC Level	Y1			Y2			Y3			Y4			Y5			Y6		
	Term 1	T 2	T 3	T 1	T 2	T 3	T 1	T 2	T 3	T 1	T 2	T 3	T 1	T 2	T 3	T 1	T 2	T 3
5																		
4A																		▓
4B																		▓
4C															▓			
3A															▓			
3B												▓						
3C												▓						
2A			▓	▓						▓								
2B			▓	▓						▓								
2C																		
1A																		
1B																		
1C																		
P8			+	+*														
P7		°	°	°														
P6	◆	+◆	°◆	◆														
P5	+° *◆	*	*															
P4																		
Interventions in place	Social skills 2 x 20 min per week	Sp. and lang. gp., 3 x 20 mins/ week Reading group 2 x week	As for term 2	Place 2 Be plus sup-port as in Y1 terms 2 and 3	CAMHS referral made													

Expected English and Maths level for age group shaded

* Child's Reading level ◆ Writing level + Maths level ° Speaking and listening level

TABLE 4.6 Example of a cumulative tracking sheet for a Year 2 child

NC/P level	Sub-level	Point score
P1i		0.5
P1ii		0.7
P2i		0.9
P2ii		1.1
P3i		1.3
P3ii		1.5
P4		2
P5		3
P6		4
P7		5
P8		6
L1	c b a	7 9 11
L2	c b a	13 15 17
L3	a b a	19 21 23
L4	c b a	27 27 29
L5	c b a	31 33 35
L6	c b a	37 39 41
L7	c b a	43 45 47
L8 (Maths only)		51

GCSE GRADE	A*	A	B	C	D	E	F	G	U
Points	58	52	46	40	34	28	22	16	0

TABLE 4.7 The National Curriculum points system

Evaluation

All these tracking systems have the added advantage of making possible something that IEPs could never achieve – allowing the SENCO/INCO or SMT to evaluate the effectiveness of particular interventions, and the progress of pupils with SEN/D in their school. They can, for example, answer the questions:

- What percentage of lower-attaining pupils and those with SEN/D met their end of year or key stage numerical targets, and how does this compare with the percentage of pupils without SEN or disabilities achieving their targets?
- Which interventions are proving effective in helping pupils with SEN or disabilities meet their numerical targets? Which aren't?
- Does RAISEonline show that the value added progress of pupils with SEN or disabilities in our school is at least as good as the national progress?
- Have we increased the percentage of pupils with SEN or disabilities meeting their numerical targets since last year, and what did we do to achieve this?

Reviewing progress

Just as effective SEN/D systems require that schools track pupil progress made as a result of additional or different provision, so it also requires a regular and frequent review schedule for individuals.

This need not mean a lot of extra work or separate SEN procedures. Our case study schools in Chapter 2 were all successful in combining review requirements for pupils with SEN/D with what they did for all pupils – twice-yearly parent meetings extended from 10 to 30 minutes for children with SEN, or Academic Mentoring days at which TAs join pupils, tutor and perhaps Head of Year to take stock of progress.

Again, these integrated systems have the advantage of keeping ownership of the progress of pupils with SEN or disabilities where it belongs – with those who are immediately responsible for their subject learning and pastoral care.

Refinements for pupils with SEN or disabilities will, however, be necessary. Reviews must, for example, look at progress across the curriculum and often behavioural, organisational, study, life and 'learning-to-learn' skills as well as progress in individual subjects. This is particularly important in secondary schools where uneven performance across subjects can often give vital clues about what helps and what hinders a pupil's learning or behaviour. The reviews must be one-to-one, unlike the group 'learning conversations' between class teacher or form tutor and target pupils used in some schools.

Review systems for pupils with SEN or disabilities should also build in a review of the extent to which pupils' classroom curricular and personal targets have been met, as well as overall numerical progress in NC levels, sublevels and P scales.

They should review not only the pupil's progress but also the effectiveness of the school's actions. Is there evidence from teachers' differentiated planning, for example, that staff are taking account of the pupil's individual needs? Have any additional interventions used proved effective, on the evidence from before and after measures and evidence from what the pupil, parents/carers and staff all think? Is further intervention necessary, and if so what types of provision from the school's provision map might be appropriate?

These review questions help hold the school to account for what it is doing to support the pupil. Review meetings also provide an opportunity to hold everyone involved (pupil, parents/carers, staff, outside agencies) to account for any actions they agreed to undertake at the last meeting or review.

Another added dimension to review meetings that involve pupils with SEN or disabilities is the cast list involved. While reviews for most students may only involve pupil, parent/carer and class teacher or form tutor, those for pupils with SEN or disabilities might also involve the SENCO/INCO, perhaps the Head of Year in a secondary school, and any outside agencies that are involved.

Finally, there may be additional work to be done with both pupils and parents/carers to secure their confident engagement in review meetings. This is discussed in Chapter 7.

The additional elements in SEN reviews mean that the SENCO/INCO may want to build on regular school record-keeping by adding additional headings or prompts. A possible set of agenda prompts is included in the toolkit section of this book.

Summary

This chapter has considered ways in which SEN-specific practices can increasingly be subsumed within whole-school systems for setting targets for pupils and tracking their subsequent progress.

It has also suggested additional features that might need to be added to whole-school systems, if they are to fully meet the very particular needs of pupils who in some way fall outside the norm. These additional features are summarised in Table 4.8 below.

WHOLE-SCHOOL SYSTEMS	SEN ADAPTATIONS
Target-setting – numerical	Use RAISEonline and local authority data to set numerical targets for pupils functioning well below age-related expectations, including those working at 'P' levels.
Target-setting – curricular	Teach class and subject teachers how to track back to identify curricular targets for pupils functioning well below age-related expectations, including those working at 'P' levels. Provide banks of targets for behaviour, study, organisational, 'learning to learn' and life skills.
Tracking progress	Monitor the impact of intervention programmes by using 'before' and 'after' data. Monitor the progress of pupils with SEN and disabilities towards numerical targets, as a group
Reviewing progress	Ensure that reviews • are cross-curricular; • include a review of the achievement of curricular and personal targets; • are individual, rather than involving a group; • involve others beyond the pupil, tutor or class teacher and parent – for example, SENCO, head of year, TA/key worker, outside agencies; • consider how effective the school's provision has proved to be; • check whether all concerned have completed the actions they undertook to take at the last meeting or review; • are preceded by work to secure the confident participation of pupil and parents/carers.

TABLE **4.8** Suggested adaptations to existing systems

Achieving targets
Adaptations to everyday classroom teaching

There are four things that make a real difference to the achievement of children with SEN or disabilities. They are:

- additional provision made by the school, in the form of time-limited, evidence-based intervention programmes to address gaps in children's language, literacy, mathematical and social and emotional learning;
- interventions that extend beyond the school and involve outside agencies, from disabled children's services to youth offending teams, in providing support to the child in the context of the family and community.
- the meaningful involvement of parents/carers and young people themselves, so as to increase aspiration, motivation and support at home;
- adaptations to everyday classroom teaching, signalled via teachers' medium- and short-term planning.

This chapter is about the last of these four. It is about whole-school systems that expect all teachers to take account of the needs of pupils with SEN or disabilities (and for that matter more able pupils, EAL learners and other vulnerable groups) when they plan their teaching, and monitor whether this expectation is being met.

Successfully embedding thinking about SEN and disabilities into teachers' planning is essential to beating bureaucracy. Like setting targets and tracking progress for all pupils, it enables schools to use everyday systems that already exist in order to provide for SEN/D, rather than separate paper trails.

IEPs were intended to be the mechanism for influencing teachers' planning. But as we saw in the case studies in Chapter 2, there is little evidence that they successfully did so. On the other hand, the case studies show that class and subject teachers do appear to make use of pupil profiles provided by the SENCO, when combined with planning formats which have an extra column, row or cell in which teachers are expected to record the differentiation that will be in place for pupils with SEN/D.

Embedding SEN and disability in teachers' planning takes time and effort, however (see Figure 5.1). First, there will need to be professional development for all staff on the basic principles. Second, it may be necessary to introduce new planning formats, or amend existing ones. Third, SENCOs/INCOs need to spend time working alongside class and subject teachers to model and coach the process of differentiated planning. Fourth, the school will need to consider building the requirement to plan for pupils with additional needs into performance management. They will also need to build in systems for monitoring teachers' planning to identify staff who may need further support or challenge.

Mapping out this four-part strategy can take care of another potential piece of bureaucracy – the requirement to produce an accessibility plan showing how curriculum access will be provided for disabled pupils. The SENCO/INCO can simply identify the actions that need to be taken (staff training, modelling/coaching, adapting planning formats and performance management) into the School Improvement or Development Plan. Government guidance has consistently made clear (Independent Review Unit, 2007) that embedding curriculum access plans into overall school development plans is an acceptable and sensible step.

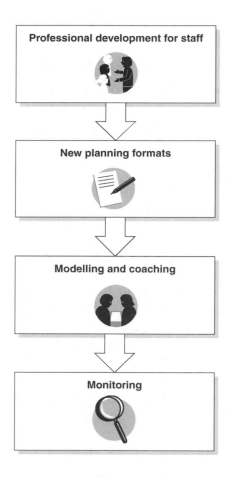

FIGURE 5.1 A four-part strategy to embed thinking about SEN

Professional development for staff

The National Curriculum (2000) statutory inclusion statement sets out three key principles essential to planning and teaching:

- setting suitable learning challenges;
- responding to pupils' diverse learning needs;
- overcoming potential barriers to learning and assessment for individuals and groups of pupils.

These principles form the basis for professional development that SENCOs/INCOs can provide for staff. They can be translated into practice and represented visually as shown in Figure 5.2.

 ## *Learning objectives*

SENCOs/INCOs can explain to staff that when planning for a class they need first to think about the range of learning objectives that they need to cover. The majority of the class will be working on an objective linked to age-related expectations. Some pupils, however, will need to work on objectives that are more advanced, others on objectives that come earlier in the progression set out in the relevant curriculum frameworks or programmes of study. This will apply even in setted classes. In many

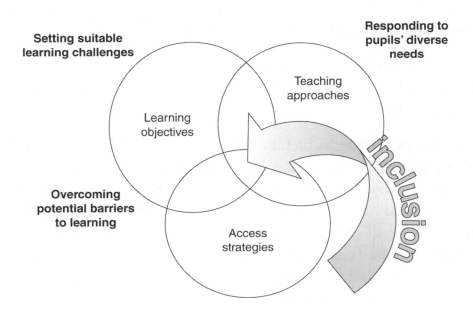

FIGURE 5.2 The circles of inclusion

schools, the range can be very great – from P3 to Level 4a in maths in one Year 3 class, for example.

Teachers plan for this range of ability in different ways. Typically, they may plan activities at three levels – for a group of pupils working below age-related expectations, a group at age-related expectations, and a group who should be expected to achieve above age-related expectations.

For some children with SEN or disabilities, and pupils who are highly gifted, there is a need for a further level of planning, often at an individual level. This should describe arrangements for those who are working well below, or well above, age-related expectations.

It is this level of planning that is often missed out, usually because teachers are uncertain about learning objectives that lie outside the usual terrain, and have not had the opportunity to work alongside an expert in planning how to help pupils achieve them. They tend to plan (Ofsted, 2004) 'how pupils with SEN could be engaged rather than on what pupils needed to learn next … this was a common reason why a significant number of pupils with SEN made too little progress'.

There is a problem, too, in the planning that many teachers do at even the three levels of below, at and above age-related expectations – the 'must/should/could' that we could call 'normal differentiation'. All too often the differentiation is based on outcomes not learning objectives. The group working at below average expectations is simply expected to produce less in terms of outcomes (a sentence instead of a paragraph, for example), while the learning objective remains the same for the whole class. Alternatively, the planning simply notes that the lower-attaining group will be supported by a TA to achieve the general class learning objective (or at least remain reasonably quiet while everyone else does).

What SENCOs will want to encourage colleagues to do is write into their planning *different* learning objectives for groups and in some cases individuals, all linked into the same overall class focus.

The former National Strategies literacy and numeracy frameworks for the primary phase, and the secondary progression maps, modelled the way in which a teacher can take a learning objective for a particular group and track forwards (for more able pupils) and backwards (for lower attaining) to find linked objectives appropriate to the needs of individuals or groups. The structure and the electronic format of those primary frameworks (still available on many schools' networks) supported such multi-level curriculum planning, and allowed teachers to easily track back through a progression strand to locate earlier, and later, learning objectives. The interactivity offered by the electronic framework enables exemplar teaching units to be amended so that teachers can add in differentiated learning objectives.

The principle of identifying different learning objectives for individuals and groups is one that staff easily grasp. Equally, the teachers will understand that planning differentiated learning objectives will give a focus to the work of additional adults providing support in the classroom. Research (Moyles and Suschitzky, 1997; Blatchford *et al.*, 2012) has shown that teaching assistants tend to focus more on helping children complete tasks successfully (what children are meant to *do*) rather than on what they are meant to *learn*. Differentiated learning objectives that are communicated to TAs can stop this happening.

Even though they see the advantages and support the principle, the idea of multiple learning objectives can still nevertheless sometimes alarm staff. How, they will ask, are they expected to teach a class of thirty children working on a number of different learning objectives?

There is no point in pretending that this is easy; better to say that it represents the peak of a teacher's skilled performance, something to work towards and something that even the most skilled teacher will not achieve all of the time. Even so, people will be able to give you examples of how, when they are in the 'exposition' phase of the lesson, they are able to drop in questions at different levels, targeted at different named pupils, or re-iterate an explanation of a concept covered last year for the benefit of pupils who are still trying to master that particular idea.

They will even more easily be able to give examples of how they design tasks at different levels for the part of the lesson when pupils are working independently or in groups – this is part of every teacher's planning repertoire. Practical help, too, is available through the former National Strategies' planning sections of the primary literacy and mathematics frameworks, which in electronic versions have direct links to resources for pupils working above, below or well below age-related expectations for any given unit of work. Table 5.1 gives an example.

In providing training to colleagues, SENCOs/INCOs will want to help them consider the assessment for learning guidance in the Table 5.1 example. The plenary part of any lesson or unit of work should also be differentiated, so as to use it to assess the success of individuals and groups in meeting particular learning objectives set for them. This too needs to be built into planning – not just what will be taught for children working outside age-related expectations, or how it will be taught, but also how it will be assessed.

Finally, SENCOs/INCOs may want to help colleagues think about ways of building children's *personal* targets into their planning. Tracked-back learning

CHILDREN'S LEARNING OUTCOMES	ASSESSMENT FOR LEARNING
I can talk about how I solve problems using counting	How did you find out how many more pencils were needed so that children had one each?
I can count up to 20 objects I know that the number of objects does not change even if I move the objects around	How many 10p coins are in the purse? How do you know you have that number/ How do you know you have counted every coin?
I can compare numbers up to 20 and say which number is bigger	Would you rather have 9 pence or 15 pence? Why?

Resource links to existing published material

Mathematical challenges for able pupils Key Stages 1 and 2

ACTIVITIES
Four-pin bowling Activity 1
Gold Bars
Snakes and ladders

Intervention programmes

Springboard unit
None currently available

Supporting children with gaps in their mathematical understanding (Wave 3)

	RESOURCE
Can only begin counting at one; inaccurately counts objects when re-arranged; has no consistent recognition of a small number of objects; lacks systematic approaches	1 YR + / -

TABLE 5.1 Primary Framework for literacy and mathematics: Year 1 Block A – Counting, partitioning and calculating Unit 1 (extract)

objectives work well for the majority of children with learning difficulties, for most of the time. However, as we saw in Chapter 4, there will be particular things that children with SEN or disabilities need to learn that are a real priority for their overall development, but may not always link to the class learning focus. As an example, the absolute priority for a child at a particular time might be to learn to take turns when sharing equipment, or to learn how to use question words when speaking. These are not targets that necessarily relate to learning objectives in a teacher's overall class planning. If a teacher was planning a mathematics lesson on measurement, for example, tracking back through the mathematics framework would not take her to learning objectives about taking turns or asking questions. It could be more important for her to think, in her planning, about how she could use the general context of the lesson to support the child's progress towards these priority personal targets. She might make a note in her planning, for example, to say that she would put the child in a group of three for a practical measuring activity, and explain to him beforehand that what she was looking for was to see him take turns with the measuring tape in the playground. If his target was to learn to ask questions using the question word 'What' she might make a note that in the plenary she would model the questions 'What did you do?' and 'What did you find out?' and then have the child put the questions to each group in turn.

Building personal learning targets into teachers' everyday planning in ways like this means that children with SEN or disabilities can do most of their learning with their peers, in the classroom, rather than be pulled out for separate IEP-related activities. It is like a child doing their special physiotherapy exercises in the context of a PE lesson, or their own special speech and language therapy activities in the context of mathematics or history.

This will not always be possible; sometimes it is simply more practical, economic and effective to provide the special learning that a child needs outside of the work of the class as a whole. An example might be a child with severe learning difficulties whose priority personal target is to learn how to cross the road safely, find the right bus home or pay the right fare. These would be occasions when separate planning would be appropriate, rather than trying to build the learning into the planning of class or subject teachers. Sometimes, we do try to stretch 'inclusion' (in the sense of being physically present in every mainstream lesson) too far.

Giangreco and his colleagues (1993) provide us with a vocabulary for thinking about planning for children with SEN or disabilities, which may be helpful to share with colleagues when providing training.

Giangreco talks about four different options for student participation in general classroom activities.

The first option he calls *same*. This describes occasions when the student with SEN can pursue the same objectives and the same activities as others in the class. The example he gives is a lesson where a class is practising songs for a concert for parents.

91

The second option is '*multi-level*'. This is where students are all involved in a lesson in the same curriculum area but are pursuing different learning objectives at multiple levels based on their individual needs. This corresponds to the idea of tracking back (or forward) through relevant sequenced objectives such as those in the former national frameworks.

The third option Giangreco calls '*curriculum overlapping*'. This occurs when a student with SEN is involved in the same lesson as the class, but is pursuing objectives from different curricular areas. This would correspond to the example of covering social/emotional or speech and language objectives in a maths lesson about measurement.

Finally, Giangreco describes an option he calls '*alternative*'. This refers to times when the regular class work does not offer reasonable opportunities to address the particular priority learning objectives for a student with SEN, and they need to be addressed discretely in a way that is not linked to the work of the class as a whole. It corresponds to the example of work on road safety and independent travel described above.

All teachers need to understand the difference between 'same', 'multi-level', 'overlapping' and 'alternative' learning objectives. They can then consider which of these options is most appropriate at any given time for a particular individual or group when planning. SENCOs/INCOs might want to help them by providing a flow chart of questions, like the one in Figure 5.3.

Access strategies/reasonable adjustments

Having explained how everyday lesson planning can note tracked-back learning objectives for children with SEN or disabilities, or provide the context for priority learning objectives that are not linked to those of the class as a whole, SENCOs/INCOs can go on to explore occasions when a child with SEN or disabilities *can* work on exactly the same learning objective as the rest of the group or class, if appropriate access strategies – or, as disability legislation frames them, reasonable adjustments – are used to overcome a barrier between the child and the learning.

A good example to give is that of a child with a visual impairment, but with no learning difficulties. Staff will readily agree that there is no reason for such a child to work on earlier learning objectives or be placed in a group of 'less able' children. If the barrier created by the visual impairment can be overcome by appropriate

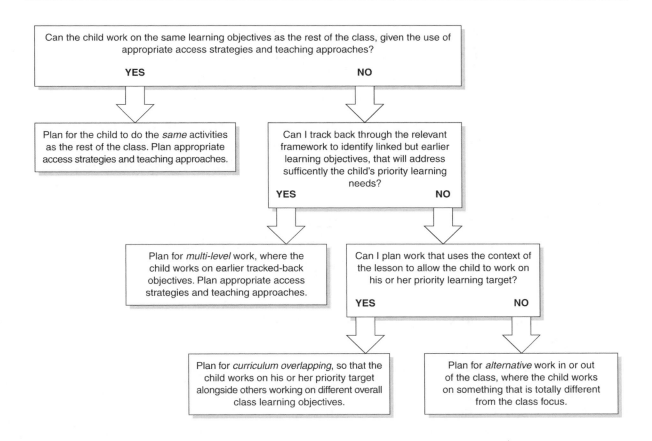

FIGURE 5.3 Questions flow chart

access strategies (by using an enlarged text, for example, or materials in Braille) the child can be expected to achieve the same learning objectives as their peers.

You could then ask staff what they would say about a bright child with behavioural difficulties – one with ADHD, for example. Does this child need work on earlier learning objectives? If he is placed with a group who are working at earlier levels (perhaps because they happen to have a TA with them), what are the implications for his learning? Are there any access strategies the teacher could use to overcome the barriers presented by this child's behaviour to his own learning, and the learning of others? Ideas might be increased opportunities to be 'up and doing' rather than sitting, building in breaks when the child can for example take a message to another class or have a brief period of exercise, or providing an individual workstation that is screened at the sides.

Finally, you could ask staff to think about a child with dyslexic difficulties, who can express himself well orally and is quick to pick up new ideas. Do they think they need to plan for different learning objectives for him in science, maths, history, geography and so on? Does his slow reading, his brief and scrappy written work

93

mean he is not capable of understanding the subject content of a lesson – or does it just mean that he needs access strategies that provide him with scaffolded or alternative means of recording, such as those described in the toolkit section of this book? Are there subjects where he might need both differentiated learning objectives *and* access strategies? An example would be in English, where the class are working on spelling, and he does need to work on earlier learning objectives but might also need the access strategy of having a buddy read instructions on a spelling worksheet for him.

Questions like these, and the discussion they will prompt, will help colleagues to be aware that many underachieving children can work on the same learning objectives as others in the class, as long as the teacher plans access strategies to overcome a barrier between the child and the learning.

The idea of using access strategies extends to the whole area of inclusion, not just to SEN or disability. For EAL learners, the barrier might be difficulty in understanding the teacher's language as she explains a task. The access strategy might be simultaneous use of the child's home language. Or the teacher might plan to 'chunk' her speech into shorter sentences, use pictures or real objects to accompany her instructions, and check on comprehension by asking the child to repeat the instruction back – all access strategies that would work equally well for a child in the class with speech and language difficulties. For gifted and talented pupils, the barrier might be the difference between the speed of their thoughts and their ability to get these thoughts onto paper. The teacher could overcome the barrier by suggesting the child uses concept mapping, for example, to get their ideas down quickly in a visual format. This strategy would work equally well for a dyslexic pupil in the class.

Access strategies should form part of every teacher's planning for personalised learning. Whenever they design tasks and activities for children, they need to be thinking about what might get in the way of learning, and be creative about ways around the barrier. What SENCOs/INCOs will want them to avoid is using just one, not very creative access strategy – that of allocating a teaching assistant to support the group who are likely to have difficulties. This is the most common access strategy used, but it places a heavy burden on the TA, who has to coax a group of children into completing tasks that have not been designed with their particular needs in mind, and may not even be addressing appropriate learning objectives. It is also something that Ofsted are now examining closely in inspections – so teachers need to consider carefully whether they are spending less time with pupils with SEN/D than they are with other pupils, whether pupils with SEN/D have opportunities to work independently, and to work with peers during lessons.

Teaching approaches

As well as planning access strategies to overcome specific barriers to learning, teachers need to think about the more general teaching approaches that are appropriate to particular types of SEN or disabilities.

Children with learning difficulties often benefit, for example, from teaching approaches which make abstract concepts real for them by making links to their everyday experiences. This is particularly so in mathematics, where building work on 'using and applying' into all lesson planning, rather than teaching it discretely, has been one of the benefits for children with SEN/D of the revised primary mathematics Framework.

These are some other examples of matching teaching approaches to particular needs:

- Children on the autistic spectrum benefit from visual approaches – props used to back up a story or an explanation, and visual timetables that give a sense of routine and help them understand what will be expected of them and when.
- Children whose behaviour presents challenges may benefit from absolute clarity about what is expected of them, and opportunities for active and interactive learning that involves them in 'doing' rather than sitting passively.
- Children with learning difficulties or those on the autistic spectrum might need tasks that are relatively closed – that is, where the task is structured for them and they do not have to invent their own ways of going about it ('Follow the step-by-step instructions on the card…'). This might contrast with the need of more able children to be set tasks that are more open-ended or extended in time ('Devise your own experiment to explore friction').

Drawing on a variety of teaching styles and approaches (open and closed tasks, short and long tasks, visual, auditory or kinaesthetic learning), matched to the needs of individuals, forms the background to planning for both teacher exposition and independent or group activities.

Planning a staff meeting or part of an INSET day

The first step, then, for SENCOs/INCOs who want to influence teachers' planning is to provide training, either at a staff meeting or as part of an INSET day, on the 'three circles' model – getting the learning objectives right, using specific access strategies/reasonable adjustments to overcome barriers to learning, and drawing on a variety of teaching styles and approaches.

Materials for such training are available on the DVD *Leading on intervention* (DfES 2006d). They are designed for primary schools but could readily be adapted by a secondary SENCO. They include a handout on the three circles model and a range of discussion questions, for example those in Figure 5.4 below.

Teachers go on to work in year group or class teams and consider a child with SEN/D or a child whose behaviour presents barriers to learning. They share an example of short-term planning they have brought with them and together identify the appropriate learning objectives for the child, any teaching styles or approaches that might be particularly effective, and any specific barriers that might need to be overcome in order to make sure the child can access the learning objectives, using a checklist of inclusive teaching strategies as a prompt. Groups feed back their best idea for an access strategy or teaching approach.

Training like this should include teaching assistants wherever possible, and should tackle the issue of communicating planning to the TA or TAs who are working with a class. In the most effective schools, TAs take an active part in departmental and lesson planning, and can often contribute a specialist knowledge about access strategies and teaching approaches that will work for a particular type of SEN or a particular pupil. They cannot be expected to provide effective support unless they know in advance what the pupils are to learn (the learning objectives for the class as a whole and for the pupils they are supporting) and what their role is to be. At Coombe Boys' school, the case study school we looked at in Chapter 2, TAs are provided with teachers' planners and a checklist of information to be stored in these. The information includes schemes of work, short- and long-term curriculum plans and class lists with annotated needs.

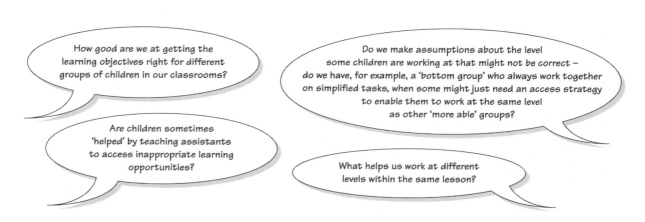

FIGURE 5.4 Example discussion questions

Planning formats

Having provided staff with a conceptual model to help them think about differentiating their planning, the next step might be to consult with them on modifications to the existing planning formats used in school.

It will be important to reassure colleagues that they are not being asked to write separate plans for all the children in a class. The former government's document *Making Good Progress* put this well:

> The personalised classroom does not entail having up to 30 separate teaching plans; it is about having one strong inclusive teaching plan which allows as much room as possible for individual engagement, targeted support, a degree of choice and respect for the range of abilities and interests in the class.
>
> (DfES 2007a)

Staff might decide that planning formats have a dedicated space (extra boxes, columns or rows) on which they can note particular adaptations they will make for pupils with SEN or disabilities, more able pupils or other groups such as EAL learners. Table 5.2 shows an example for the secondary phase; Table 2.2 in Chapter 2 shows one for the primary phase.

Alternatively, staff might decide to add a blank version of the three overlapping circles to the school's planning format, so that they can write in any learning objectives different from those for the class as a whole, any particular teaching approaches they will use to meet the needs of individuals, and any access strategies/ reasonable adjustments required (Figure 5.5).

Another idea might be for the SENCO/INCO to add a standard extra box to the planning format, containing a list of inclusive teaching strategies applicable to a wide range of special or individual needs. When planning for a particular class, the class or subject teacher simply has to reflect on needs present in the group and tick or highlight the strategies they want to make sure they use. A possible model for this is provided in the toolkit section of this book.

A final option is simply annotating existing printed plans by hand or electronically, to note the adaptations that will be made to meet the needs of particular groups or individuals. Figure 5.6 gives an example, for an ICT unit of work in a class which includes children with speech and language needs, children with difficulties in cognition and learning, and several highly able pupils.

TEACHER:			SUBJECT: English	Date
Class: 9 L	NOR: 23	Grouping: mixed ability	NC Levels: 2–7	

Unit of work: Study of Key Stage 3 Shakespeare text	

Objectives (WALT)	Outcomes (WILF)
Read and understand key scene from text Explore characters and what motivates them	Brief monologues (soliloquies) that give a good picture of what the opinions and feelings of one character are Complete reading of key scene from set text; understanding of what has happened and why

Activities	Differentiation (SEN/G and T/EAL)
Starter Paired recap on previous lesson's reading – key actions/characters. Q and A by teacher. **Main** Use IWB to display a usual wedding and contrast with play. Display still from movie – identify main characters. Individuals choose one character and write brief monologue exploring the character's thoughts and feelings in the scene. Paired work – read and comment on each other's monologue. Complete reading of scene with individuals taking parts, up to Leonardo's losing control.	Pupils to work in their buddy (mixed ability) pairs Ask Qs using 'infer', 'speculate' to challenge more able Give Ian, Parin, Anthony a copy of the last IWB slide (the still) with starter ideas in boxes for each character – students to choose one and complete in the box. Dan to work with Robbie – Robbie scribe. Pupils to work in regular (ability-matched) pairs.

Plenary What will be the effect of the scene on events to come? Last IWB slide – have students add thought bubbles for all main characters.	

Assessment opportunities Use plenary to check understanding for 5 target pupils	

Homework Edit your monologue in the light of others' comments/what actually happened in the scene	Ian, Parin, Anthony instead to read next two scenes in Comic Book Shakespeare (www.shakespearecomics.com) in preparation for next lesson

TABLE 5.2 Lesson plan

Unit: ....   **Date:** ....   **Year group:** ....

Key learning objectives: ....

Learning outcome for unit: ....

Planning for inclusion – note here differentiated learning objectives for different individuals and groups, and the teaching approaches and access strategies you will use to overcome barriers to learning.

Differentiated learning objectives

Teaching approaches

Access strategies

Session	Shared learning and teaching	Independent learning	Plenary	Assessment criteria	Guided learning
1					
2					
3					

FIGURE 5.5 Example planning format

The process of planning for individuals in the context of the class became easier as tools such as the interactive planning tool within the electronic Primary Framework became available. Such tools allow teachers to do multi-level planning by pulling down into their planning objectives from earlier or later year groups. They allow teachers to cut and paste in questions at different levels, which they can use to assess whether individual children have reached learning objectives. Plans that are saved from year to year can readily be amended to include teaching approaches and access strategies appropriate for the particular needs of 'this year's class'. Those teaching approaches and access strategies can be cut and pasted across from subject

Medium-term Plan   Subject: ITC Branching databases (Flexi Tree)   Term: Spring

Key Questions/Activity List	Resources	Teaching and learning intention and how it will be assessed
Show the class a selection of about eight materials, such as marbles, water, oil, salt. Tell the class that you are thinking of one of the objects, and that they must work out which one it is by asking 'yes/no' questions, such as 'Is it a solid?' Discuss which questions work well and point out that questions about small numbers of objects are unhelpful if the answer is no. Encourage them to use questions which divide the set of objects into two. Show the class how to create a tree diagram of branching questions, which can be used to identify each object. Do on IWB. Divide the class into mixed ability groups; give each group a tree diagram challenge. e.g. use a tree diagram to separate the Tudor monarchs.	Selection of about six materials such as marbles, water, oil, salt. 'Big' and smaller paper trees.	The children will be able to create Y/N questions to categorise information.
Create a branching database in order to create a database to classify different organisms, e.g. Lives on land?	Seven different organisms Pics from science week. Paper tree. Labels, wordbank.	The children will be able to use their knowledge of branching databases to create a database to classify organisms

ML, NG To relate back to science and use appropriate vocabulary.

ML, AW – HA in history. Higher order questions What if …?

Plus group of TP/KS/MM/ML G/JH/RLG

JH RLG practise yes/no questions about people and sort selves before joining the group.

TP KS MM MLG to do four objects with CT support.

ML, NG include more organisms (with obvious similarities) in order to make the task more challenging. Where would you put a frog? Why? ML …?

JH, RLG – to have time prior to session with ICT buddy with 1:1 support in setting up a branching database (and after, to consolidate).

JH, RLG, TP, KS, MM, MLG with CT recap on pics from science earlier in term linked to animal attributes and habitats. Sort 4 on paper tree before transferring onto computer (labels, spellings provided).

Figure 5.6 Planning annotated for children with SEN and more able

to subject, saving time and helping to ensure that ideas added to one plan as a result of a discussion with the SENCO/INCO or an outside agency will be applied more widely.

When thinking as a staff about how they want to record differentiation on their planning, it is important to avoid people making a rod for their own backs by trying to record every detail of the inclusive teaching approaches they use with a class. Planning is there to guide teaching and assessment, and what goes on it should only be what the teacher needs as a prompt. A teacher who has taught a number of children with autism, for example, is likely to have internalised the sorts of strategies that will be useful and will automatically use visual supports and closed rather than open-ended assessment tasks. The teacher does not need to annotate their planning to that effect. A teacher new to autism, however, might need to record explicitly on her planning a reminder to herself to do these things.

In general the minimum that might be recorded by all teachers is:

- the appropriate tracked-back (or -forward) learning objectives for a particular group or, if the class contains children working well below age-related expectations, for one or two individuals;
- the different tasks that groups or individuals will be set, including any different homework;
- what will happen in the plenary to enable children working on different objectives to demonstrate their learning;
- one or more questions the teacher will use to assess understanding.

 ## Modelling and coaching

Agreed inclusive planning formats can be helpful in guiding teachers towards appropriate differentiation. As ever, however, it is the *process* used to support teachers' planning that is more important than what ends up being written down. The most productive processes involve a collaborative planning process, like that used in the very interesting Lesson Study approach (wwww.lessonstudy.co.uk). Here, a group of teachers from different subject areas, which can usefully include the SENCO, plan a cycle of lessons together and observe pupils' response. SENCOs can also work individually with class or subject teachers, listening to the outline of what they want to teach and making suggestions about learning objectives, teaching approaches and access strategies that are appropriate for children in the class who have SEN or disabilities.

The examples that follow show how this can be done.

PLANNING EXAMPLE

Planning collaboratively with a Year 3 class teacher

A Year 3 teacher was planning work on speaking and listening, using a unit in which children discuss different scenarios for an ending to a novel they have been reading (*The Battle of Bubble and Squeak* by Philippa Pearce), and decide which is the most plausible. The lesson objective was to use the language of possibility to investigate and reflect on feelings, behaviour or relationships. Children were going to discuss how to talk about things which 'might' happen, using words like 'may', 'might', 'could', 'perhaps', then work in groups to talk about different endings to the story, and have a spokesperson to report on their discussion.

The class contained a number of children with speech and language difficulties, so their teacher asked for the SENCO's help in planning adaptations she could make to meet their needs.

The first step was to consider whether the teacher would need to track back to earlier learning objectives for some children. Two of the children were able to express themselves only in simple sentences, and had been assessed as working at P6–7 in speaking and listening. The SENCO suggested that an appropriate objective for them would still involve the language of prediction, but at a simpler level – learning to understand and use words like 'guess', 'I think', 'I don't know'.

SENCO and class teacher then discussed how this learning objective could be brought in to the lesson introduction, in which the teacher was going to explain to the children that we use different language to talk about things which might happen, rather than things we are sure about. The teacher wanted then to ask the class questions about what they had done in the morning before they came to school, and what they might do after school – using language like *'Are you sure?'*, *'Is that definite?'* to generate vocabulary use which expresses possibility.

The teacher thought she could bring in the learning objectives for the children with language difficulties here. With the help of the SENCO, she decided to use a covered box right at the start of the lesson and ask the children if they knew what was in it, then produce two pictures and ask them to guess which one might be inside the box. This would allow her to use words like 'guess', 'know', 'don't know', 'think'.

The next step was to think about any access strategies that children with SEN might need after the lesson introduction. The SENCO suggested that she might use play people and small models, or a story sack of concrete objects to support her recap of the *The Battle of Bubble and Squeak* so far, as the language would present a barrier to the children with communication difficulties, and also to EAL learners in the group.

For the group work part of the lesson, the teacher planned to give each group a different story prediction/ending to work on, and ask them talk about how likely their ending might be, using the clues from the story so far. She wanted the children with communication difficulties to take part, so that they could have access to the role models provide by other children's language, but decided to give them a clear role – that of timekeeper for their group.

In the plenary she wanted to return both to the overall class learning objective and to the specific objectives she had planned for the children with communication difficulties. The SENCO suggested that she might hold a class vote on which of the different possible endings would be the one in the final chapter of the book. The spokesperson for each group would hold up a card with 'their' ending drawn on it, and children would be asked to go and stand by the ending they thought most likely. First, though, she would ask the children with communication needs to 'guess' which ending would win, encouraging them to repeat and complete the sentence 'I guess that … '. For other children, she would use the language of 'predict', 'might', 'perhaps' and so on.

PLANNING EXAMPLE

Planning collaboratively for a Year 7 history lesson

This class was a mixed ability Year 7 group, in which eight pupils had learning difficulties and two had been formally identified as dyslexic. They had been learning in history about Native Americans. The school's SENCO had allocated time to work intensively with members of the history department, modelling for them how planning could be adapted to take account of a range of SEN and disabilities. He sat down with the teacher working with this Year 7 group and established what the learning objective was for the class – on this occasion to understand how important the buffalo was to the survival of the Native Americans. They agreed that this objective was appropriate for all the children, including those with learning difficulties, as long as appropriate teaching approaches and access strategies were used.

Multi-sensory teaching approaches are important for children with difficulties in cognition and learning, and this was easy to plan as staff had already had training on using visual, auditory and kinaesthetic methods. The teacher had therefore already planned to use a lot of visual support – a PowerPoint presentation on the interactive whiteboard that illustrated key information.

The SENCO suggested that the teacher have a list of key words on the wall ('nomadic', 'tribe', 'buffalo' and so on) and that she reinforce these in the whiteboard presentation for the benefit of children with reading difficulties.

The lesson was to involve children in writing down what they thought each part of a buffalo (hide, fat, teeth and so on) might be used for. The SENCO suggested supporting those with learning difficulties here by using a buddy system. The teacher would use a seating plan that paired children who found writing difficult with those who wrote fluently (but might not always have good ideas). Children would be asked to talk in these buddy pairs then have the better writer record their initial ideas, to feed back in the class discussion.

Managing to get homework down quickly can be a problem for dyslexic children, and understanding what they have to do in their homework a problem for children with general learning difficulties. The SENCO had been working for some time with staff to get them to spend more time explaining homework, and to give it to children in handout form rather than expecting them to copy it down quickly from the board at the end of the lesson.

He discussed how this could happen in the history lesson, with the teacher perhaps giving the children a homework sheet in the middle of the lesson, and rehearsing with them what they would have to do. This was a good point to suggest, too, that handouts on buff paper using a font like Arial would add to their readability for dyslexic pupils. The SENCO and teacher looked together at how the homework handout could be differentiated by providing some pupils with a box of key words on their sheet, or by giving them part-completed sentences to finish.

The SENCO also suggested that, in the part of the lesson where pupils had discussed their initial ideas on the use of various parts of the buffalo, watched a further presentation from the teacher, and were writing up their learning, some children might use a laptop with software installed that enabled text to be read aloud. The laptop would be provided by the learning support department.

SENCO and teacher then briefly discussed ways of involving children with learning difficulties in a plenary. The SENCO learned that this teacher regularly used strategies to help less confident children answer questions. In this lesson, for example, he planned to make sure that lower-attaining children had their chance to come up to the whiteboard and drag words into the right places in sentences about the buffalo – but if they struggled, would be ready to offer them the chance to 'phone a friend' or 'ask the audience'.

The advantages of a collaborative planning process like the one used in these examples are that the process makes strategies for children with SEN and disabilities live and real for class and subject teachers. The conversation is about the specific content of what the teacher is actually going to work on with a class. The ideas generated are therefore likely to be used, and remembered. Training provides the groundwork, but collaborative planning translates ideas into action.

Collaborative planning also leaves something behind. Every minute the SENCO/INCO invests in it will have a pay-off far beyond the children involved in the immediate piece of teaching. The joint planning provides the teacher with ideas they can use again and again in the future, even when the SENCO/INCO is not supporting them directly.

For children with the more common types of SEN or disability, like general learning difficulties, specific learning difficulties or mild behaviour difficulties, the SENCO/INCO may not need to invest very much time before teacher colleagues are able to incorporate appropriate differentiation into their everyday planning. The strategy sheets provided in the toolkit section of this book may be all they need to keep them going.

Where children have less common or more complex needs – for example, children with sensory impairment, or those with severe learning difficulties who will function at or below Level 2 of the National Curriculum throughout their school career, the involvement of the SENCO/INCO or outside agencies will continue to be needed. A primary class teacher working with a child who has little or no sight, for example, should expect to be able to sit down with a specialist teacher of the visually impaired and look in advance at medium-term planning, so that the specialist teacher can advise on access strategies and help in the preparation of appropriate resources.

Similarly, if a child has severe learning difficulties and is working at levels very significantly below those of the class as a whole, there will be a need to identify in medium-term planning those learning opportunities in which the child can profitably take part, working on either tracked-back learning objectives linked to those of the class as a whole, or on separate objectives (curriculum overlapping).

The examples that follow illustrate this process.

PLANNING EXAMPLE

Planning collaboratively for a Year 4 science lesson

This example describes how a teacher planned for a Year 4 class with diverse needs that included one child with profound and multiple learning difficulties. In science, he was planning work on temperature, involving the use of an electronic thermometer/probe. The children were to predict then measure the temperature of various liquids. Clearly the science learning objectives were not relevant to the needs of Shamina, the child with profound and multiple learning difficulties, whose learning was at a very early developmental level.

The teacher had access to advice from a teacher from a local special school and discussed with her how he might adapt his planning. The specialist teacher used the idea of curriculum overlapping, to show how the child with profound learning difficulties could be involved in the class activities, but for the primary purpose of pursuing objectives from other curriculum areas – in this case, communication. The objective would be for Shamina to begin to link the words 'hot' and 'cold' with the relevant sensory experience. Appropriate teaching approaches for a child working at this level would need to be based on concrete materials that provide a strong sensory stimulus.

The class teacher suggested that they use two hot water bottles, one filled with hot and one with icy water. A TA would work with Shamina and three other children, encouraging them to first let Shamina feel each of the hot water bottles and hear the words for each of them, then try to engage her in anticipation (an early cognitive forerunner of prediction) by saying 'Ready, it's going to be cold' or 'Ready, it's going to be hot'. The more able children would then predict the temperature in each of the bottles and measure it with a probe. Assessment would involve the TA in using a camera to record Shamina's responses, looking for any sign of anticipation.

PLANNING EXAMPLE

Planning collaboratively across the curriculum

Globetown Action Zone, a partnership between five schools in East London working to raise standards through support for vulnerable groups, received funding for a curriculum development project. They decided to use the funding to work on differentiated planning with subject faculties in one secondary school. Teachers' planning had so far differentiated only down to NC Level 3 in Year 7, but not below this.

The project used skilled teachers with prior experience in the relevant faculty, and often with early years and primary teaching experience also. These teachers were asked to 'track' each scheme or unit of work and prepare lesson-by-lesson plans for work appropriate for pupils working below Level 2 when they moved to secondary at the age of 11. The schemes of work now take pupils with learning difficulties from P scale levels in Year 7 through to Year 11 work that can potentially consolidate Level 3 and begin Level 4. Maths, geography, history, RE and English are covered.

In maths, for example, a Year 8 scheme of work involved the class in working on position (coordinates), straight line graphs and expressing simple functions in words. For one lesson these objectives were tracked back (using multi-level planning) to the use of everyday words to describe position and direction. Pupils with learning difficulties worked on the key words 'column', 'row', 'left', right' and 'position' using a game they played in pairs – each moving counters on a grid and answering the question 'What's your position?' The planning includes questions that the class teacher can use to involve everyone during the plenary, such as 'Can you write instructions using shorthand, for example 2R (move 2 squares to the right)?'

In geography, a potentially challenging lesson on tectonics was made accessible by planning for pupils with learning difficulties to use a simple instruction sheet to construct an 'edible earth' consisting of crust, mantle, outer core and inner core, using three different colours of ice cream, nuts and edible silver spheres. In the plenary they had to identify each part as they ate their edible earth, sharing it with the class.

In history, a Year 9 scheme of work on women at work in World War I involved the class in studying the impact of the war on the changing roles of women. In planning for differentiation, it was decided that pupils with learning difficulties could access the same learning objectives as the class, as long as particular teaching approaches and access strategies were used. These involved adding picture supports to information sheets, in the form of black and white photographs of women as bus conductors, nurses, farm workers and so on. Worksheets were simplified and supports provided in the form of sentence starters and picture–word matching activities. The teachers also took the opportunity to develop work on a key life skill for pupils with learning difficulties (writing a CV and job application) in parallel to the main history objectives (curriculum overlapping again). Pupils had to choose a job that supported the war effort and construct a letter of application using cut up sentence starters and key job vocabulary. Pupils also constructed their own CV using a digital photograph of themselves.

Table 5.3 shows some of the resources that were developed to support this history scheme of work.

Resources for Year 9 History scheme of work

Globetown Action Zone and Morpeth School

Topic: Women at work in World War I 1914–1918.

Lesson 1: What jobs did women do in World War I?

Main lesson objective	• To understand the importance of women in World War I
Key words	• Jobs, employment, transport, factories, farms, nursing
Activities for pupils with learning difficulties	• Read through fact sheet on World War I • Explain that at this time only men could do manual jobs. However when the men went to war women were needed to carry out the jobs previously done by the men. Harvest was completed by women, nurses cared for soldiers, and women worked in factories and took over the transport • Look at pictures and discuss the work that is going on • Match the sentences to the pictures.
Resources	• Information sheet • Worksheet 1 • Set of laminated pictures • Set of laminated sentences
Plenary	• Ask the children what job they would have volunteered for if they had been alive in 1914–1918

Lesson 1

Information Sheet

Woman at work during World War I

(1914–1918)

What jobs did women do in World War I?
During World War I, nine million men were mobilised in Britain and the Empire. The government needed women in Britain to carry out manual tasks.

- Women found employment in transport. They drove buses and trams
- They worked in nursing
- Women found work in factories making ammunition
- Women had to work on farms to harvest the food
- Some women had to drive trucks

These were all jobs that only men had done before the war. Women proved that they could do these jobs as well as the men.

Lesson I

Worksheet 1

Woman at work during World War I:

- Look at the pictures and discuss what you can see.
- Why are the pictures in black and white?
- What are the jobs that the women are doing?
- Can you match the sentences to the pictures?
- What job would you have chosen to do?

TABLE **5.3** Resources for Year 9 History scheme of work: Globetown Action Zone and Morpeth School

Lesson 2
What job would you apply for to help in the War?

Main lesson objective	• (Class) To understand the types of jobs that supported the war effort • (Pupils with learning difficulties) To write an application for a job using curriculum vitae
Key words	• Jobs, employment, transport, curriculum vitae, farms, nursing.
Activities for pupils with learning difficulties	• Discuss with the pupils what job they would like to do to support the war effort • Remind them that this would be the first time women would be allowed to work in manual jobs • Read through Worksheet 1 • Explain that Worksheet 2 gives words and sentence starters to help with their writing • Pupils to cut out and match words and then complete own writing • Pupils will fill in curriculum vitae (Worksheet 3) giving information about themselves
Resources	• Information sheet • Worksheet 1 • Set of laminated pictures from week 1 • Digital photo of each pupil • Worksheet 2. Cut up words • Worksheet 3
Plenary	• To share writing with the class

Lesson 2
Worksheet 1

• When you want to get a job it is necessary for you to complete an application form
• Once you have decided which job you would like to do then you will have to complete a CV. This is short for curriculum vitae
• A CV gives employers information about you
• It will give information on your name
• When you were born (Date of Birth)
• Your home address or your school address
• What type of person you are
• Any qualifications
• If you have any hobbies or interests it is important to write these down as well

Remember you can choose a job from the pictures that you have in front of you.

TABLE **5.3** continued

Lesson 2

Worksheet 2

| I would like to be a |
| I would be good at |
| because |
| I am |
| hardworking |
| kind |
| caring |
| nurse |
| truck driver |
| bus conductor |
| farm worker |
| motorcyclist |

Lesson 2
Worksheet 3
CV
Name: Photograph:

Date of Birth: (day, month, year)

Address:

My hobbies:

What job would you like to do?

TABLE **5.3** continued

Monitoring

So far we have looked at how a SENCO or INCO might provide training for colleagues on how to plan for a range of needs in their class, and how to support this through opportunities for collaborative planning – for modelling and coaching. Ideally, there would also be opportunities from time to time to follow up collaborative planning with review. 'How did the lesson go?' the SENCO might ask. 'How did those with SEN or disabilities respond? What worked and what didn't? What strategies might you want to use again or apply in other subjects or with other age groups?'

If change is to be embedded, however, it will also need to be monitored, and built into existing performance management systems. Teachers might for a period all have a target to increase the amount and quality of differentiation in their planning. This could form part of the school's curriculum access plan or (better and less bureaucratic) part of a section of the school development or improvement plan concerned with increasing curriculum access.

Monitoring is relatively straightforward. From time to time the SENCO/INCO looks at a sample of planning drawn from across the school, and provides feedback to individual staff and an overview for the senior leadership team and subject leaders of issues arising from the monitoring exercise. The subject or whole-school issues unearthed will feed into school self-evaluation and the SEF. Any issues relating to individuals feed into performance management and the provision of extra training and support. A suggested monitoring proforma is provided in the toolkit section of this book.

Finally, the school will want to know whether its improved planning is feeding through into teaching. Whoever is monitoring teaching in the school – members of SMT, subject leaders, the SENCO/INCO when gathering specific evidence on SEN/D for the school's self-evaluation – will need to check whether there is a clear read-through from planning through to what they see happening in the classroom for children with additional needs.

6 Achieving targets
Mapping additional provision

So far, we have looked at a number of key elements of our essential bureaucracy-busting kit that provides the alternative to writing individual plans for every child with SEN or a disability – at Personal Profiles, whole-school target-setting and tracking systems, and differentiated curriculum planning. In this chapter we tackle another element, provision maps.

Provision maps were described in *Special educational needs and school improvement* (Gross and White, 2003), and further guidance outlined later in publications such as the National Strategies' materials *Leading on inclusion* (DfES, 2005c), *Leading on intervention* (DfES, 2006d) and *Effective leadership: ensuring the progress of pupils with SEN and/or disabilities* (DfES, 2006a). It is not the intention to repeat this information here. For those who may not be familiar with the concept, this chapter will briefly summarise what a provision map is and the function it fulfils, but the main focus will be on what has been learned since more and more schools began to take on provision mapping. We will look at what to do to keep the process of developing a provision map as simple as possible, how to build in new developments in quality interventions, and how to move from effective provision mapping to effective provision management.

What is a provision map?

A provision map is a way of describing the provision that a school makes for children with additional needs, over and above inclusive class or subject teaching, using additional targeted time from teachers, teaching assistants or volunteers.

Table 6.1 provides an example of a primary provision map, and Table 6.2 a secondary map. Provision is best mapped by year group (although in very small schools it might be mapped by phase) and by types of provision – literacy interventions, mathematics interventions, interventions to boost oral language skills, motor coordination or social, emotional and behavioural skills. It can also be helpful to subdivide literacy and mathematics provision into 'Wave 2' and 'Wave 3' interventions. This will distinguish the provision made for different target groups – those who are working just below age-related expectations and can be expected to catch up with their peers as a result of a tightly structured programme of small group support delivered by adults working to a script (Wave 2), and those for whom the gap is wider, and who will need one-to-one

PROVISION	YR	Y1	Y2	Y3	Y4	Y5	Y6
Language intervention	Narrative group intervention	*Talking Partners*				*Language for thinking group*	
Literacy intervention	Phonological awareness group	*Reading Recovery FFT Wave 3 ELS*	*Project CODE*	Y6 buddy readers (*Better Reading Partnership*)	Y6 buddy readers (*Better Reading Partnership*)	*Further Literacy Support* Paired reading programme Reciprocal teaching	Paired reading programme
Maths intervention			*Numbers Count 1stClass@number*	*Numbers Count*	Teacher and TA – Primary Strategy Wave 3 materials	Teacher and TA – Primary Strategy Wave 3 materials *Springboard 5*	Teacher and TA – Primary Strategy Wave 3 materials
Motor Coordination programme	Weekly breakfast motor skills group plus home programme						
EAL provision	Home language support and additional language work for early stage learners	Home language support, pre-tutoring and additional language work for early stage learners	Home language support, pre-tutoring and additional language work for early stage learners	Small group language enrichment and pre-tutoring for children at later stages of learning EAL	Small group language enrichment and pre-tutoring for children at later stages of learning EAL	Small group language enrichment and pre-tutoring for children at later stages of learning EAL	Small group language enrichment and pre-tutoring for children at later stages of learning EAL
1–1 counselling /solution focused work with Learning Mentor	Estimated 3 pupils per year group						

PROVISION	YR	Y1	Y2	Y3	Y4	Y5	Y6
Small group SEAL work	*Nurture group*	*SEAL* silver sets	*SEAL* silver sets *Circle of Friends*	*Pyramid Club* *SEAL* Silver sets	*SEAL* Silver sets	*SEAL* Silver sets	Transition group
In-class support							
Attendance / extra curricular support	Walking bus Monday after-school club					Learning Mentor programme targeting attendance/ engagement	Learning Mentor programme targeting attendance/ engagement
Gifted and talented provision				After school clubs with secondary buddies			
Other	1–1 work with TA on programme devised by speech and language therapist	1–1 TA work with child with ASD on social scripts	1–1 TA sensory programme supervised through outreach from SLD special school	1–1 work with TA on programme devised by speech and language therapist	ASD social skills group		

TABLE **6.1** Example of a primary provision map

PROVISION	Y7	Y8	Y9	Y10	Y11
Targeted literacy intervention	Literacy progress units – 4 groups (pupils <L4) Reading and Writing Challenge with librarian – 5 pupils	Reading and Writing Challenge with librarian – 5 pupils			
Targeted maths intervention	Springboard 7 (pupils <L4) – 5 groups	Maths Challenge 1–1 with maths TA			
Targeted language intervention	ELCISS vocabulary and narrative group			Words for Work programme with business mentors	
Further SEN literacy intervention	Toe by Toe programme 1–1 with teacher (pupils <L3) Early morning reading club	Paired reading programme organised by Inclusion Coordinator, involving disaffected Year 10 as tutors – approx. 18 pupils involved on a rolling programme Lunchtime literacy computer programmes, in library	Lunchtime literacy computer programmes, in library	Lunchtime literacy computer programmes, in library 1–1 tuition with undergraduate volunteers	
Further SEN mathematics intervention	SEN teacher – Primary Strategy Wave 3 materials with 7 pupils	SEN teacher – Primary Strategy Wave 3 materials with 6 pupils		1–1 tuition with undergraduate volunteers	
EAL provision	Grammar for Writing – group of advanced bilingual learners- English teacher with support from EMA teacher	Home language support and additional language work for 2 children at the early stages of learning EAL	Home language support and additional language work for 4 children at the early stages of learning EAL	Additional language work and academic tutoring for an estimated 3 new arrivals	Additional language work and academic tutoring for an estimated 3 new arrivals
1–1 counselling	Via Learning Support unit (LSU) team - estimated 12 pupils per year group				
Focus group work to develop social, emotional and behavioural skills	Nurture group for 8 pupils entering Y7	Circle of Friends for 3 pupils	SEAL friendship skills focus group and 2 anger management groups run by LSU team Lunchtime club		

PROVISION	Y7	Y8	Y9	Y10	Y11
1–1 mentoring to increase aspirations/engagement with learning	*Learning Challenge 1–1 with Learning Mentor Buddy system Y7–Y12 organised by Learning Mentor*	*Learning Challenge 1–1 with Learning Mentor*		Learning Mentors work on programme targeting attendance/engagement Success group for Black Caribbean boys	Learning Mentors work on programme targeting attendance/engagement
In-class support for individuals	*Kalam, Jamila, Jenny, Cameron, David*	*John , Rafiq, Attia, Brendan*	*Stephen, Adam, Parvis, Aki, Jahangir, Sedef*	*Gareth, Brooke*	*William B, Patrick, Travis, Sara*
Out of school support	Homework /ICT club	Homework /ICT club	Homework /ICT club Outdoor activity programme for targeted pupils	Study support tutorials ICT room group	Study support tutorials ICT room group
Gifted and talented provision	Specialist lunchtime enrichment clubs		Mentoring by university students		
Other	1–1 work with TA on programme devised by speech and language therapist- *Cameron* 1–1 TA work with child with ASD on social scripts, *David* Touch typing – 2 pupils (20 mins, during registration)	1–1 TA work with child with ASD on social scripts *Anthony, Rafiq, Brendan* Social skills group work with this group	1–1 TA sensory programme supervised through outreach from SLD special school *Beth*	Tailored curriculum group of 12 – Youth Awards, vocational programme, Certificate of Achievement in English and Maths	

TABLE 6.2 Example of a secondary provision map

or very small group support from a specialist teacher or highly trained teaching assistant able to provide learning experiences tailored to the assessed needs of the child (Wave 3). Schools that make extensive provision for children with social, emotional and behavioural needs often find it helpful to subdivide their provision in this area into 'Wave 2' and 'Wave 3' also.

It is good practice to include in a provision map all the different types of additional provision a school makes for children – those in need of booster or catch-up provision, those with identified SEN/D, those who are EAL learners, those who are gifted or talented, those with behaviour difficulties and those who are vulnerable for other reasons. This saves the time, paper and effort that might be spent on constructing separate maps for different types of need. It recognises the overlap between needs, in which a child with autism taking part in a social skills group might also require support as an EAL learner. Most importantly, it allows the school to achieve an overview of all the additional needs in each year group and make a coherent plan to meet them.

In so doing, it enables the SENCO /INCO to follow the general principle that children with SEN or disabilities are better integrated systems that personalise learning for all children, rather than separate systems that are driven by SEN categories and procedures.

Steps in developing a provision map

The steps involved in developing a provision map are shown in Figure 6.1.

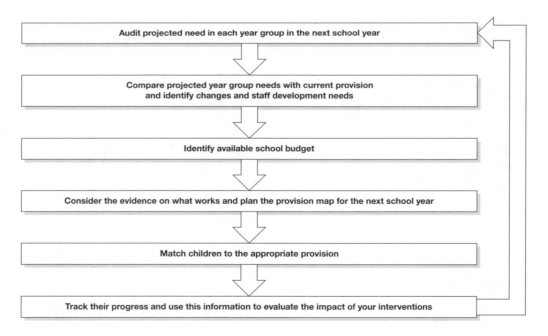

FIGURE 6.1 Steps in developing a provision map

Auditing the projected need in each year group in the next school year means listing types of provision you could make: literacy, mathematics, language, social and emotional, motor coordination, EAL/EMA, attendance, extracurricular, and gifted and talented provision, and an 'other 'heading to cover very individual arrangements made for children with less common types of SEN/D. Then under each you write the names of children for whom that additional provision would be desirable. It is helpful if on your lists (perhaps using a particular colour) you distinguish those for whom additional provision is essential (your 'MUST' group) – for example, children with Statements or an Education, Health and Care Plan specifying a particular provision, or children at a very early stage of English language acquisition. Next, enter in another colour those who have the next highest call on available provision (your 'SHOULD' group). These could be children whose difficulties impact very significantly on their own or others' learning or those who have the potential, with relatively little help, to catch up with their peers and achieve age-related expectations in social and emotional learning, literacy or mathematics. Finally, enter the names of children for whom you make additional provision, if the budget allows, but for whom the priority is lower (your 'COULD' group).

Comparing projected year group needs with current provision and identifying changes and staff development needs means looking at the audit you have done for each year group for the coming school year and noticing differences between the audit and current needs and provision in that year group. Is there going to be an increase in children in Year 1 who need provision to develop their speech and language skills, for example, that might mean introducing a new intervention and training up staff (in advance) to implement it? Will there still be a group needing a Year 3 literacy support programme, or not? What does the incoming Year 7 look like in terms of need for literacy progress units, maths Springboard 7 and Wave 3 mathematics support? Does it contain a number of children on the autistic spectrum, and if so what are the implications for provision and staff development? Does next year's Year 9 have a large group of pupils who according to current tracking are making poor progress across the board because of lack of engagement with learning, and if so is there a need for a mentoring programme?

Identifying the available school budget means pulling together different funding streams, such as a core amount from the school's base budget, delegated SEN funding, the Pupil Premium and any other local or national funding for priorities such as early intervention or behaviour support. It will be necessary to ring-fence any funding that is allocated through a Statement of SEN or Education, Health and Care Plan which specifies that the child must receive a fixed number of hours of TA support or other specified provision. Otherwise, funding streams should be combined so as to achieve the best possible fit to the priorities identified in the audit. Coherently planned provision which draws together a range of funding sources is more likely to achieve positive outcomes than piecemeal use of pockets of money.

The next step, *considering the evidence on what works*, means making choices about what interventions you will put on next year's provision map, drawing on information provided nationally, by your local authority, from your own research and reading and from your evaluation of interventions used previously in school.

Once the map has been drawn up and the new school year has begun, precise tracking information can be used to *match children to the appropriate provision*. This process will be easier, and fairer, if you have established clear entry and exit criteria for each of your provisions. Finally, 'before' and 'after' measures can be used to *track children's progress* as a result of the intervention, and this information used to *evaluate the impact of each provision*. This in turn feeds back into the provision mapping cycle, helping to inform your choice of interventions in the future.

What are provision maps for?

A provision map is fundamentally a management tool, based on auditing the needs of year groups, deciding as a result what provision is needed in which year groups, and using this to determine budgetary and staffing arrangements. Its main value is 'the strategic view that it gives, and the opportunities that it then affords to carry out some intelligent, and evidence-based planning for predicted needs, rather than simply reacting on an individual basis' (Cochrane, 2006).

Developing a provision map helps the school to manage different funding streams coherently to target particular patterns of need in different year groups. Priorities are established and made transparent, so that staff can see, for example, why the TA who was formerly attached to their class full-time now needs to work differently, running time-limited interventions in a number of year groups. Provision maps help schools to avoid situations where in one class there might be a teacher and three TAs, each attached to support individual children, while next door in a parallel class the teacher is struggling alone with no additional support. They also help schools to check the overall pattern of their provision, and make sure children do not become demoralised by repeating very similar interventions year after year.

Another advantage of provision maps is the basis they provide for systematic evaluation of the impact of each intervention that has been planned through the map. Combined with data on pupil outcomes, the map gives substance to the school's SEN/D self-evaluation and will be helpful to Ofsted inspectors. For parents, the map provides very useful information about what they can expect the school to provide for their child, putting flesh on the bones of the 'local offer' required under the 2011 SEN and Disability Green Paper (DfE, 2011b).

From the standpoint of this book an even more important advantage of provision maps is that SENCOs/INCOs and class teachers can avoid the need to write particular provisions down over and over again on a series of IEPs. Provision for individual children can be recorded (as at Stocksbridge High School, one of the case study schools in Chapter 2) by simply highlighting on a copy of the school's provision map the provision a particular child is receiving, dating the map and storing it with the child's records. This personalised map will provide good information for parents/carers and increase parental confidence that their child's needs are being comprehensively met.

Provision maps as a management tool are mainly a way of planning strategically for children with high-incidence (more common) types of additional need, and for planning the provision over which the school has control – that which it makes from its own budget, including any delegated SEN funding. For the majority of children, therefore, it will be sufficient just to highlight a standard, whole-school provision map when recording the provision made for that child.

Provision maps are also mainly about planning targeted intervention – time-limited group or one-to-one programmes used in class or on a withdrawal basis, rather than planning for general in-class support. This is because the evidence for the efficacy of such generalised support for children with the more common types of SEN is weak (Giangreco *et al.*, 1997; Gerber *et al.*, 2001; Howes, 2003), with recent large-scale research at the Institute of Education in London (Blatchford *et al.*, 2012) finding that for pupils with similar prior attainment, social class and SEN status there was a negative relationship between the amount of TA support received and academic progress – in other words, the more TA support a child receives, the less progress they make on average. Schools are in general better advised to spend their money elsewhere.

Some children, however, such as those with physical impairments or medical conditions or severe BESD, do require in-class support. So as to have all the information about the child in one place, these very individual arrangements can be recorded in the 'other' column on the provision map. The same column can be used to record the support provided by external agencies.

Keeping it simple

There is something about SEN/D that seems to make us manufacture complexity where none need exist. With provision maps, what started as a simple planning tool for school managers has degenerated in many local authorities into yet another bureaucratic burden. These are some examples:

- Provision maps that include Wave 1 class or subject teaching, and try to list every single adaptation that teachers make to meet particular types of SEN/D.
- Provision maps written individually for every child, aimed at showing exactly what is being done to meet their needs, and often running alongside IEPs.
- Provision maps which must be submitted annually to the local authority, with each provision costed, so as to 'prove' that the school has spent every penny of its delegated SEN budget.

Let us consider each of these common mistakes in turn.

It can be useful as a one-off professional development exercise for a staff group to collate a list of teaching approaches and access strategies that they already use to support children with particular needs – dyslexia, for example, or autism, or language difficulties. Such an exercise enables teachers to reflect on what they are already doing well, to learn from others' ideas, and produce one collated ideas list of which they will have ownership, and therefore be more inclined to use. It will energise everyone because it follows the best principles of managing any sort of development or change – identifying what people are already doing that works, so as to do more of it in the future, more often and more systematically.

But why go to all the trouble of writing all these strategies on a provision map that is produced annually, and will become so long and complex that it loses its usefulness? Instead, the SENCO/INCO might want to develop the school's own bank of computer-held strategy sheets for each main type of SEN or disability, drawing on the ideas from the toolkit section of this book as well as those generated by staff. Once on the school's networked system, staff can quickly look up the strategy sheets when they want help in knowing how to plan differentiated learning and teaching for a child in their class.

Next, it is important to avoid turning provision maps back into another form of IEP by writing one for each individual child. This misses the point of provision mapping altogether. The questions a provision map seeks to answer are these:

? How many children have we in each year group who need additional interventions for language, literacy, mathematics, social and emotional learning and so on?
? Where do the greatest priorities for additional provision lie?
? How can we best deploy additional adult and peer support so as to meet these priorities?

? What particular interventions will we choose to use, on the basis of their impact?

? Looking at our tracking data from last term/year, which provisions have had the desired impact, and which ought we to review?

These are very different questions from the more familiar 'What does this individual child need in the way of extra support?' which might lead a SENCO to begin by constructing a provision map for each child. That was the question to which we were led by an IEP-driven system. And an IEP-driven system led us to patterns of provision based mostly on attaching TAs as if by Velcro to individual children, to provide generalised in-class support or teaching geared around three or four IEP targets.

As we saw in Chapter 1, such a system failed to serve our children well, and failed to serve the SENCOs and teachers who drowned in paper while struggling valiantly to make it work. It is essential that provision maps do not replicate the weaknesses of the past. We need to construct them on a whole-school basis, to plan the provision in year groups, not for Saleem or Sam or Sarah. We can print and date a copy, highlighting on it the provision that Saleem receives, so as to have an ongoing child-level record on file. We can add to it the very individual arrangements, like help with toileting, and a physiotherapy programme that Sam might need. We can add to it the multi-agency support – speech and language therapy, advice from a specialist VI teacher, advice from a teacher in a local special school – that Sarah might access. We can, as we will see later in this chapter in the section on evaluation, add provision columns to the pupil-level data held in RAISEonline, and print out individual provision records. But we must start our provision planning with a proactive, strategic, whole-school focus rather than ad hoc child-by-child arrangements.

Finally, what about costing provision maps? It is not uncommon now for local authorities to require schools to produce costed maps. The Audit Commission has provided a tool to help with this. This is seen as helping the local authority fulfil their current statutory duty of ensuring that appropriate provision is made for children with SEN/D, by making sure that schools are using all their delegated SEN funding for its specified purpose.

There is not a single headteacher, however, who cannot by canny accounting demonstrate that their school is spending not only what the local authority have provided to meet SEN/D in the school's budget share, but far more besides. Almost any arrangement, such as running smaller class groups or sets, providing each class with its own TA, having extra adults around to keep order at lunchtimes, having extra pastoral staff to enable a school in a difficult area to run smoothly, or buying extra computers can be allocated to a school's notional SEN budget and its provision map if the school so chooses. The definition of what constitutes SEN/D provision is so wide as to be meaningless. And in a sense accounting for spending is an irrelevance: what matters is the impact that the school's spending choices have on pupils. If the school chooses to spend its SEN budget on refurbishing the staffroom, and can demonstrate that the attainment and well-being of pupils with SEN or disabilities improves, then the local authority has a poor case for challenge.

Unless your school has developed a sophisticated IT system that holds data on average hourly staffing costs and does the necessary calculation, costing a provision map is a lot of work. That work should not be undertaken to fulfil someone else's purposes if those purposes can be met in other more sensible ways. This is the case for local authorities' current duty to hold schools to account for the progress of pupils with SEN or disabilities. Providing data on pupil *outcomes* is a more sensible way of meeting that purpose.

It may be useful to highlight or print a provision map for an individual child and cost it, if you have to give evidence at a Tribunal or need to convince a parent that you are fully allocating funding provided through a Statement or Education, Health and Care Plan. Otherwise, the only reason for costing a whole-school provision map is if doing so will meet your *own* school purpose, to raise standards and promote pupils' well-being. Here, there may be a case for costing different provisions so that you can do a cost–benefit analysis – that is, compare the costs and impact of different provisions to see which gives best value for money (the highest impact at the lowest cost). An anger-management group run by a Learning Mentor, for example, might prove to have an impact as great as that of one-to-one counselling from a clinical psychologist for the four individuals involved, but provide better value for money because the unit costs of a Learning Mentor are very much lower than those of a clinical psychologist, and because the pupils work as a group rather than one-to-one.

Even here, however, schools may want to be cautious. In the example above, they would need to be sure that the pupils were comparable – that those working with the Learning Mentor in this case had needs just as great as those working with the clinical psychologist. One also needs to be aware that analysis that considers only *immediate* benefits and immediate costs can sometimes lead to unhelpful conclusions. Consider, for example, the Head Start programme, which provided intensive pre-school intervention for disadvantaged children. Immediate analysis showed costs to be high and the differential benefits (when compared to outcomes for similar children not involved in the programme) to be limited. It was only when the Head Start children were followed up to adulthood and found to be much less likely to have dropped out of school or to have been involved in crime, that the benefits became clear. This long-term cost–benefit analysis showed that for every dollar spent on the programme, over seven dollars was saved by society.

A study carried out in this country (Every Child a Chance Trust, 2009) makes a similar point. Here, researchers compared the costs of providing the intensive, one-to-one teacher-led Reading Recovery programme to six-year-olds with literacy difficulties with the costs incurred by schools and society if the children's difficulties remained unaddressed. The one-off cost of providing Reading Recovery was £2610 per child (at 2009 prices) – much more expensive than an intervention delivered by a TA or delivered in a group. Yet the same six-year-old receiving less expensive but also less effective provision would cost their junior school £2390 in special needs support over the course of Key Stage 2, and the secondary school £3850 over the course of Key Stages 3 and 4 – over £6,000 in total. With the longer-term costs of crime, ill health and reduced employment opportunities also taken into account, the researchers estimated a return on investment of between £11 and £19 for every pound spent on Reading Recovery.

Special educational needs that are not effectively addressed carry life-long consequences for individuals and for society. Cost–benefit analyses can be misleading if the benefits assessed are only short-term, and if the cost–benefit analysis focuses only on the costs and benefits for the institution rather than on the wider issues of every child's right to the best possible future.

Developments in provision mapping

Extending your provision

One notable development in provision mapping in recent years has been the extension of the range of provision that is planned for. Early provision maps were often dominated by provision for pupils with literacy difficulties, with perhaps a nod to numeracy and speech and language provision. Now, a primary provision map might include four or five different literacy interventions, one or more maths interventions, an oral language scheme, a social use of language programme and the use of social stories for children on the autistic spectrum, perhaps a motor coordination skills programme, and a range of provision for children who need extra help to develop social, emotional and behavioural skills. In the secondary school, there might be a small Year 7 nurture group for vulnerable pupils, a range of one-to-one mentoring programmes, study support, learning to learn courses, skilled counselling or cognitive behaviour therapy and social skills groups, as well as the usual literacy and mathematics catch-up interventions.

125

An important growth area is provision for pupils with BESD. The development of a 'universal' curriculum framework to teach all children social and emotional skills (the SEAL primary and secondary resources) has allowed us to apply a 'Waves' model, originally devised for literacy and numeracy, to social and emotional learning (Figure 6.2). Schools are encouraged to identify pupils who with just a little help can catch up with their peers in this area of learning, as a result of taking part in a structured group work programme, and are able to draw on a range of guidance and materials (DfES, 2005b, 2006c; DCSF, 2007b – available at www. sealcommunity.org) to help them plan, deliver and evaluate such groups. These Wave 2 developments throw into sharp focus the needs of pupils who require intervention that is much more intensive and personalised – a Wave 3 intervention delivered by a highly skilled professional, often in a multi-agency context where there is work not only with the pupil but with the family and in the community. Provision for children with attendance problems is beginning to figure on provision maps too – like the school that has organised a 'walking bus' to pick up the 20 children who used to be late or attend irregularly.

FIGURE 6.2 Waves model: behaviour/emotional health and well-being

Another set of opportunities for increasing the range of provision comes through the wider offer developed in extended schools initiatives. The features of an extended school (childcare, study support, parenting support, community use of facilities, access to multi-agency support) prompt us to think about how these elements can be used to enhance the school's provision map. How for example, can school-based literacy and numeracy intervention be enhanced by the addition of work with families such as family literacy and numeracy courses? How can school-based BESD provision be enhanced by parenting programmes, or by the involvement of a voluntary organisation providing youth groups in the community? How can the extra *time* provided by the extended schools concept (before and after school and in the school holidays) help us overcome the problem of how to fit interventions into a crowded school day, and how to avoid pupils missing out on a broad and rich curriculum while they are having help with basic skills?

The national Achievement for All programme is another source of ideas for provision aimed at building pupils' self confidence and self-efficacy – the belief that they can make valuable contributions and take charge of their own lives.

At Caludon Castle School in Coventry, for example, a pupil Faculty Ambassador scheme was introduced, to help improve targeted pupils' engagement with learning. The role of the Faculty ambassador was to meet and greet new pupils, support the transition of incoming Year 6 pupils, contribute to curriculum development, carry out observations of English lessons and provide feedback. Ambassadors were chosen through open recruitment, but two pupils with SEN (both with social difficulties) were personally invited to take part. Ambassadors met with the English teacher leading the scheme every two weeks, to practise a range of social skills. The initiative was very successful in improving the confidence, attendance and independence of the pupils with SEN who were involved.

Another development in Achievement for All schools has been the development of carefully planned and targeted before- and after-school clubs, like those at Frederick Bird Primary, described in Chapter 2, or at Stanley Road Primary in Oldham. Here, staff set up a programme of courses run by teachers, TAs and external providers, in everything from cooking and gardening to street dance and sports. Children can build up credits to a national award within the Children's University scheme.

Provision maps for clusters of schools

Another new aspect of provision mapping is the idea of clusters of schools coming together to pool funding, map needs and plan shared provision. A secondary school and its feeder primaries, for example might share a speech and language assistant who works across the schools, a parent support adviser, a primary mental health worker and a Reading Recovery teacher.

CASE STUDY

Headteachers of secondary schools and their link primary schools in County Durham meet half-termly to discuss SEN/D priorities and how best to spend funding delegated by the local authority. Provision funded this way and shared by a cluster includes a speech and language assistant, a parent support worker and the Lexia literacy intervention programme.

(Leadership that promotes the achievement of students with special educational needs and disabilities, Chapman *et al.,* National College for School Leadership, 2011)

Defining effective provision

Another development in provision mapping is the greater sense we now have of which provisions have the greatest impact on children's progress.

Research evidence for the impact of different provisions was summarised in *SEN and school improvement (*Gross and White, 2003), and updated in the former National Strategies' *Leading on intervention* materials (2006d). Since then, further research has been published and is incorporated into a summary table (Table 6.3). The table lists the interventions that schools can use with some certainty that they will have the desired effect.

Moving from provision mapping to provision management

Constructing a provision map is one thing. Making sure that the provision it describes proves effective is another. Like IEPs, provision maps run the risk of sitting in someone's drawer or on their laptop, to be pulled out when Ofsted come but not in between.

Key to making provision maps effective are the processes which link the map to tracking information. Tracking too can become meaningless paperwork – 'fantastic folders of pupil tracking, kept in the deputy head's office but nothing done about them', as one school put it. Linking your provision map to tracking information means that the map can be regularly adjusted to meet changing needs.

Also key are the systems that are in place to monitor the quality of the provision, and to evaluate its effectiveness. The steps involved are shown in Figure 6.3.

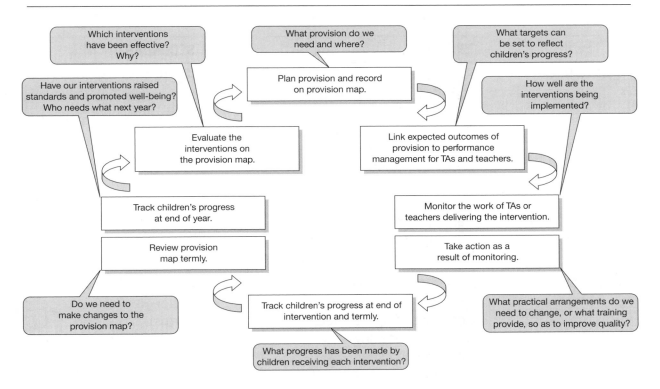

Figure 6.3 Provision management

Linking provision to performance management is a relatively new area. Although we are used to linking the progress of a class or classes to teachers' performance management, and monitoring the quality of classroom and subject teaching, many schools are only just beginning to identify clearly the outcomes they expect for groups of children taking part in intervention programmes, and link these to performance management targets for the adults involved. Usually, this will be a teaching assistant who is delivering the intervention – but it is also important, in primary schools, to make similar performance management arrangements for the class teacher. This is because with an intervention it is essential that the class teacher retains overall ownership, with the TA working under his or her direction and very good links made between the work the children do in the intervention programme and the work they do in class.

It is important, too, that adults delivering intervention programmes are observed from time to time. Such monitoring has several purposes. It enables a SENCO/INCO or other manager to check that the intervention is being delivered in the way intended by those who originally constructed and evaluated the programme. We know from research (Beard *et al.,* 2005) that such 'fidelity to the programme' is both highly important, in terms of programme impact, and relatively rare. Training has an immediate impact on the way we teach, but most of us are programmed to return to our default settings (the way we behaved before we had the training) over time – unless we have top-up training, observation and feedback.

	PRIMARY	**SECONDARY**
LANGUAGE	Key Stage 1 Narrative, Key Stage 2 Narrative (Black Sheep Press) Languageland (Black Sheep Press) Talk Boost (www.ican.org.uk) Language for Thinking (Speechmark) SPIRALS (Routledge) Talking Partners (www.educationworks. org.uk) Reading for Meaning (readingformeaning.co.uk) Language4Reading (www.ican.org.uk)	ELCISS (Speechmark) Secondary Talk (www. educationworks.org.uk)
READING[1]	Acceleread, Accelewrite ARROW Better Reading Partnership Catch Up Literacy Direct Phonics Early Literacy Support (ELS) ENABLE Family Literacy Fischer Family Trust Wave 3 Further Literacy Support Lexia Paired reading, paired writing (www. literacytrust.org.uk) Phono-graphix TM Project X Code Reading Intervention Reading Recovery Reciprocal Teaching Read Write Inc One-to-One Phonics Tutoring Kit Read Write Inc Fresh Start SIDNEY Sound Discovery Sounds-Write THRASS Toe by Toe	Academy of Reading Better Reading Partnership Corrective Reading Catch Up Literacy ENABLE PLUS (KS3) Fresh Start Literacy Acceleration Paired reading Read Write Inc Fresh Start Sound Training for Reading THRASS Toe by Toe
READING COMPREHENSION	Inference Training Reading for Meaning Reciprocal Teaching	

Note

1 See Brooks, G. (2007) *What works for pupils with literacy difficulties*. London: DCSF and www.interventionsforliteracy.org.uk for further information on the reading, writing and spelling programmes in this table

TABLE 6.3 What works in school-based intervention

	PRIMARY	SECONDARY
SPELLING	Acceleread, Accelewrite ARROW Cued Spelling ENABLE One-to-One Interactive Assessment and Teaching Improving Spelling through Teaching Morphemes Individual Styles in Learning to Spell Lexia Multisensory Teaching System for Reading (MTSR) Phono-graphix Reading Intervention RITA Sound Discovery Sounds Write THRASS	Literacy Acceleration THRASS Read Write Inc
WRITING	Family Literacy Further Literacy Support Paired Writing Rapid Writing Reading Recovery	
MATHEMATICS	Catch Up Numeracy (www.catchup.org) Family Numeracy (www.skillsfor families.excellencegateway.org.uk) firstclass@number (everychildcounts. edgehill.ac.uk) Mathematics Recovery (www. mathsrecovery.org.uk) Numbers Count (everychildcounts. edgehill.ac.uk) Numicon Closing the Gap and Numicon intervention Programme (Oxford University Press) Peer tutoring (www.york.ac.uk/iee/ research/t_peer_learning_paired_ maths.htm and The Paired Maths Handbook, David Fulton) Rapid Maths Supporting pupils with gaps in their mathematical understanding – Primary National Strategy Wave 3 mathematics (www.teachfind.com and www. lancsngfl.ac.uk/ curriculum/math/index.php?category_ id=461)	Peer tutoring (http://www.york.ac.uk/ iee/research/t_peer_ learning_paired_maths. Htm)

TABLE 6.3 continued

	PRIMARY	**SECONDARY**
LEARNING / WORKING MEMORY DIFFICULTIES	Jungle Memory (www.junglememory. com)	Jungle Memory (www. junglememory.com)
PARENTING PROGRAMMES FOR CHILDREN WITH BESD	FAST (Families and Schools Together) (www.familiesandschools.org) Family Links Nurturing Programme (www.familylinks.org.uk) Contact local specialist services for advice on the programmes below: Empowering Parents, Empowering Communities The Incredible Years (3–12 years) Mellow Parenting Positive Parents Spokes Triple P	Contact local specialist services for advice on the programmes below: Group Teen Triple P The Strengthening Families Programme for Parents
SOCIAL AND EMOTIONAL LEARNING	Good Behaviour Game (www. interventioncentral.org/behavioral-interventions/schoolwide-classroommgmt/good-behavior-game) Nurture group (www.nurturegroups.org) PALS (Playing and Learning to Socialise) (www.inscript.com.au/pals) Pyramid Clubs (www.continyou.org.uk/ school/pyramid) SEAL group work (www.teachfind.com) School Home support workers (www. schoolhomesupport.org) Some mentoring schemes such as Chance UK (www.chanceuk.com) Stress reduction Place2Be (www. theplace2be.org.uk), A Quiet Place (www.aquietplace.co.uk) Therapeutic Story Writing, (www. therapeuticstorywriting.com and www. youngminds.org.uk) Story Links (www.storylinkstraining .co. uk and www.youngminds.org.uk)	Aggression Replacement Training (ART) (www.aggression replacementtraining. org) Alternative curricula e.g. Skill Force (www. skillforce.org) Fairbridge (www. princes-trust.org.uk) School Home support workers (www. schoolhomesupport.org) Some mentoring schemes such as Chance UK (www. chanceuk.com) and some learning support units School-based counselling (www. barnardos.org.uk; www.nspcc.org.uk; www.relate.org.uk)

TABLE **6.3** continued

	PRIMARY	**SECONDARY**
SOCIAL AND EMOTIONAL LEARNING	Contact local specialist services for advice on the programmes below: Circle of friends Cognitive behavioural/social skills groupwork such as Dinosaur School, anger management FAST Track Music therapy Play therapy Peer mentoring/buddying Relaxation training	Contact local specialist services for advice on the programmes below: Cognitive behavioural/ social skills groupwork such as anger management, SEAL group work Music therapy Peer mentoring/ buddying Relaxation training
ADHD	Attention training computer games (www.gamesforlife.co.uk) Contact specialist advisory services for advice on the interventions below: For moderate difficulties, group-based parenting programmes and small-group or individual cognitive-behavioural/ social skills programmes as for BESD For severe difficulties or in cases of lack of response to parenting/small group programmes, drug treatment in addition	Attention training computer games (www.gamesforlife.co.uk) Contact specialist advisory services for advice on the interventions below: For moderate difficulties, group-based parenting programmes and small-group or individual cognitive-behavioural/social skills programmes as for BESD For severe difficulties or in cases of lack of response to parenting/small group programmes, drug treatment in addition

TABLE **6.3** continued

133

	PRIMARY	SECONDARY
AUTISM	Contact specialist advisory services/ speech and language therapists for advice on these interventions: Augmentative and Alternative Communication Cognitive-based social skills training Circle of friends and other forms of peer-mediated support Intensive Behavioural Interventions Intensive adult–child interaction Sensory integration Structured small group play activities e.g. Lego therapy Social stories, Comic strip conversations (www.thegraycenter.org) Social Communication Inference Programme (SCIP) TEACCH Therapeutic touch (massage)	Contact specialist advisory services/ speech and language therapists for advice on these interventions: Augmentative and Alternative Communication Cognitive-based social skills training Circle of friends and other forms of peer-mediated support Sensory integration Social stories TEACCH Therapeutic touch (massage)
DEVELOPMENTAL COORDINATION DISORDER	Contact occupational therapists for advice on this intervention: CO-OP (Cognitive Orientation to Daily Occupational Performance)	Contact occupational therapists for advice on this intervention: CO-OP (Cognitive Orientation to Daily Occupational Performance)

Sources and further information

Brooks, G. (2007) *What works for pupils with literacy difficulties*. London: DCSF

Case-Smith, J. and Arbesman, M. (2008) Evidence-based interventions for autism, *The American Journal of Occupational Therapy*, 62, 4

Copps, J. *et al.* (2007) *Lean on me: mentoring for young people at risk*. London: New Philanthropy Capital

DCSF (2008) Targeted mental health in schools – using the evidence to inform your approach: A practical guide for headteachers and commissioners. London: DCSF

Dowker, a. (2004) *What works for children with mathematical difficulties*. London: DfES

Dyson, A. *et al.* (2010) *Narrowing the gap in educational achievement and improving resilience for children and young people with additional needs*. London: C4EO

Goodall, J. *et al.* (2010) *Review of best practice in parental engagement*. London: DfE

Higgins, S. *et al.* (2011) *Toolkit of strategies to improve learning*. London: The Sutton Trust

Hill, A. *et al.* (2011) *Evaluation of the Welsh School-based Counselling Strategy*. Cardiff: Welsh Government Social Research

National Institute of Health and Clinical Excellence (NICE) (2008) *ADHD: diagnosis and management of ADHD in children, young people and adults*. London: National Collaborating Centre for Mental Health

Paterson, E. *et al.* (2010) *Count Me In*. London: New Philanthropy Capital

Stewart-Brown, S. and Schrader, A. (2010) *Home and community based parenting support programmes*. Warwick: Warwick Medical School

Weare, K. and Nind, M. (2011) Mental health promotion and problem prevention in schools. *Health Promotion International*, 26, S1

TABLE **6.3** continued

Observation of interventions will also inform the professional development that should underpin any performance management cycle, and enable any practical problems to be spotted and resolved. The TA or teacher may be working in a noisy place, for example, or have children arriving in dribs and drabs to their session, without the materials they need, or opportunities for liaison between the TAs and class teacher may be limited. Picking these practical issues up early will make the adult delivering the programme feel valued and enable them to make the most of the precious time they have with the children with whom they work.

The Toolkit section of this book provides an exemplar framework for monitoring the quality of interventions, that allows for professional development needs to be identified and practical problems resolved.

Also in the Toolkit are a set of proformas for use when setting up an intervention programme. The basic framework was originally developed by Sheffield local authority, and appears on the former National Strategies' *Leading on intervention* CD (DfES, 2006d). Additional proformas for setting up a range of commonly used interventions are provided here; others can be developed, using the basic model, for any intervention in use in your school. The proformas support the management cycle of planning, developing, monitoring and evaluating provisions in Figure 6.3: they describe the entry criteria for the intervention, the expected outcome (exit criteria), how and when delivery will be monitored and the evaluation method that will be used. Essentially, they enable SENCOs/INCOs to manage the school provision for children with additional needs, once they have mapped the provision that is needed.

Another time-saving tool for evaluating the school's provision comes from the use of RAISEonline. The pupil-level data function on RAISEonline allows a school to hold and import data about each of its pupils – name, gender, date of birth, SEN status, Free School Meals status, ethnic origin. To the basic spreadsheet a school can, using the custom attributes button, add further columns, one for each of the provisions on the school's provision map. Putting a 'Y' in the relevant columns allows for a personalised printout of the provision received by each child, if you want to use this as an alternative to highlighting a paper version of your whole-school provision map.

More importantly, however, recording each child's provision on a database enables you to evaluate the impact of your provisions. You can, for example, use the filtering function to pull out only those pupils who have received a particular intervention, such as anger management groups, and print out their exclusion data, attendance data, end of Key Stage test results and results of any additional assessments (such as QCA optional tests or reading ages) that have been entered onto RAISEonline.

You can refine your evaluation by, for example, pulling out only boys who have had a particular provision, or only girls, or only those in a certain year groups, or with a particular type of SEN/D.

You can even, if you use a system like that developed in Surrey schools, look at intervention outcomes by the member of staff delivering the programme. Surrey's tool allows a SENCO to enter on a spreadsheet the name of the intervention, the person delivering it, and the children taking part with details about them (free school meals status, type and stage of SEN, whether they have EAL and so on). There is a column in which to enter the expected outcome of an intervention in terms of points score gains or behaviour change. Then, for each child, the SENCO can enter a green judgement (if the child exceeded the expected outcomes), an amber judgement (if the child met the expected outcome) or a red judgement (if the child did not meet the outcome). For any intervention or intervention provider, the percentage of children involved who met or exceeded the expected outcome can be calculated. The same calculation can be made for pupils eligible for free school meals and receiving the Pupil Premium, for children with different types of SEN/D, for EAL learners and so on.

Such sophisticated uses of data provide a powerful tool for evaluating a provision map, and promise much for the future in terms of reducing the workload involved in proper evaluation.

7 | Working in partnership
Parents, pupils and outside agencies

Working with parents and carers

Working effectively with parents and carers is the key to reducing bureaucracy. If parents are confident about what is being done to support their child, they do not need pieces of paper. They can be your greatest ally in reducing bureaucracy, or – if you get the relationship with them wrong – they can undo all your efforts. Not least, they can exercise their legal right to request a statutory assessment for a possible Statement of SEN/Education, Health and Care Plan that will generate a blizzard of paperwork for you and the local authority.

So it is essential that in making any changes to the way you manage SEN and disability in school, you do this with the full support of parents and carers.

Systems for involving parents/carers

Ideally you will begin by finding out, perhaps through a questionnaire or focus group discussion, how parents/carers feel about your current procedures. They may be happy – but they may not. Research shows that parental involvement remains a real challenge for schools. Pinkus (2005) researched the experiences of 14 parents in four local authorities as they 'worked in partnership with professionals to meet the needs of their SEN children', and found that parents often felt that they only attended meetings to listen to what professionals had to say. Their perception was that decisions had already been made, for example, when they were asked to sign IEPs that had been written before the meeting started. Many parents find the paperwork involved in SEN full of jargon, and are aware that some of the child's teachers may not even read it, particularly when the child changes class or school. Significantly, what they want and do not always feel they get is information on what they can do to help their child with learning.

A study by Lindsay *et al.* (2010), in which parents of children with SEN/D were interviewed, sums up elegantly what it is that parents really want:

> What gave parents confidence that their child's school could meet
> their child's needs was very simple: that teachers and/or senior leaders,

preferably both, were willing to meet with them and to hear their story and their views about their child; that teachers listened and took seriously what they communicated about their child; that often relatively simple adaptations were made to accommodate their child's learning needs (e.g. alternative ways of recording what they knew); that their child's strengths were recognised and communicated to child, peers and parents; and that the social and emotional impacts of learning difficulties were recognised and addressed.

If your own research shows that parents and carers have concerns about current systems, you will find it easy to explain why you are making changes, such as no longer having IEPs for all children with SEN/D. You might want to invite parents to a meeting to explain any changes; you will certainly want to provide all of them with information in leaflet form. The Toolkit section of this book provides a possible model for you to build on.

You will want to make clear the advantages of the new approach – for example, the expectation that class or subject teachers build a knowledge of the child's individual needs into their everyday planning. Parents/carers will also be very interested to see the school's provision map, with entry and exit criteria for each additional intervention, so that they know what provision they can expect for their child.

It is very important to find out, too, about any worries your parents/carers may have. These will be particular to your setting but might be about having less contact with you as the SENCO/INCO, if meetings to review progress are more often to be led by the class teacher or form tutor. You will need to be clear what arrangements there will be for others (such as you, or a head of year, or the child's key worker in school) to routinely join review meetings involving pupils with SEN/D or behaviour difficulties. You could also make clear that there will be no change to the kind of informal communication lines (telephone contact, drop-in times and so on) that parents/carers usually value far more than the more formal contacts).

Parents/carers will want to know not just what you are stopping doing, but also what you are planning to do instead. It will be helpful for you to explain your plans for:

- involving them, as the experts on their own child, in providing information and feedback to the school;
- making sure all relevant staff are aware of their child's needs;
- setting targets;
- reviewing and reporting on progress;
- making additional provision for the child;
- providing ideas on how they can help their child at home.

In other chapters we have seen how these areas can be addressed in non-bureaucratic ways. Parents can be given a highlighted provision map so that they know exactly what provision their child receives. They can provide information about their child, and contribute to pupil-held personal profiles, in the ways described in Chapter 2. They should have sent home to them every term the (differentiated) targets that their child will be working on in class, or see these recorded in the child's Learning Log or planner.

Ideally the targets for all children in the class will be linked to information on how the family can help the child achieve them. Some schools, for example, post on the web the learning programmes for the week, with some suggestions about how parents/carers can help at home. Others put a poster on a door or window where parents bringing or collecting their children will see it. At Owler Brook primary in Sheffield, each classroom has a shelf outside the door displaying objects and books about the topic the class is working on each week.

Some schools put together activity bags linked to the learning targets for children to take home at weekends. For example, a Reception Year child with SLCN whose curricular target was to use verbs in speech took home 'verb bags' such as a collection of objects (like toy cars) that would invite the use of the verb 'push'.

Alternatively, the school might simply give younger children a daily sticker with a suggestion for the parent – 'Today we have learned about floating and sinking. Ask me to tell you about it'. Older children might construct their own messages and write them on stickers, or record them on Talking Tins.

Really useful materials for home activities developed by the National Strategies are available on the Teachfind website (www.teachfind.com), in the form of leaflets for parents of primary children (search for Using curricular targets in Year 2, and Year 6) and web-based, printable guidance for parents of secondary-aged children (search for Progression Maps). An example is shown in Table 7.1.

Parents'/carers' involvement in reviews of progress might, for some children with more complex SEN/D, take the form of specially convened meetings. But for many children they will take place at regular parents' evenings – perhaps with more time allocated to the meeting than might be standard for other pupils. Or they may take place at special academic tutoring days, like those at Coombe Boys' school in the case study in Chapter 2, where parents, pupil and form tutor meet together on an appointment basis, joined where necessary by specialist colleagues.

In between reviews, the most effective schools use a range of strategies, including the internet, to keep parents/carers in touch with how their child is doing. Cardinal Wiseman secondary school in Birmingham, for example, provides parents/carers

YEAR 2 READING: STORIES	Home activities
I can use a contents list and index and tell a friend what a book might be about by looking at the cover, title and illustrations.	Use a TV listings guide to choose programmes that you would like to watch together.

YEAR 2 MATHEMATICS: MEASURING	Home activities
I can estimate the lengths of different objects, compare their size and measure them, and compare their length.	Have your child stand in a doorway in your house. Say that the doorway is roughly 2 metres high. Ask your children how many things they can see that are taller/shorter than 2 metres.

TABLE 7.1 Taking an active interest in your child's learning

with password-protected access to regularly updated information on their child's academic progress, conduct log and attendance record. All pupils have targets that are reviewed termly; progress against these targets is regularly tracked and assessment information placed in the e-portal. Parents who do not have internet access receive printed versions of assessment information, and pupils also put their targets (on sticky labels) in their homework diaries.

ICT is also used to good effect at Eggbuckland College in Plymouth. Here, pupils all have an electronic individual learning plan. The e-ILP can be added to by pupils and teachers, and can hold anything from targets to action plans to personal blogs. It forms the basis for the school's twice-yearly review days, when parents come into school for three-way meetings with their child and the form tutor.

At South Dartmoor College in Devon, there is a similar system of personalised appointments. The college allocates a day a week each February for these reviews. Much effort goes into making sure parents/carers make and keep appointments; where necessary they are reminded by phone or an Education Welfare Officer (EWO) visit. As a result, attendance at the review days has risen from 70 per cent to almost 100 per cent. Parents/carers of Key Stage 4 pupils have subject-specific meetings, but in Key Stage 3 the meeting is with the form tutor. The school use SIMS Parents' Gateway to provide information on progress in all subjects; the tutor and parents can call up the data on-screen and discuss it together.

Nationally, however, we have a way to go before the potential of ICT to support parental engagement is fully exploited. A BECTA (2010) study found that only 25 per cent of parents received information about their child's learning via online tools. But the learning platforms with personal access and information for each pupil that are now in place in many schools are now making it easier to use electronic systems like those used at South Dartmoor and Eggbuckland.

Learning platforms allow parents to see their children's marks and assignments, records of behaviour and attendance, and a range of other information about what the child is studying. At Grays Infant and Nursery School in Newhaven, the use of learning platforms has been taken to a high level. Every child has their own e-portfolio space entered by clicking on their photograph. The space holds data on the child's attainment, targets, activities and achievements. Staff are given regular time to upload information and photographs – for example, for a child where a target agreed with parents was to 'build confidence in class and group situations', a TA or teacher might upload a photograph of him succeeding in a PE lesson.

To help them understand and use the system, parents and carers were invited into school (with a crèche and doughnuts provided) to go online and see how it worked. A film was also made to support them. They soon concluded that 'It's just like Facebook', and now regularly log on, helped by the school's system of sending a 3G-connected netbook home once a week where the child does not have internet. One powerful benefit has been enabling distant dads to keep in touch with their child's learning.

One can easily imagine that practice like this will grow, so that welcoming, highly visual systems like these will be where the targets and other information that would once have been on an IEP will be held in future, with the child's class teacher or tutor updating the information at regular intervals.

Helping parents/carers to help their child – whole-school approaches

As we have seen, the biggest gap for parents/carers in our current SEN procedures is their failure to support them in knowing how best to help their child in the areas where they are experiencing difficulty. Equally, we know how fundamental it is for the child's progress that there is home support for learning. Influential research (Desforges and Abouchaar, 2003) has shown that where parents/carers are involved, on average children's attainment will be 15–17 per cent higher than where they are not involved.

The type of involvement that brings these gains is not about 'coming into school' – attending school events, turning up at parents' evenings, helping in class and so on. What makes the difference instead is what Desforges calls good at-home parenting. This means the provision of 'a secure and stable environment, intellectual stimulation, parent-child discussion, good models of constructive social and educational values and high aspirations relating to personal fulfilment and good citizenship'. A key element of this is the quality of the 'home learning environment' (Sylva *et al.*, 2003): the extent to which parents/carers talk to and play with their child, take them on outings, read to them, teach nursery rhymes and songs, play with numbers and letters and so on. And this is not dependent on the social class or educational level of parents and carers; as Sylva says, 'What you do is more important than who you are'.

How can we help all families provide this sort of good at-home parenting? It is clear that the SENCO/INCO cannot achieve this by working on their own. Involving parents/carers of children with SEN or disabilities, or of EAL learners or other vulnerable groups, needs to build on an existing ethos which conveys to parents/carers that they are valued partners rather than potential troublemakers.

An ethos like this is often tangibly conveyed in some schools, whilst absent in others. It can be conveyed by asking families what they want – Earlswood Infant School in Redhill, for example, surveyed parents and found that 61 per cent didn't have a computer; they did not want courses but did want internet access, so the school set up its own internet café. Another school, at parents' request, introduced drop-in sessions with the school nurse.

A parent-friendly ethos can also be conveyed, for example, by the school entrance hall, where local radio might be playing (rather than Mozart), where the reading matter on the table in the comfortable waiting area includes *Hello* magazine as well as the school prospectus. There will be information in community languages, and posters inviting parents to join in a range of activities, some of which are deliberately unthreatening to a parent whose own experience of learning may hitherto have been negative – everything from nail art, stress workshops, massage, art and craft and ICT through to Dads and Lads Saturday sport and Maths4mums through the more 'academic' curriculum workshops and full Family Learning courses. A good example is the work of Candleby Lane Primary School in Nottinghamshire, where families were offered free breakfasts of bacon and sausage cobs to encourage them to come in to school; in the first term only a handful of parents turned up, but within a few years numbers had risen to 350, with the breakfasts followed by workshops on 'how to help your child'.

Care will be taken that parents' and carers' first communications with school are not about any difficulties their child may have. A relationship will have been built up long before this, that focuses on sharing information about the child as a person and a learner (not a 'special needs child'), and which celebrates strengths and successes, for example by sending home 'praise postcards' to let parents know when things have gone well.

In these schools special efforts will be made to reach out to fathers. Fathers' involvement in their child's learning is strongly related to educational attainment and adjustment, particularly for boys (Flouri and Buchanan, 2002). In the teenage years, one study showed that 90 per cent of boys who felt that their father spent time with them and took an active interest in their progress were confident and successful. By contrast, 72 per cent of those who said their fathers rarely or never did these things fell into the group with the lowest levels of self-confidence, and were more likely to dislike school and get in trouble with the police.

The case studies below give examples of the kind of imaginative work schools have done to engage parents in children's learning. They represent the type of practice the SENCO/INCO, as part of the school leadership team, will want to develop in their school.

CASE STUDY

1 Birley Spa

Birley Spa Primary School in Sheffield used the Index for Inclusion (CSIE, 2002) to undertake a self-evaluation of inclusive cultures, policy and practice. As part of this review they surveyed parents, and used the information gained to re-shape aspects of the way they work with the community. Parents were involved in working groups to tackle issues such as communication. A support group was set up for parents who might have concerns, for example about bullying, but did not initially feel confident to talk to staff. Every day there are as many as 80 parents and carers in the school, providing volunteer support in classrooms, attending courses as adult learners, or helping with childcare for the many adult education courses available. These cover subjects requested by local people, such as ICT. Adults who take part in these courses are supported to progress, where they want to, to obtain qualifications at the local college.

CASE STUDY

2 Arbourthorne

At Arbourthorne Primary, also in Sheffield, a concerted drive to improve the relationship between the school and parents led to the appointment of key staff to lead the work – a Deputy Head and a Learning Mentor, who spent time chatting to parents, inviting them in for coffee, and going into the playground every day to invite reluctant parents in to watch a lesson. Children and families were given special interactive homework that involved them in working together; this project was given high status, with parents actively involved in providing feedback and helping shape future work. The school arranged opportunities for parents and children to work together in school with visiting artists, and organised a range of courses in and out of school including ICT, book-keeping, and Basic Skills literacy. After two years the school had established a group of parents who by now were very comfortable in school and in supporting their children's learning. These parents now organise themselves and decided on the next steps, which have included setting up a very successful Credit Union, running a fruit snack shop in school, the establishment of a PTA, and regular curriculum workshops where teachers explain what children will be learning, what homework will be involved, and how parents can help.

CASE STUDY

3 Cooper's Lane

Cooper's Lane Primary School in Lewisham devised a 'Dads Matter' scheme. A group of fathers and male family figures have been meeting once a month in a local pub or restaurant to plan a strategy to encourage fathers to become more involved with their children's learning. Support is particularly targeted at families of children with behaviour difficulties, because of the lack of positive male role models many of them have experienced. The group planned trips, home reading activities, fun homework tasks, and a 'Bring your dad to school day', when dads would come in and use their talents and interests to work with children. One father, for example, brought in his motorbike to show to the boys. About 60 fathers took part in the first year of the scheme, which had a marked impact. Fathers became much more confident to come into the playground and into school, and there has been a reduction in behaviour problems among the target children.

CASE STUDY

4 Marner Primary

Marner Primary in Tower Hamlets employs two home support workers and runs an ever-increasing range of clubs, workshops and groups for parents. There is a cookery group, an embroidery group, family days out, a parent and child Chatterbox Club run by a TA who has been trained by a speech and language therapist. Strengthening Families parenting groups have proved very popular; parents often want to continue once the course finishes so one group has gone on to become a SEAL group. Maths is a focus for the school, which has taken part in the local authority's Bead String Project of home activities, and also in the very successful Ocean Maths programme in which parents and children engage in practical and enjoyable maths activities together through workshops and specially designed homework that children and parents can share.

Where schools set up initiatives like these they are providing the essential backdrop against which the SENCO or INCO can build their own targeted work with families of children who have SEN or disabilities.

This backdrop is particularly important where children have behavioural, emotional and social difficulties. Research shows that support for their parents in developing their parenting skills can have a huge impact (Furlong *et al.*, 2012). But the parenting programmes that work, such as those listed in Chapter 6, can easily feel stigmatising and uncomfortable for parents/carers. Very few schools succeed by simply inviting targeted parents to attend a parenting course. There is a potential stigma about such courses, and a feeling amongst most parents that they should somehow automatically know how to bring up a child, that acts as a powerful deterrent. Schools have to work hard to overcome these barriers. Where they are successful, it is usually because they have built up 'parental capital' by offering parents range of non-threatening and enjoyable activities. These, as we have seen, help create the climate where parenting skills courses can be offered as a natural progression for parents/carers who are already confident in coming into school. After that, a good way in is to offer SEAL Family Learning workshops (DfES, 2006b) to *all* parents/carers in a non-stigmatising way, then follow this up with more intensive work with some.

The need for parents to have a 'safe' way in to involvement with the school is illustrated by the experience of a group of schools in the town of Winsford in

Cheshire. Deprivation levels are high and children's language and communication skills poor on entry to nursery and school. The schools implemented an initiative called Talking Boxes, in which children and their parents are invited to decorate a sturdy wooden box which they then fill with objects that are special to the child. Each child has the opportunity to bring their box into class and tell everyone about their special things.

The schools have found this a good way of getting parents to come into school. 'We would never have got them in for literacy or numeracy', they say. 'But decorating a box – everyone felt they could do that'.

Helping parents/carers of children with SEN or disabilities to help their child

The extended schools agenda is involving more and more schools in whole-school effort to involve parents/carers. Given this backdrop, what more can be done to support parents/carers of children with SEN or disabilities?

Overcoming barriers

First, SENCOs/INCOs will need to make special efforts to draw some of these parents into what the school has to offer. Many experience particular barriers to involvement. Their own experience of education may make them anxious or angry when coming in to school or talking to teachers. They may themselves have low literacy or numeracy levels which make it difficult for them to help their child. Their feelings about their child's difficulties are often those that cause awkwardness in their relationship with the school. They may simply get tired of hearing yet another teacher tell them their child has problems.

But as Klein (2000) puts it, 'Parents don't exist solely as the receptacles of bad news about their children's problem behaviour or poor attainment'. The best SENCOs/INCOs understand this and go out of their way to overcome barriers and provide extra nurturing for parents as well as pupils. At Coombe Boys', the case study school in Chapter 2, the SENCO put time and energy into making that all-important first contact with parents/carers. If they would not come to school, she would visit them at home, together with an Education Welfare Officer. In the first meeting she would highlight specific positives about their child, and introduce them personally to a person in school (one of the TA team, for example) whom they could contact at any time. After the first meeting she would nurture the relationship by being available in person or on the phone when parents needed to talk, by checking with them when any changes were proposed to the child's pattern of support, and by offering practical help. All parents of children with SEN or disabilities in Year 7 were invited to a coffee morning at the start of the school year. There, they heard about the school support systems and could chat informally with the school's educational psychologist, transition worker, Head of Year and SENCO. Through measures like these Coombe were able to achieve 100 per cent parental attendance at review meetings.

A primary school in Bristol, serving one of the most deprived areas of the city, achieves 95 per cent attendance at parents' evenings. The school day starts early and finishes late – with breakfast clubs and after-school clubs covering family literacy, numeracy and mother tongue classes where parents learn alongside their children. There are also sewing, art, gardening and health classes and every subject coordinator runs sessions explaining how their subject is taught. Families take part in maths trails, drama workshops, musical sessions and various environmental and geographical trails. Drop-in sessions are available for parents with pre-school children and there are pre-nursery home visits for all. Parents are always welcome in school, helping in classes and sitting on working groups. They work with the children on computers, with art activities, literacy-based lessons and in after-hours clubs.

Parents' evenings are where initial discussion about a child with SEN takes place, and if parents do not attend then someone in school will try to catch them later: 'We missed you at parents' evening – how about popping in tomorrow after school?' Teachers stress the positives: 'He did a fantastic piece of work on robots. Why don't you come in and see his books – you'll be pleased'. Class teachers have an informal chat to parents before any sort of formal letter about SEN goes home, and the SENCO follows up with another chat. The school will always telephone a parent who is known to have literacy difficulties, rather than write to them. The SENCO has set up a support group for parents of children with SEN or disabilities. The group meets once a week for coffee; parents might watch a video on how to help your child at home, borrow reading books or make a game to play with their child.

Practice of this kind challenges our assumptions that some parents will never be able to become involved or support their child's learning.

'Achievement for All' structured conversations

Further evidence to challenge assumptions has come from the national Achievement for All (AfA) initiative. Working with parents is one of AfA's key strands, and the idea of a 'structured conversation' developed for the programme has fundamentally changed the relationship between schools and parents of children with SEN or disabilities.

The structured conversation is a meeting of about an hour, held two to three times a year initially, between the parents/carers of pupils with SEN, the pupil themselves where appropriate, and a key teacher in school. The key teacher will be the class teacher in a primary school; in a secondary school it is often the form tutor.

These teachers receive a half day's training in how to hold a conversation structured around four stages: explore, focus, plan and review. They learn how to use basic counselling skills – active listening, paraphrasing and summarising, how to ask open rather than closed questions, how to agree targets and develop a plan of action, and how to summarise the discussion and clarify next steps.

The aim of the conversation is to really listen to the parent's point of view, to understand what they see as the key barriers to their child's learning, what they think has worked well in the past, their aspirations for their child and the provision they would like to see in place. As one teacher said, the conversation provides 'designated time to get to know what parents feel and take on board their hopes and aspirations for their children'.

The AfA initiative as a whole has been outstandingly successful. An external evaluation (Humphreys and Squires, 2011) found that 37 per cent of the 28,000 primary and secondary aged children with SEN or disabilities involved in the pilot scheme, made progress as great as or greater than that made by all pupils nationally in English, and 42 per cent in maths. Persistent absence reduced by 10 per cent. As we saw from the case studies in Chapter 2, the initiative has a number of elements and the structured conversation is only one of them. Nevertheless, the external evaluation found that schools perceived it to be the most successful element of the programme.

The proportion of AfA schools reporting excellent relationships with parents increased over the two years of the pilot from 12 per cent to 48 per cent. Those reporting poor relationships fell from 11 per cent to 1.5 per cent. In terms of sustainability, more than 90 per cent of participating schools said they intended to continue to use the structured conversation model after the conclusion of the funded pilot. Some planned to extend the training to all staff so that the principles of listening to parents rather than talking at them could be embedded into regular systems such as parents' evenings.

The structured conversation is not a development to be undertaken likely. It is not just a matter of individual teachers having training; to be successful, it requires 'fidelity to the programme' (that is, implementing the model exactly as it was designed to be used), and leadership from the top. The evaluation of AfA found, for example, that where the person leading AfA in the school was the headteacher, parent participation in a full three structured conversations per year was on average

55 per cent, compared to 32 per cent where the lead was the SENCO and 30 per cent where it was a class teacher.

The data from AfA schools demonstrate that it is possible to engage almost all parents and carers of children with SEN or disabilities in joint planning for their child. The number of schools who reported not being able to complete a single structured conversation with at least one of the child's parents was very small and reduced by nearly one third over the course of the pilot.

In part, this was because parents felt valued and listened to. As one teacher said, 'I think the strategy of getting parents to talk about their child first rather than us jumping in is interesting, you know, I think that's a really good idea that we can fly with'.

Schools also used a range of strategies when inviting parents to take part in a structured conversation, including:

- texting parents to remind them of the meeting time and using text messaging for any ongoing communication, including sending 'good news' home;
- phoning more reluctant parents to reassure them about the purpose of the meeting;
- providing a structure for parents, with questions for them to think about in advance – how do you feel your child is progressing? what has been their biggest achievement this year? do you think anything has got in the way of them making progress?
- offering a range of times to meet, covering the whole day from 8am to 7pm;
- encouraging reluctant parents to bring another key person in the child's life, such as a grandparent or older brother or sister;
- picking up the parents or conducting the conversation on home visits.

CASE STUDY

5 Bromesberrow

Bromesberrow is a small rural primary school in Gloucestershire, drawing its intake from a traveller site and a nearby town. Traditionally, Romany traveller pupils from this site do not attend school after the age of 11, retaining a strong historically embedded mindset that children should stay close to the family and (especially girls) engage in domestic activities. The majority of mothers do not read and write well and academic aspirations for girls are very low.

As part of the AfA initiative, the school worked hard on structured conversations aimed at encouraging mothers to come into school more often and increase their aspirations for their children. Initially, the headteacher and a class teacher visited Traveller sites to hold the conversations. They also set up family literacy classes on the site for mothers and their children.

In a recent round of structured conversations all pupils but one were represented. The school has seen noticeable impact on children's learning. Parents' and children's aspirations are changing; one child in Key Stage 2, for example, is beginning to talk for the first time about the possibility of going to secondary school.

Achievement for All (2012) Anthology Pilot 2009–2011

The growing use of strategies to reach out to reluctant parents reflected the value schools felt they got from the structured conversations. These were some of their observations:

The structured conversations give you a wide picture of each child and actually some of the children were very active at home, and doing a whole variety of things. One child in particular, she's a really skilled musician and we didn't know that.

It challenges the concept that some students have that parents were only brought in when a student was in trouble. Our key teachers have been at pains to speak to students and say 'you are not in trouble – we want to celebrate how well you are doing and we want your parents to come in.' They feel really special that this is happening about them and they are really proud and they will go and seek out their key teacher and say 'I haven't forgotten it is next week'. And it is really positive.

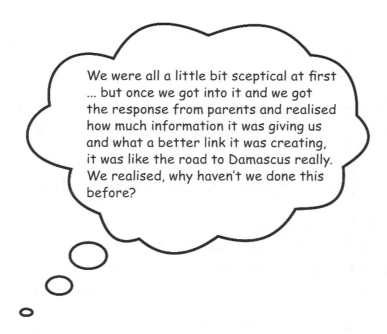

We were all a little bit sceptical at first ... but once we got into it and we got the response from parents and realised how much information it was giving us and what a better link it was creating, it was like the road to Damascus really. We realised, why haven't we done this before?

Schools were often able to use the information from structured conversations to re-shape their provision and to put parents in touch with the support systems they might need. One school arranged a family care worker to visit the home of a child with severe disabilities, another planned drum lessons in school for a pupil with BESD so as to build on his interests and talents; another planned evening classes for parents as they had learned that there was a demand for this.

A final key benefit of structured conversations was – as befits the theme of this book – engaging class and subject teachers in seeing themselves as in charge of the progress of children with SEN/D, rather than the SENCO or a TA. As one SENCO said, 'I used to run all the IEP meetings and then I would feed back to the class teacher, I have now got class teachers running the structured conversations and they are coming back to me. So it is actually a much better management structure'.

Person-centred planning

Another growing trend is the involvement of not only parents but as many as possible of the significant adults in the child's life, using the highly visual and engaging techniques of person-centred planning (Murray and Sanderson, 2007; DH, 2010). In person-centred planning, meetings might for example include the child, parents, perhaps grandparents, older or younger siblings, neighbours, friends, teachers, support staff, social workers – all those who care about the child and his or her future.

The person who is facilitating the meeting asks everyone, including the child, about their ambitions for the child. What is it they most want for them in the future?

The facilitator records these and then asks 'Which of these is the most important to you and the child?' There is discussion and the agreed aspirations are charted in the form of pictures at the end of a large, long strip of paper on the wall.

Next comes discussion of the steps on the way to achieving the ambition, which are also charted, along with obstacles or worries, and the actions that all those who care about the child can take.

Person-centred planning enables children and their supporters to identify for themselves:

- what's working, and needs to stay the same;
- what's not working, and needs to change;
- what really matters for the child or young person themselves, and to others;
- how each person who cares about the child can help them achieve their goals.

The group might then meet three or four times a year to review the plan and evaluate progress. The aim is to reduce dependency on 'agencies' to provide support, by mobilising the energy and commitment of the people around the child – their natural 'circle of support'.

Ongoing support for parents

Having engaged parents, including those who may have been anxious or reluctant, the next challenge is to find ways to provide them with ongoing support. Good ideas from schools include:

- inviting a group of parents whose children have the same type of SEN/D, or are in the same year group, to get together on a one-off or regular basis;
- having a drop-in 'surgery' session at a fixed time each week that is convenient for parents;
- linking a parent or family with another with a child with similar needs in a buddying relationship – someone you can always ring up, for example, if the child has forgotten what the homework was meant to be;
- running a link parent scheme, where a group of parents whose children have already transferred to a secondary school continue to attend activities for Year 6 parents so as to support families over the transition;
- having a room or space specifically for parents of children with SEN or disabilities, with information leaflets, videos and access to helpful websites and helplines such as the local parent partnership service, Contact a Family, Young Minds, Dad Talk and Family Matters;
- setting up a shared electronic forum where parents can access information such as factsheets on dyslexia or ASD, and comment on local initiatives;

- having staff and families undertake training together, for example on alternative and augmentative communication;
- identifying a TA or Learning Mentor as the key contact for a given number of families, as happens for example at the outstanding Priestnall Secondary School in Stockport, where a TA might take the role of key worker for about five pupils.

Involving parents in interventions

Having built bridges and forged relationships, the next step for the SENCO/ INCO – and one which applies equally to parents/carers who are keen to come into school and knowledgeable about their rights – is to have systems that provide clear information about the provision available in school, and involve the parent/carer in decisions to use a particular intervention or to review its impact. This was one of the learning points for schools involved in AfA. As one parent said, at the start of AfA, 'We had a meeting in January when they asked us what we wanted for Chris. We were not aware of what was available so you can't really ask for something when you don't know if it's available or not'.

Given the government's plans for parents in future to have more control over decision-making and funding, including access to personal budgets, this shared awareness is becoming ever more essential.

This is where the provision map is such a helpful tool, particularly if it is combined with clear information about the entry and exit criteria for each provision.

Wherever possible, each intervention should have parental involvement built into its design. Examples of this are:

- the 'take-homes' in Early Literacy Support (ELS);
- the ideas for home activities in the Primary Strategy 'Supporting pupils with gaps in their mathematical understanding' materials;
- the 'Special delivery' parcels of games and activities sent home to families of children involved in the post/letter-themed 1stClass@Number numeracy intervention programme;
- the Incredible Years parent programme that runs parallel to the Dino Dinosaur social skills group work intervention programme for 4–8-year-olds.

The provision planning proformas in the Toolkit section of this book signpost the importance of parental engagement within each intervention; if you are developing a planning proforma for an intervention of your own, it will be useful to think about and record this element.

Some interventions ask parents/carers to sign up to a semi-formal contract that sets out what the school will deliver, and what the parent is asked to do in return. The well-known Reading Recovery literacy intervention, for example, relies on the child being in school daily for their 12–20 week series of lessons. Where children have attendance problems, there will be a chat with the parents about the investment the school is making in the child for this very intensive and expensive intervention, and the effects if the child misses sessions. The message is 'If you can get your child to school we will make sure they get their daily lesson and they will learn to read really well'. Parents are invited to watch a lesson and the teacher will spend time with them afterwards to discuss what they saw. Parents also sign up to work with their child every day on the Reading Recovery 'homework'. This is carefully planned so that it does not ask parents/carers to do anything that might cause difficulty. They simply hear their child read one or more short books that the child can already tackle well independently, and help the child re-construct a cut-up sentence they have written and already re-assembled and re-read several times in their lesson in school.

The Numbers Count intervention programme follows a similar pattern of parents observing lessons and doing simple work with their child at home. The case study below illustrates what can be achieved.

CASE STUDY

6 Bankside

At Bankside Primary in Leeds, Kauser Jan was struck by what she learned about parents' attitudes to mathematics when she met them to explain the Numbers Count programme. 'It was a revelation', she says. 'If I talked about literacy they were animated and confident. But not in maths – they would say "I'm no good at maths", or "I was useless at maths at school"'. Kauser realised that they needed to be shown that they know much more about maths than they think they do – that maths is all around us and part of everyday life. She also realised she might need to use the same sort of strategies with parents/carers as she does with the children she teaches, strategies that would empower them and give self-belief.

Kauser tries to ensure she is out in the playground before and after school to chat to families. She shows them where her office is and makes clear they can come in at any time to watch a Numbers Count lesson or talk to her. Children were asked who they would like to come and see their good progress. In one case mother, father, grandfather and an older sibling all visited, and the lesson became a family event. Children are often asked to choose their take-home activities: 'What would you most like to take home to help you learn?'

Kauser sends home personalised *Every Child Counts* newsletters to parents/carers every two or three weeks. The newsletters describe what the child has been working on and include comments from observations of lessons by the family or other visitors to the school.

Kauser also wanted to find a way to celebrate families' contribution and hard work. She decided that parents/carers, as well as children, would have a graduation ceremony and receive a certificate thanking them for the help they had given their child. The ceremony takes place at a whole-school assembly. Afterwards Kauser takes parents/carers into the Numbers Count room and shows them examples of what the child could do 'before' and 'after' their programme. The children had made huge gains, often a 13-month gain in number age over a three-month period. These gains are discussed with the family, and the next steps – exit plans, three- and six-monthly follow-up assessments – are outlined.

In a challenging context, Bankside has succeeded in involving every parent/carer of children involved in Numbers Count. The secret, Kauser feels, is 'making parents feel comfortable, having face-to-face contact and using a translator where necessary'. Persistence is often called for. When she had not succeeded in making contact with one family, Kauser spoke to a Family Support Team Mentor who lives in their community and asked the worker to pop round to the house and invite the family in to school.

Also vital is making families feel valued. The message to parents/carers is that the Numbers Count intervention programme would not work without them – that as parents/carers they deserve thanks. It is this sense of genuine, equal partnership that, more than anything, accounts for Bankside's success.

Workshops and courses

Finally, the SENCO/INCO will want to build on the provision the child receives in school with linked, targeted workshops or courses which will model for the parent the ways in which they can help the child at home. Although IEPs were meant to guide parents on how to help, they do not – according to parents – seem to have succeeded. Often the ideas written on them are too general: 'Hear Jack read every day' can leave the parent wondering how exactly they should do this. What is more helpful is a practical demonstration. An example for literacy might be a Paired Reading workshop for a group of parents in which they learn how to follow a very simple procedure – first the parent and child read simultaneously out loud until the child signals (for example by knocking on the table) that he wants to read by himself, then the child reads independently until they get stuck or make a mistake, when the parent joins in until the child signals again, and so on. Another alternative is to train parents as Better Reading Partners, using the scheme developed by Bradford local authority.

At Bankside, the case study school featured earlier, a natural progression to general confidence-building was to develop maths workshops to build parents' skills. Kauser and Gemma Scholes, a Numbers Count teacher from another school, developed a series of five, weekly parent workshops covering Numbers, Counting, Models and Images, and Addition and Subtraction. They also devised a set of leaflets such as things to do with number cards, and things to do with a number line.

Bankside developed its own customised courses, but there are plenty of off-the-shelf courses – workshops that provide practical demonstration – available to schools. Table 7.2 shows some of the activities that could be offered, many of them by local authority Family Learning services. All have robust evidence of impact (Goodall and Vorhaus, 2011). The SENCO/INCO's role is to bring together a group of parents whose children have similar provision in school, for shared sessions where they can both learn new techniques to help their child, and also provide each other with mutual support. Often the sessions include 'take-home' elements; for example, some schools have developed Paired Maths schemes, with a stock of games coded according to the maths skill or concept involved and with an accompanying card to highlight the kinds of mathematical language the game could bring out. Parents borrow a game or two each week, and record how play went in a home-school book.

Such workshops and courses can be really successful with lower-attaining pupils. Evaluations of Family Literacy and Numeracy courses for parents of 3–6-year-olds, for example (Brooks, 1996, 1998; Brooks and Pahl, 2008) showed that the proportion of children whose low reading level would leave them struggling in school fell from 67 per cent to 9 per cent, and the proportion whose even lower reading level would leave them severely disadvantaged for learning fell from 24 per cent to 9 per cent. Progress in number and mathematical language was also good. Equally, parenting skills courses can halve the rate of severe behaviour problems (Scott *et al.*, 2001; Lindsay *et al.*, 2008; Furlong, M. *et al.*, 2012), with improvements maintained up to ten years later (NICE, 2006).

A recent very successful import to the UK is the Families and Schools Together (FAST) programme. This eight-week after-school programme is offered to families with 3–8-year-old children. Families sit at family tables and eat together. Parents are coached by a trained volunteer in how to give instructions and have the child

SPECIAL EDUCATIONAL NEED	COURSES FOR PARENTS/CARERS
Learning	Campaign for Learning *Learning to Learn* parent/child workshops.
Literacy	Paired reading workshops. SHARE: workshops for small groups of parents that provide ideas and resources for learning activities to share with their children at home. INSPIRE: a programme widely used in the West Midlands to encourage parents to be involved in developing their children's literacy skills. Family Literacy: aims to raise standards of literacy for both parents and children. Keeping up with the children: introduces parents to the way their children are taught literacy in school, so they can be confident in supporting them. Spokes parenting programme: a programme aimed mainly at improving behaviour in Y1 children, but also helps parents support their children's literacy development.
Language	Locally run Family Learning programmes such as Family Talk.
Mathematics	SHARE: workshops for small groups of parents that provide ideas and resources for learning activities to share with their children at home. INSPIRE: a programme widely used in the West Midlands to encourage parents to be involved in developing their children's numeracy skills. Keeping up with the children: introduces parents to the way their children are taught mathematics in school, so they can be confident in supporting them. Family Numeracy: aims to raise standards of numeracy for both parents and children. Ocean Maths: parent-student workshops alongside carefully planned programme homework activities. Primary and secondary.
Social and emotional skills	Family SEAL: workshops involving both parents and children, supporting parents in understanding their child's SEAL learning at school and applying ideas from SEAL to relationships in the home. Primary and secondary. FAST (Families And Schools Together): an after-school programme for 3 to 8 year old children and their families, designed to improve relationships within and among families. Parenting skills courses such as Family Links Nurturing Programme, Incredible Years, Triple P, Group Teen Triple P, Mellow Parenting, Positive Parents, Spokes.

TABLE 7.2 Courses and workshops for families

follow them. Children then go off to play while parents discuss issues of their choice in groups. At the end there is a 15-minute special play session in which each parent plays with their child, coached to follow the child's lead. An evaluation found that the programme reduced teacher-rated emotional and behavioural difficulties in the classroom by 46 per cent and also raised attainment compared to children whose parents just received behavioural parenting pamphlets (Lexmond *et al.*, 2011).

Another idea is to invite a parent in to work with their child and a teaching assistant in school once a week, or to have a TA or Family Support/Home School worker implement a time-limited home visiting programme. For young children with significant learning difficulties, the Portage scheme provides an outstandingly successful model. Here, a specially trained Portage worker visits the home once a week to model for the parent the games and activities that will help the child achieve specific next steps in their learning – whether it be language and communication, or motor skills, or cognitive development. A home visiting scheme has also been used for early literacy skills; one small-scale research study (Feiler, 2003) used a TA to visit parents of reception children once a week for about an hour, and showed that the children supported caught up with their peers by the end of the year. In Sheffield, the REAL project involved teachers undertaking around one home visit per month over 18 months to two years. Children were five at the time the first visits started. Teachers were released for half a day a week to work with eight families each on a range of language and literacy activities. Children whose mothers had no educational qualifications showed significant and enduring gains compared to a control group who did not receive the intervention (Brooks and Pahl, 2008).

Involving pupils

Pupil involvement was flagged up as a fundamental element of effective SEN practice in the 2001 SEN Code and accompanying Toolkit (DfES, 2001a). Yet, two years after the Code and all the training that accompanied it, Norwich and Kelly (2004), in a survey of over 400 SENCOs, found extreme variance in school practice. Most pupils with SEN were consulted at some time in respect of IEP reviews, but the number of IEPs made it impossible for this to happen every time. In 2009, a study by Jane Goepel noted little overlap between the IEP targets set for children by their teachers and the children's perceptions of their own need, concluding that 'while some children may be willing to engage with IEP targets that are teacher-initiated, children whose voice is overlooked are in danger of becoming disengaged from learning' (Goepel, 2009).

There has been a great deal of excellent work done since then on how to seek the views of children and young people with learning and communication difficulties, and how to prepare pupils with more complex needs to take an active part in annual Statement reviews and Transition reviews. Yet the DfE's *Support and aspiration: progress and next steps* document (DfE, 2012a) expressed ongoing concerns about inconsistencies in pupil involvement:

> We want to give greater control to disabled children and young people themselves – to make them the 'authors of their own life stories'. Currently, across the country, participation for disabled young people or those with SEN is patchy. For some areas it is a real strength and is reflected in the quality of services and the levels of confidence that young people have in them. But that is not the case everywhere.

The involvement of pupils with high-incidence types of SEN remains tokenistic. The volume of IEPs which schools have tried to manage has meant that they have become formulaic – a piece of paper rather than a record of dialogue and joint planning involving pupil, parent/carer and the school. As such, pupils are often not involved at all, or if they are the involvement may be no more than putting their signature to targets that the adults have already dictated, and reports of progress in which they have had little or no say.

What, then, can the alternative SEN/D systems suggested in this book, based on intensifying for some pupils the whole-school systems for personalising learning that are used for all pupils, offer in terms of pupil involvement?

The offer is significant. It is significant not least because it is based on a cultural shift we are seeing in many schools, following the insights provided by Assessment for Learning theorists and practitioners. Assessment for Learning, as we saw in Chapter 3, encourages teachers to help children take responsibility for their own learning, playing a part in assessing their own progress and deciding what they need to learn next. In some schools, pupils actually *lead* reviews with their parents and tutors, contributing their own views on how they are doing before asking others to comment. All this is a far cry from educational models of learners as passive receptacles of subject knowledge imparted by adults, which have held sway in many secondary schools in the past.

The changing culture in schools, then, forms the backdrop for improved participation for pupils with SEN or disabilities. And the case studies in Chapter 2 show how schools can build on this backdrop, by involving pupils in setting their own targets (some personal, some academic), in taking part in regular review meetings held at parents' evenings or academic mentoring days, in contributing to a personal profile that they use to let staff know what their particular needs are and what forms of support they find helpful.

In schools involved in Achievement for All, for example, pupils have Pupil Passports with headings 'I am good at … ', 'I am interested in … ', 'I enjoy… ', 'I don't like …', 'It helps me when … ', 'I want to improve … ', 'My friends are… ', 'I need to sit with … '. The Passport can include three targets derived from a termly structured conversation involving the pupil, parents and the class teacher or form tutor, and might have a section called 'My successes' in which teachers can comment on achievement or progress against the targets, and pupils can reflect on what skills they used to make progress in achieving them

The growth in person-centred planning offers another opportunity to empower children and young people. There are a number of useful tools available to structure and visually record discussions with young people about their views and feelings (see, for example, the Person Centred Planning website for Central Lancashire, and the website of Inclusive Solutions). Good ideas include a wall chart with a big horizontal arrow and speech bubbles to record 'What's working', 'What's not working', 'What's important'. 'What will a good life look like'. There are 'Circles of Support' maps to record the important people in the child's life, 'Good day, bad day' charts to capture the child's experiences, 'What people like and admire about me' charts, 'Where I want to be' charts, 'Daily routines that are important to me' charts.

Person-centred planning or thinking requires a mind shift that genuinely hands responsibility to the child or young person. Meetings are theirs, not yours. The child or young person is asked where they would prefer people to sit, for example, and what they want recorded, in what colour pen, with whom information can be shared. This is a far cry from standard practice in schools, so good training is necessary for all those involved.

Children and young people will not respond to efforts to involve them, moreover, without specific help from SENCOs/INCOs. Pupils who have for so long had the label 'SEN' applied to them by others, rather than being asked how they want to be identified and discussed, are not necessarily ready to hold their own profiles or tell adults what they need in the way of help. A legacy of shame and stigma lies between the children we are now identifying as 'special needs pupils' and those of the future, who may be part of a culture where all pupils are encouraged to identify their strengths and weaknesses, and understand that they may all need a little extra help from time to time. The intensification of 'normal' systems used for all pupils is one way of achieving this kind of culture. Another is work with all pupils, and with staff, to promote disability awareness and disability equality, and on the effects of stigma, teasing and name-calling.

This can be followed up by specific mentoring of individual pupils by disabled older peers and adults – to help them define themselves confidently as disabled and articulate equally confidently what they need and don't need from those around them. The aim is that all children and young people with SEN or disabilities can be as clear as the young man with ASD who manages his difficulty in handling two-way conversations by telling everyone 'You will have to tell me when I've talked to you long enough because I won't know'.

SENCOs'/INCOs' involvement in training pupils in self-advocacy, and creating a climate where pupils can ask for what they need as of right, is vital in beating bureaucracy. In the end, those who are best positioned to make sure their needs are met are pupils themselves. It is the pupils themselves who are always there, in every teaching and learning situation, with every supply teacher for the class, in every part of the extended school day. If we can help them communicate their needs, many of the elaborate and paper-driven SEN systems that we have designed to fulfil this communication role may become redundant.

Involving outside agencies

Some of the bureaucracy in SEN/D is about trying to protect the interests of pupils and parents. As we have seen so far in this chapter, there may be more effective ways of achieving this than bits of paper that surface from time to time and are then forgotten.

Another function of bureaucracy, however, is one of gate-keeping and rationing limited resources. Psychology services, learning and behaviour support services, speech and language therapists and social services use paperwork to try and manage an open-ended demand for services that they are simply not staffed to meet.

Understandably, these agencies have to ration what they provide, for example by providing them only where the school itself can show that it has made substantial efforts to understand and help the child from its own resources, before asking for outside help. The result is often a set of complex referral forms, a different one for each agency, accompanied by requests for copies of recent IEPs. Quite rightly, too, external agencies require information in order to gain a good picture of a child's profile and needs, and what has been tried so far to help them. On this they can build their own interventions.

SENCOs and INCOs are not in control of the systems used by outside agencies, unless their school or cluster is directly commissioning and paying for the service – a growing trend. Where this is not the case they can seek to influence agencies' systems. Increasingly, groups of professionals work in a locality with a defined group of schools. There is often an opportunity for headteachers and SENCOs/INCOs to sit on local management groups or panels that help to develop the local systems that will allocate time and manage referrals

One helpful development that SENCOs/INCOs can seek to bring about in their own area avoids referral forms altogether by having regular in-school multi-agency meetings. These can take various forms. They may be formal and infrequent, like the ones described in the case studies in Chapter 2. Or they may be smaller and more frequent – for example involving a monthly hour with the school's EP, EWO and school nurse, at which actions for previous meetings are reviewed and four or five children or families discussed in depth. Other agencies can be invited when their presence will be relevant to a particular child to be discussed.

If it is not possible to influence outside agencies' referral systems so that referrals stem from face-to-face contact rather than forms in triplicate, SENCOs/INCOs should try to insist that there is just one multi-purpose form used by all agencies. They can also circumvent the form by copying existing paperwork they hold on the child, rather than starting afresh. They might, for example, copy:

- the latest pupil personal profile;
- a highlighted provision map showing the provision the child receives;
- recent tracking data.

The only thing they might need to add to this is a very clear description of what they want from the agency. Is it assessment to help clarify needs? Is it training for those working with the child in school? Is it direct therapeutic input that no one in the school has the skills (or could acquire the skills through training) to provide? Is it support for the family? Is it simply extra resources?

A welcome development that involves outside agencies, parents, pupils and schools together with (potentially) lots of face-to-face contact and little bureaucracy is the Team Around the Child (TAC) approach, pioneered in the Early Support Programme for pre-school children with significant SEN/D and now being developed for school-age children too. The approach is demanding of human resources and it remains to be seen whether there will ever be sufficient multi-agency input and availability of key workers coordinating the services a family needs. Nevertheless, it has the potential to reshape the review and planning process for children with the greatest needs, replacing the current exchange of written reports (which often duplicate information and add little to the understanding of those who actually teach the child) with a system of meaningful dialogue that is genuinely responsive to the child's and family's needs. As the government has said (DfE, 2012a), it is important to 'ensure that professionals' time is maximised in front-line service delivery rather than producing reports'.

Schools also have to fall in with the requirements of the Common Assessment Form (CAF). It remains to be seen whether the bureaucracy involved in the CAF – now with versions running to 18 pages or more – proves over the top in relation to the benefits it brings. Evaluation (Easton *et al.,* 2011) is positive, finding that CAFs have enabled earlier intervention and supported multi-agency working. Teacher surveys present a less optimistic picture, with reports of more paperwork, delays in accessing services and minimal progress towards interagency working (Ellis *et al.,* 2012). It may be that the CAF process will achieve its aim of making sure that no child falls through the net, but equally we should not be surprised if overstretched and fallible human beings still fail to communicate, despite a form and database to help them do so. Meanwhile, a suggestion to SENCOs/INCOs might be that they avoid being seduced by an elegantly designed CAF into spending hours and hours inputting information that no one else will really look at. As ever, it would be wise to be clear with local colleagues what the school's information is needed for – what the purpose of providing it is – and seek ways of meeting the purposes rather than necessarily the bureaucracy around them.

8 | Making the change

It will be clear by now to those reading this book that its theme is not only a reduction in bureaucracy, but also a fundamental re-think in the way we manage SEN and disability in schools.

This kind of re-think will involve a lot of people in school in changing the way they do things. It means changing SEN/D from a bolt-on activity undertaken by a few, to an integral aspect of whole-school systems for all pupils.

The difference between these two approaches is brilliantly captured in a National College of School Leadership publication (Chapman *et al.*, 2011) on leadership that promotes the achievement of pupils with SEN/D (Table 8.1).

It will not be enough, however, for the SENCO/INCO to announce to colleagues that in future there will be a whole-school approach with fewer IEPs, and that they will be expected to take more responsibility for the targets, progress monitoring and strategies used to support pupils with SEN/D. Change, alas, is not that easy. As Everard and Morris (1990) say:

> Implementing change is not a question of defining an end and letting others get on with it: it is a process of interaction, dialogue, feedback, modifying objectives, recycling plans, coping with mixed feelings and values, pragmatism, frustration, patience and muddle.

This chapter suggests a process a school might want to use to manage the change and overcome some of the difficulties inherent in any change in 'the way we do things here'. It is based on the work of theorists like Michael Fullan (2001) and presented as a series of principles you might want to use to develop your own plan for change in school.

SEN/D as bolt-on activity ⟹	SEN/D as an integrated aspect of whole-school systems
Conceptualisation: task of SEN viewed as the preserve of specialists	Conceptualisation: task of SEN/D viewed as whole-school
Values: individual values and the emergence of subcultures	Values: a shared commitment to inclusion
Approaches to teaching and learning: individual problem-solving approaches used to support the achievement of students with SEN/D	Approaches to teaching and learning: collaborative, problem-solving approaches used to support the achievement of students with SEN/D
Resources for support: used to strengthen SEN/D discrete provision	Resources for support: potentially available to all pupils and used for flexible provision and individual planning
Specialist leadership roles: a few staff take on formal and informal leadership activities to support the learning of students with SEN/D	Specialist leadership roles: highly distributed, with staff taking on formal and informal leadership activities to support the learning of all students
Approaches to integrated services: problems are referred to specialist services outside the school	Approaches to integrated services: services beyond the school are used to enhance the flexibility of provision

TABLE 8.1 Moving to a whole-school approach

Source: Chapman et al., 2011, National College of School Leadership

KEY PRINCIPLES

Managing change

1 The change process works best when it offers a change that meets people's needs, offering them a chance of solving a problem for them or the institution.

2 The process of change must be owned by and negotiated with those involved in it.

3 Those managing the change should try to involve as many people as possible, but make sure that they involve people who have power.

4 Those managing the change must consider who else has the power to block the proposed change.

5 Those managing the change must consider what resources will realistically be needed for the new system to work, and make sure these are built into the school development plan.

6 Effective change requires a blend of pressure and support.

7 In the implementation phase of any change, people need continued repetition of what will happen, reminders through several channels, and patient explanation of the details.

8 Once a change has been implemented, it needs to be 'institutionalised' or embedded.

1 The change process works best when it offers a change that meets people's needs, offering them a chance of solving a problem for them or the institution

The first principle of successful change is that the people involved see it as necessary, linked to needs in their institution rather than imposed arbitrarily from outside. In relation to beating bureaucracy, this might mean that you need to begin by investigating, as part of your school self-evaluation, how stakeholders (staff, pupils, parents, you as coordinator) really feel about your current SEN/D systems. It also might mean collecting evidence about the impact of your current systems. Are pupils with SEN or disabilities doing well in your school? What do the data show? What national data might you present to staff about, for example, the impact that prevailing bureaucratic models of meeting SEN have actually had on children's progress? Chapter 1 will help you here.

This kind of self-evaluation will allow you to demonstrate to stakeholders that there really is a problem – one that they have helped to identify.

2 The process of change must be owned by and negotiated with those involved in it

People will adopt new systems with energy and commitment if they have had a say in creating them. Once you have presented relevant information from your self-evaluation (which will almost always show that people are spending a lot of time on paperwork that isn't felt to benefit children), you will need a way of involving stakeholders in coming up with alternative systems to meet the functions we identified in Chapter 3:

- identification;
- assessment;
- communication;
- identifying priorities and setting targets for learning or behaviour;
- identifying strategies, in the classroom and elsewhere, to help the child achieve targets;
- reviewing progress and celebrating success;
- engaging parents and carers;
- coordinating the actions to be taken by the school and outside agencies;
- informing decisions about the allocation of resources;
- supporting transition.

You might want to do this by setting up a small working group, with representation from parents, pupils and staff. Or you might want to ask for time at a primary staff meeting, or secondary faculty meetings, and with a focus group of parents, to ask for people's ideas.

3 Those managing the change should try to involve as many people as possible, but make sure that they involve people who have power

Successful change is not possible in any institution if the people in positions of power or influence are not behind it. This means of course that you can do nothing without first seeking the support of the headteacher and other senior managers. Your self-evaluation information will be powerful here, but there may be anxieties or resistance – perhaps a worry that parents will be upset and complain if they no longer have the apparent security of an IEP, or perhaps a wish to maintain the status quo because the current bureaucratic systems meet the local authority's needs and secure additional resources for the school (through Statements or Education, Health and Care Plans, for example). You need to identify in advance what these concerns or issues might be, and plan the reassurances you will give – about how you are taking parents with you in moving to a new system, for example, or how changes in the local authority resourcing system mean that the drive for Statements is no longer of such relevance.

Most important, you need to demonstrate to senior leaders the impact on attainment that can follow a move from a bolt-on SEN/D system to an integrated whole-school system. The impact data from the Achievement for All programme (see Chapter 7) will help you here.

4 Those managing the change must consider who else has the power to block it

Everard and Morris (1990) divide those involved in change into four groups:

- those who are ready to oppose the change;
- those who are willing to let it happen;
- those who are willing to help it happen;
- those who are willing to make it happen.

This means making sure that you enlist those who you think will really want the change to happen as allies from the start – for example, as key members of each subject department in a secondary school, or key parents who have influence on others. It also means you need to think carefully about who might be worried about your new ideas, how you can respond to their worries, and how you can make sure you involve them actively in the planning. The chart in Table 8.2 below may help.

5 Those managing the change must consider what resources will realistically be needed for the new system to work, and make sure these are built into the school development plan

Successful change is often demanded but rarely achieved without the provision of at least some additional resources. In relation to new SEN/D systems, it will be helpful to ask staff, at the stage when you are working together to agree the new system, to identify the resources they will need to make the change work. The resources identified will most likely be time, for staff INSET and for staff to take a new look at differentiation within their medium- and short-term planning. Time will also be needed for you to work alongside colleagues to support improved practice.

These are some ways in which schools have created time:

- In one school, the head instituted a curriculum day when she brought in a team from outside the school to work with the children on creative projects. This freed up staff to work in phase teams on differentiated planning.
- In another school, twice-termly staff meetings are set aside for phase-based curriculum planning.

CONCERN	POSSIBLE STRATEGIES
Class teachers: • The more children I have with IEPs, the more TA support I will get in my class • Doing all this brings more resources through external agencies and Statements/Single Plans • It will mean more work for me	• Show how the audit of needs and provision map provides the fairest match of resources to need • Point out the changed national policies on school funding and the 'local offer' (the provision that must be made from schools' budgets and that which comes from the local authority and partner agencies) • Offer to work alongside the teacher to help with planning and target-setting • Show how time will be provided to support this • Work in stages; try out the new system with just one willing year group or faculty, for example, and get them to report back
Parents: • The teachers won't know my child has SEN/D • My child won't get the help they need • I won't know what is happening for my child and how they are doing • I won't be involved in helping my child at home	• Involve parents and pupils in devising a format for a personal profile for pupils with additional needs • Show how the provision map works • Show examples of differentiated classroom planning • Ask parents to comment on your planned systems and formats for tracking and monitoring progress • -in times, structured conversations and review meetings • Provide information on the workshops and courses provided in school
SENCO/INCO: • Without the security of IEPs, I won't have a handle any more on what is happening, and staff won't use strategies/make an effort to meet SEN/D	• I can monitor what is happening by looking at plans and through classroom observation and talking to pupils
All • It may not work	• Build in an abort button – we will try the new system till x and then review it – if we aren't happy we can go back to the old system

TABLE 8.2 Strategies to address concerns

169

- Another school established a buddy system for planning. Foundation Stage and KS1 teachers were paired with KS2 teachers, so that they could help them plan work for older children working significantly below age-related expectations.
- Another school reduced the SENCO/INCO's teaching load for one year, so as to free him to work with subject colleagues in a cycle that involved joint planning, teaching and review.

6 Effective change requires a blend of pressure and support

Good ideas are not enough on their own. If change is to happen, people need both ongoing support and also in some cases an element of pressure. Pressure can be exerted through the school's regular performance management systems – through targets set for all staff, and outcomes monitored not just by the SENCO/INCO but by other senior managers. Support, as we have seen, can take many forms – INSET, buddying, opportunities for staff to observe each other's teaching, opportunities to look at the targets set for pupils across different classes and subjects, and opportunities to work alongside the SENCO/INCO or with outside agencies.

Effective support means not expecting staff to become experts in personalisation overnight. The ideas in this book ask a lot of them. They will need to plan for a range of learning objectives in one class, use access strategies and varied, inclusive teaching approaches, and help pupils set and review both academic and personal targets. It will work best if you start small, perhaps getting to grips with tracking backwards and forwards in objectives frameworks to identify appropriate learning objectives before asking staff to think about access strategies. And the SENCO/INCO can help staff use simple systems to help themselves change their practice, as in this example:

> One SENCO suggested to colleagues that they identify two or three inclusive teaching strategies for lower attaining children, and for their highest attainers, that they wanted to use more often. They then put these up on post-its on the wall, so as to remind themselves throughout the day. 'Make it personal' (i.e. link an explanation to pupils' own real-life experience), 'Chunk my instructions', 'Teach the key vocabulary I'm using' were examples of strategies staff chose for themselves. They also decided that to stretch higher attainers they wanted to ask more higher order questions using words like 'deduce', 'predict', 'infer', so put these up on post-its too and set themselves a target of asking at least one or two in each session.

Another great idea is to support teachers in making changes by identifying a small pot of money that they can bid into, for resources they feel they need in order to develop their practice. At Hampstead School in London, staff were asked to identify a key performance indicator that could be monitored, then to bid for relevant support. Some staff bid for cover time to enable them to plan with specialists, others chose to go to conferences or buy books to extend their learning about SEN/D, others bid for teaching resources or to make a video for new teachers in their department.

7 In the implementation phase of any change, people need continued repetition of what will happen, reminders through several channels, and patient explanation of the details

Telling people once about a change is not enough. The SENCO/INCO will need to put round written and e-mail reminders, circulate examples of good practice in target-setting, hold competitions for the best piece of differentiated planning, speak to individuals, and set a date when she or he will be 'coming in to see how it's going for you and what I can do to help'.

Change can sometimes seem elastic, able to be put off to another day when things are less busy (which of course they never are). There is nothing more motivating, therefore, than having a date by which action must be in evidence, and nothing more helpful than occasional reminders of what has already been achieved by others.

8 Once a change has been implemented, it needs to be 'institutionalised' or embedded

Institutionalising change means building it into the system in ways that will survive changes of leadership, changes of staff or just the dip in energy that follows the initial enthusiasm involved in doing something new.

As Huberman (1983) said, 'New practices that get built into the training, regulatory, staffing and budgetary cycle survive; others don't'. In relation to SEN/D systems this means embedding the new way of working into relevant policies (not only SEN/D, but also curriculum, assessment and professional development policies), into planning formats, into information for parents, into job descriptions, performance management systems and induction for new staff.

A final check

Once you have made a plan for introducing, implementing and embedding changes to your current SEN/D system, it will be useful to run a final check using the chart in Table 8.3.

The chart identifies five key elements that need to be in place if a complex change is to be successful – vision, skills, incentives and resources.

Where there is no clear vision for what needs to change, and what the new system will look like, the result for all involved (staff, parents, pupils) will be confusion. This points to the need to spend time on self-evaluation, sharing the outcomes and identifying with all stakeholders how they want things to be in the future. People need 'the big picture' – the background and context for the proposed change, and how things will improve as a result.

Where there is a vision, incentives and resources but those who will have to implement a change do not have the skills they need, there will be high levels of anxiety. This points to the need for a really good plan for any INSET staff will need. This might be in Assessment for Learning, or in understanding and using data to track and monitor progress, or in inclusive planning. It also means thinking about the skills that pupils will need, and any necessary development work to help them become confident partners in setting and reviewing targets for their personal and academic development, and communicating to others what their needs are and what forms of support they find helpful.

Where there is vision, and professional development, and resources but no incentives there will be resistance (often subtle, but nevertheless powerful) amongst parents and colleagues in school. The way round this is to highlight very clearly what everyone has to gain from the new system. For parents, this will be better progress for their child – with teachers really having to think about how to teach them rather than handing responsibility over to support staff – and clarity about what extra provision their child can access, over and above the all-important inclusive class and subject teaching. You will need to provide many parents with

VISION	+	SKILLS	+	INCENTIVES	+	RESOURCES	=	CHANGE
	+	SKILLS	+	INCENTIVES	+	RESOURCES	=	CONFUSION
VISION	+		+	INCENTIVES	+	RESOURCES	=	ANXIETY
VISION	+	SKILLS	+		+	RESOURCES	=	RESISTANCE
VISION	+	SKILLS	+	INCENTIVES	+		=	FRUSTRATION

TABLE 8.3 Managing complex change

Source: Adapted by Richard Vila, Bayridge Consortium Inc. from Knoster, 1991.

the evidence, summarised in this book, that the ways of managing things that they have come to expect (attaching TAs to children as if by Velcro, and working on three or four SMART targets) have not, according to national data and Ofsted, led to improved outcomes for pupils with SEN/D – indeed, rather the reverse. The same arguments can be used to provide staff with incentives to make the change: new systems will mean improved outcomes for children, reflected in the school's self-evaluation and evident to Ofsted, and linked to rewards inherent in the performance management system. There may be other incentives too, that a creative staff group can come up with as a way of celebrating the effort everyone has put in to make the new system work.

Finally, where there are incentives, coupled with vision and skills, but not enough resources (time or money), the result will be frustration – a familiar scenario for the education staff who have been asked to implement a thousand new initiatives over the last ten years, not all of them adequately funded. As we have seen, proper discussions with senior leaders in school about what time and resources will realistically be required, for the initial preparation period and when the change is implemented, will help reduce staff frustration.

Change and the SENCO/INCO

In all the work you may do with parents, pupils and colleagues to bring about changes in the way SEN/D is managed in your school, it is important to remember also that a new system may represent considerable change for you too, as SENCO or INCO.

Fundamentally, what you will become is less of a manager of paper and meetings, and more of a strategic manager, and a leader of inclusive teaching and learning in your school.

You might want to reflect on what proportion of your time you currently spend on each of these broad activity headings:

- SEN Code of Practice procedures – IEPs, reviews, records, reports, meetings.
- Contributing to year group/subject curriculum planning.
- Monitoring – observing lessons and providing feedback.
- Managing TAs or other staff.
- Supporting school-based staff professional development and work with parents to help them support their child's learning.
- Strategic management of SEN/D – school self-evaluation (including analysing data on the progress and participation of children with SEN/D), planning and evaluating additional provision, contributing to the school improvement plan.

- Teaching children with SEN/D.
- Linking with outside agencies.
- Organising resources.

If you record the proportion of time spent on each of these as a chart, it might, perhaps, look like the one in Figure 8.1, with by far the most time spent on processes that research has shown to be least effective in their impact on children's progress. Reducing the number of IEPs in the school should enable you to shift the emphasis, so that your chart might look more like the one in Figure 8.2. Alternatively, if strategic management is really not your thing, and someone else in school carries out that role for inclusion, you could shift the time pattern so that you spend more time teaching children with SEN/D directly, using some of the evidence-based intervention programmes described in Chapter 6, or more time supporting family learning and parenting groups or workshops, as described in Chapter 7.

Managing inclusion is a team job, not the role of a single individual. It is up to you and your school to determine how the various roles in relation to SEN and disability are fulfilled, and what your part will be. But shifting away from paper processes to focus on teaching and learning will have big implications for you, whatever the new pattern of your time. It represents a change, and the same conditions that apply to whole-school change apply also to you. You may have a vision for how you want your role to develop in the future, but it is useful to reflect also on what you need in terms of skills, incentives and resources. The incentive of reducing fruitless paperwork may be sufficient, but you may also want to have the effort involved in managing that change recognised and rewarded through your own performance management. You will perhaps be able to articulate to senior leaders the differences you see in your future role, and enter into discussions about how they will be reflected in management structures and pay scales.

Resource implications for your changed role should not be excessive. A reduction in bureaucracy is intended to change the way you use existing time, rather than require lots more. But you will need resources in the form of time at staff meetings or INSET days to introduce staff to new systems, and time identified in their timetables to work with you as you support them in developing their inclusive teaching practice.

Finally, there are likely to be substantial skills implications in a change of role for you. Table 8.4 provides a skills audit to guide you in planning your own professional development. Courses or school-based support on all of this should be available from your local authority, from independent providers, from teaching and leading practice schools, or from higher education institutions.

A SEN Code of Practice procedures –
    IEPs, reviews with parents, reports, meetings
B Contributing to year group/subject curriculum planning
C Monitoring – observing lessons and providing feedback
D Managing TAs or other staff
E Supporting school-based staff professional development and work
    with parents on how to support their child's learning
F Strategic management of SEN – School self-evaluation
    (including analysing data on the progress of children with SEN),
    planning and evaluating additional provision, contributing to school
    improvement plan
G Teaching children with SEN
H Linking with outside agencies
I Organising resources

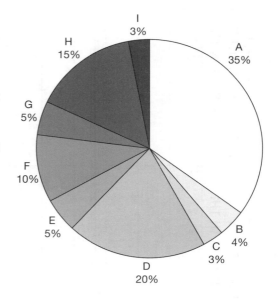

FIGURE 8.1 How do I spend my SENCO/INCO time?

A SEN Code of Practice procedures –
    IEPs, reviews with parents, reports, meetings
B Contributing to year group/subject curriculum planning
C Monitoring – observing lessons and providing feedback
D Managing TAs or other staff
E Supporting school-based staff professional development and work
    with parents on how to support their child's learning
F Strategic management of SEN – School self-evaluation
    (including analysing data on the progress of children with SEN),
    planning and evaluating additional provision, contributing to school
    improvement plan
G Teaching children with SEN
H Linking with outside agencies
I Organising resources

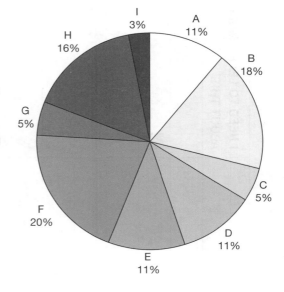

FIGURE 8.2 How do I spend my SENCO/INCO time?

Conclusion

Making change happen is difficult. So, however, is the everyday job of SENCOs/
INCOs and classroom teachers as they struggle to implement the bureaucratic
procedures that currently occupy most of the time and energy available to meet the
needs of children with SEN or disabilities. Because of this, change is essential.

Readers of this book will by now understand how fundamental are the changes
proposed in the way we manage SEN/D in schools. The theme may have been

✓ Tick the column that best fits you

KNOWLEDGE, SKILLS, UNDERSTANDING	I NEED TO LEARN MORE ABOUT THIS	I FEEL PRETTY CONFIDENT IN THIS	I CAN SUPPORT OTHER SENCOS/INCOS IN THIS
Inclusive classroom planning and teaching			
Assessment for learning			
Interpreting and using data on pupil progress			
Provision mapping			
The evidence base for different intervention programmes			
Evaluating the quality and impact of intervention programmes in school			
Providing support to other adults (TAs, learning mentors) delivering intervention programmes			
Undertaking classroom observations and feeding back to staff			
Monitoring planning			
Coaching colleagues			
Providing INSET			
Training pupils in self-advocacy			
Providing workshops and running groups for parents, to help them support their children's language, literacy or mathematics learning			
Providing workshops and running groups for parents, to help them support their children's social and emotional development			

TABLE 8.4 Skills audit for the SENCO/INCO

how to beat bureaucracy – but it has also been how we might get a better deal for children with SEN or disabilities through the changes we make to our systems. It has been about recognising that, as Charles Desforges (2007) says:

> From the learner's point of view, if educational change does not happen in classrooms then it does not happen.

It has been about shifting effort away from paper and meetings that happen outside the classroom and have little impact on what happens inside it, onto placing more of the responsibility for meeting individual needs back with the class or subject teacher.

This will only work if we make it easy for these teachers to take on this shift of responsibility. It will only be manageable if the systems we ask them to use for pupils with SEN or disabilities are the *same* as they use for all the class – embedded in their regular target-setting, assessment and curriculum planning processes.

Taken to the limit, these new systems may eventually mean that, while retaining the concept of disability, we can dispense with the more nebulous concept of 'special educational needs' altogether, and simply think about how learning can be personalised for a whole range of children who from time to time require extra responsiveness from us, for all sorts of reasons linked to the experiences they are going through. So far, the notion of special educational needs and the elaborate and separate bureacracy around it have only served on the whole to marginalise pupils and make them 'someone else's problem'. Integrated, personalised systems will mean they make better progress.

Bureaucracy, it is interesting to reflect, is what others ask of you. *Systems*, however, are what you devise for yourself and your own setting. Schools like the ones in our case studies show us that more effective systems are possible. Such schools would not claim to have beaten bureaucracy, but they do feel they have held it at bay. Where there is paperwork, it is paperwork that the school sees as meeting the particular needs of their children – not paperwork done for its own sake with little impact on learning. Staff may be working just as hard as ever, but they feel that the actions they take now make sense and will make a difference. As one SENCO put it, 'It's how you *feel* about the time not the actual time that matters'.

The schools described in this book have found new meaning in what they do, as a result of changing the way that key people, particularly the SENCO or INCO, spend their time. Personalisation, provision mapping and new SEN funding systems have created the context that makes this possible. It is up to us all now to follow their lead.

Beating bureaucracy toolkit

The materials in this section are available to download from
www.routledgeeducation.com/resources/fulton

Information for Ofsted and other outside agencies

We agree with Ofsted (2006, *Inclusion: Does it matter where pupils are taught?*) that
what makes most difference to higher outcomes for pupils with SEN/D is effective
teaching, target-setting and tracking by their class and subject teachers.

We have therefore tried wherever possible to support pupils with SEN/D through
our regular whole-school systems for setting targets for all pupils, and monitoring
their progress. It is our policy to write and review separate individual education
plans (IEPs) only for children with low-incidence, complex learning difficulties or
disabilities, where a number of different agencies are involved.

Much of the evidence of the impact of our support for pupils with SEN/D, and the
systems that support that impact, is therefore located within regular school systems:

- tracking data on pupil progress;
- differentiated curriculum planning;
- pupil-held personal and academic targets.

In addition, evidence can be found in the following SEN/D-specific systems:

- Provision map.
- Evaluations of the interventions in our provision map.
- Data on overall participation of pupils with SEN/D in extra-curricular activities.
- Data on the overall destinations of pupils with SEN/D on leaving our school.
- Data on the overall exclusions and attendance of pupils with SEN/D, and their
  experience of bullying.
- Cumulative overview/record of progress for each individual pupil with SEN/D,
  linked to the provision they have received, the extent of parental involvement
  and their access to wider opportunities such as extra-curricular activities.
- Personal Profiles/Passports for individual pupils.

- Records of structured conversations with parents.
- Parent workshops listed on our website.
- Strategy sheets for staff, with strategies they can use for main types of SEN/D.
- SEN/D self-evaluation audit and action plan (including current Accessibility Plan and whole-school CPD plan). Our self-evaluation includes summary of progress data, information from work scrutiny and classroom observation, information from pupil and parent surveys, information from evaluation of interventions.
- Details of performance management and professional development of teaching assistants, linked to pupil outcomes.
- Governors' monitoring and evaluation programme for SEN/D.

Our systems to ensure the progress and well-being of pupils with SEN/D are set out below.

PURPOSE OF AN EFFECTIVE SEN/D SYSTEM	HOW THE PURPOSES ARE ACHIEVED IN OUR SCHOOL
Identification – ensuring that children's needs are identified	Class and subject teachers track pupil progress closely and identify pupils requiring support Parental concerns expressed to teacher or SENCO are followed up Class/subject teachers use checklists to screen pupils with weak reading or spelling for dyslexia We screen all pupils with literacy difficulties or behaviour difficulties for speech, language and communication needs
Assessment – ensuring that assessment takes place, to better understand the barriers to learning and how they might be overcome	SENCO trains/coaches colleagues in involving the pupil in identifying strengths, difficulties and what helps SENCO uses appropriate tools to assess pupils with literacy, numeracy, behaviour difficulties SENCO uses information from outside agencies' assessments to develop strategies for pupils with low-incidence/complex needs
Communication – making sure that all relevant staff and outside agencies know what the child's needs are and what should be done to support them	We use pupil-held personal profiles/passports that record strengths, difficulties and what helps SENCO provides training for pupils in how to communicate their needs
Identifying priorities and setting targets for learning or behaviour; involving pupils	We use pupil-owned targets set together by the class or subject teacher and the pupil

PURPOSE OF AN EFFECTIVE SEN/D SYSTEM	HOW THE PURPOSES ARE ACHIEVED IN OUR SCHOOL
Identifying strategies, in the classroom and elsewhere, to help the child achieve targets	SENCO provides strategy sheets for staff SENCO and school-based behaviour/SEAL specialist act as consultant to colleagues on what works for lower-attaining pupils, pupils with SEN/D and those with behavioural, emotional and social difficulties
Tracking, monitoring and reviewing progress	Assessments are used before and after an intervention Standard school tracking systems use P levels as well as NC levels and sublevels
Engaging parents and carers – agreeing priorities and targets with them, making sure they know what is being done to help their child and to what effect, suggesting ways in which they can support their child's progress	Our SEN/D policy contains clear provision map showing the extra provision and what entry levels entitle a child to access that provision. We meet parents/carers at least twice a year to share information on the child's progress SENCO and curriculum specialists run workshops for parents/families and implement projects (such as paired reading) for specified groups
Coordinating the actions to be taken by the school and outside agencies, and evaluating their impact	Internal provision and external agency involvement are recorded on a cumulative overview/record of progress for each pupil, alongside progress tracking data and data on behaviour and attendance The impact of interventions on our provision map is evaluated through before and after measures We gather and analyse data on the participation of pupils with SEN/D in extra-curricular activities
Informing decisions about the allocation of resources – extra adult time and/or physical resources	We use a detailed provision map to plan additional provision
Supporting transition – making sure that information about the child's needs is passed on as they move from one class or setting to another	We pass on pupil personal profile and record of additional provision (highlighted, dated provision maps and cumulative overview/record of progress)

Information for parents and carers

Dear Parent

This letter is for parents and carers of children with special educational needs or disabilities. It explains how we will help your child at X school.

We want to make sure that everyone in school understands your child's needs. So we will work with you and your child to write a Communication Passport/Personal Profile that will go to everyone who teaches Y. The Passport/Profile will say what Y is good at, what s/he finds difficult, and what helps him/her to learn.

When teachers plan their lessons they will think about what exactly your child needs to know and learn, what teaching approaches will work best, and what they need to do to overcome any barriers that will stop your child learning. You are very welcome to look at examples of teachers' planning. We will also make sure you know about your child's individual targets, which they set with their teachers.

If you would like to help your child reach these targets through home activities we can suggest ideas. Sometimes we organise special events in school – like how to help your child with literacy, or social and emotional learning – that we hope you will come to and find useful.

Y may also have extra one-to-one or small group help with language, literacy, maths, social and emotional or coordination skills. Our school 'provision map' shows what help we provide in each year group. We would like you to see this map. If your child needs this extra help, it will be for a fixed period of time. We will assess progress before and after this extra teaching so that we can tell you what difference it has made.

Class/subject teachers assess each child's overall progress once a term. Progress will be discussed at parents' evenings twice a year. At these meetings we want you to tell us about anything that will help us do a better job to help your child.

But please don't wait for parents' evenings if there is anything you would like to discuss. Just get in touch – your contact person is Z, tel:

With best wishes,

Communication passport

Child's photograph

NAME:

D.O.B.:

SEN/D stage:

SEN/D support began:

Areas of concern:

WHAT AM I GOOD AT?

WHAT DO I FIND HARD?

WHAT SHOULD TEACHERS AND OTHER PEOPLE IN SCHOOL DO TO HELP ME?

Personal profile

Name: **Form:**

SEN stage:

Personal profile

Strengths and interests

Areas of difficulty

Strategies

Class handover profile

Class average Sept 2012

SA	RA

Class list	Reading – progress 11/12	Writing – progress 11/12	Maths – progress 11/12	Spell Age	Read Age	SEN STATUS				G&T	EAL	Looked after	Free school meals	Summer born	Poor attendance	Other issues e.g. bereavement
						School Stage	ST'MT	SEN TYPE								

Legend:

2 sub-levels progress made

1 sub-level progress made

0 sub-levels progress made

Cumulative tracking and intervention record

Expected English and maths level for age group shaded

* Child's reading level • Writing level + Maths level ° Speaking and listening level

NC LEVEL	Y1 Term 1	Y1 Term 2	Y1 Term 3	Y2 Term 1	Y2 Term 2	Y2 Term 3	Y3 Term 1	Y3 Term 2	Y3 Term 3	Y4 Term 1	Y4 Term 2	Y4 Term 3	Y5 Term 1	Y5 Term 2	Y5 Term 3	Y6 Term 1	Y6 Term 2	Y6 Term 3
5																		
4A																		▓
4B																		
4C															▓			
3A												▓						
3B																		
3C																		
2A									▓									
2B																		
2C																		
1A							▓											
1B																		
1C																		
P8																		
P7																		
P6																		
P5																		
P4																		
Interventions in place																		

Progress review meetings with parents and pupils (SEN or disability)

Pre-meeting information for class teacher or form tutor to gather

✓ Notes of last meeting

✓ Progress against termly National Curriculum sub-level targets/P levels in the core subjects

✓ Achievement of curricular and personal targets

✓ Progress in relevant behavioural, organisational, study and 'learning-to-learn' skills

✓ 'Before' and 'after' assessments showing impact of any interventions used (literacy, language, mathematics, social and emotional, motor coordination, other)

✓ Evidence of differentiation of class/subject teacher planning

Agenda

- Have we all completed the actions we agreed at our last meeting?
- How good is x's progress against termly National Curriculum sub-level targets/P levels in the core subjects?
- Is x achieving his/her curricular and personal targets? How good is progress in relevant behavioural, organisational, study and 'learning-to-learn' skills?
- What has been the impact of any interventions we have used? Are any further interventions needed?
- How have we adapted our classroom planning to meet x's needs?
- What is helping x to make progress?
- What is getting in the way?
- What can we do about it?

Notes

Actions agreed

Date: Signed:

Inclusive planning format

Unit: .... Date: .... Year group: ....

Key learning objectives: ....

Learning outcome for unit: ....

Planning for inclusion – note here differentiated learning objectives for different individuals and groups, and the teaching approaches and access strategies you will use to overcome barriers to learning.

Differentiated learning objectives

Teaching approaches

Access strategies

End of Unit Review of inclusive strategies used

What went well?

Even better if …

SESSION/ LESSON	WHOLE CLASS LEARNING AND TEACHING	INDEPENDENT LEARNING	GUIDED LEARNING	ASSESSMENT CRITERIA	PLENARY
1					
2					
3					
4					
5					

Medium-term plan

YEAR:　　　　　　**TERM:**

HIGHLIGHT THE INCLUSIVE TEACHING STRATEGIES RELEVANT TO THE CLASS
CHOOSE ONE OF THESE STRATEGIES TO FOCUS ON AS PART OF YOUR PROFESSIONAL DEVELOPMENT

Plan seating taking into account needs of pupils with sensory impairment, distractible pupils
Avoid background noise
Check light source in front of me not behind
Face pupils when speaking
Cue pupils in to what I am going to talk about and cue again when the topic changes
Clarify, display and refer back to new or difficult vocabulary
Break long instructions down into chunks and say one at a time
Check for understanding of instructions – ask pupil to explain them in their own words
Jot instructions down on post-it notes or ask a pupil to do this for a study buddy
Use visual supports – pictures, concrete objects, visual timetable
Pitch questions so they are relevant for learning objectives at different levels
Give time/support before responses are required – personal thinking time, partner talk, persisting with progressively more scaffolding until child can answer correctly
Use buddying for seating and paired / partner work –more settled pupil paired with a child who finds concentration difficult, more able with less able
Plan pre-tutoring by TA for individuals/groups, where this will help them to access the lesson
Make sure TA knows learning objective for any pupil(s) they will be supporting
Use encapsulation – tell class the three main points lesson will cover, teach them, recap on them at end of lesson

Make tasks more open/closed for different individuals and groups, according to need
Plan tasks as extended or short for different individuals and groups, according to need
Clearly explain and model tasks – check for understanding, task cards or boards as reminders, make time available and expected outcomes clear
Provide resources to help pupils be independent – write down and leave up instructions after saying them, keep relevant material from whole-class session on display, provide word lists or mats, dictionaries of terms, glossaries, maths resources such as number lines
Vary pupil groupings according to purpose and learning objective
Make arrangements such as buddying, adult support, audio recording where necessary to ensure that pupils can access written text / instructions
Plan alternatives to written recording for those who find this difficult – role play, drama, making posters, video recording, audio recording, dictating to a study buddy, mind mapping, card sorts, matching labels to diagrams or pictures
Use large print worksheets (12–14 point Arial), cream/buff paper
Use alternatives to copying notes from the board e.g. photocopy transcript of another pupil's notes
Provide scaffolding for writing – writing frames, clue cards, choice of words to fill in blanks
Plan use of ICT as an access strategy – speech or sign-supported software, on-screen word banks, predictive word processing, annotating print-outs of IWB pages
Give pupils opportunity to feed back in plenary in variety of media
Give pupils time to copy down homework or provide it on a sheet

UNIT (Weeks)	LEARNING OBJECTIVES (for pupils above/at/below and where appropriate well above/well below age-related expectations)	CHILDREN'S TARGETS (for pupils above/at/below and where appropriate above/well below age-related expectations)	SUCCESS CRITERIA						FOCUS OF USE AND APPLICATION
1									
2									
3									
4									
5									

Review of key strategy used as part of your professional development

What went well?

What did you notice about the impact?

Even better if ....

Strategy sheet: attention deficit hyperactivity disorder (ADHD)

Please use the highlighted strategies with . . . (Pupil) in . . . (Form)

Seat pupil near the front with their back to the class, between two good role models and well away from areas other pupils need to walk through.
Establish a quiet place where pupil can go to work.
Allow pupil to fiddle with a piece of Blu-Tack, rubber band, squeeze ball or another chosen object.
Make tasks short, with frequent breaks and opportunities to move around.
Give instructions simply and clearly. Make sure the pupil is looking at you first. Check that he or she has understood them.
Use a kitchen or sand timer to help pupil complete a task in a specified period of time.
Aim for a ratio of four positive comments to one negative and teach pupil how to reward themselves: 'You managed to concentrate on your work very well just then; give yourself a pat on the back.'
Devise a private signal system to let the pupil know when they are off-task or behaving inappropriately.
Use a planned reward system.
Teach a relaxation strategy like slow breathing and cue pupil when they need to use it.
Teach/use clear classroom routines, e.g. have all pupils hold an object when it is their turn to talk. Display classroom rules and routines for pupil to refer to. Illustrate them visually – for example, use a traffic-light system to indicate whether pupils can talk or not, or symbols for different noise levels (partner voices, group voices, classroom voice, playground voices).
When pupil is misbehaving: ● Say what you want him or her to do, rather than what you don't – 'N, I want you to keep your hands in your lap' instead of 'N, stop bothering P'. ● Label the behaviour but not the pupil – not 'You big bully' but 'N, bullying is not allowed in our school'. ● Remind pupil of a rule, rather than telling them off – 'N, our rule is we put up our hand to answer', or make a point of praising a pupil who is keeping the rule – 'A, I like the way you put your hand up when you knew the answer'. ● Use the language of choice, reminding pupils of the consequences of the various behavioural choices open to them.
To help pupil work independently: ● Actively teach core routines for certain tasks, having pupil practise them with progressively less help until they can quickly tell you and show you what they have to do if you ask them to do that type of task. ● Give independent tasks that have previously been modelled for the whole class. ● Give clear guidelines: 'I expect you to have produced at least three lines by ten past ten; I will be asking you then to share these with your writing partner.' ● Use visual prompts in the form of pictorial task cards. ● Provide support in the form of writing frames, word mats, relevant classroom displays, and prompts such as a card with ideas for 'Five things to do if you are stuck with your work'.
Ask another pupil or a small group to buddy the pupil who is having difficulties, praising them when they achieve easily reachable behavioural targets.

Strategy sheet: autistic spectrum disorder

Please use the highlighted strategies with ... (Pupil) in ... (Form)

Prepare the pupil before the session/lesson by outlining what it will be about.
Support oral presentations/explanations with charts, diagrams, pictures, real objects or mime.
Set tasks with clear goals and write worksheets in step-by-step form.
If pupil becomes anxious allow him/her to remove self to an agreed calm-down area.
Seat pupil in an area of classroom free from busy displays and distractions.
Teach/use clear classroom routines, e.g. have all pupils hold an object when it is their turn to talk. Display classroom rules and routines, illustrated by pictures, for pupil to refer to. Illustrate them visually – for example, use a traffic-light system to indicate whether pupils can talk or not, or symbols for different noise levels (partner voices, group voices, classroom voice, playground voices).
Use a visual way of showing the pupil what they/the class will be doing, such as a sequenced series of pictures (a visual timetable), clockface divided into sections, or written list.
Use timeline of events → → that branches ↕ to show where pupil will have to make choices.
Use short simple instructions. Give one at a time and check for understanding. Repeat instructions in same words rather than different ones. Write instructions down as a list for pupil to tick off when completed.
Use pupil's name before asking a question or giving an instruction.
Avoid or explain metaphorical language and idiom like 'pull your socks up', 'it's raining cats and dogs', 'in a minute'.
Explain any changes of routine to the pupil in advance.
Involve the pupil by asking direct, concrete questions at their level of understanding.
Support writing with writing frames, templates (e.g. writing up a science experiment), mind maps, gapped handouts.
Allow pupil to work alone rather than in a group where possible. If in a group, give clear roles within the group and put the rules and roles into writing.
Use visual prompts on cards or photos, or consistent non-verbal signs (sit, look, listen, hand up, wait, quiet) to show pupil the social behaviours expected.
Prevent repetitive questioning by giving pupil a set number of question cards to give you each time they ask a question – when cards are gone, no more questions.
Don't ask the pupil to talk or write about imagined experiences.
Avoid tasks which depend on empathy (e.g. in literature, history, geography, PSHE and citizenship).
Set explicit and clear expectations e.g. how many lines to write, how many questions to answer, how long to listen (use timer).
Put a green 'start' dot on the pupil's book and a line to show where to finish. Use in and out boxes for work to be done and work that is finished.
Provide pupil with a symbol card to display when he or she wants help.
Expect to teach pupil social skills e.g. what to say/do when praised, how to ask for help. Always tell the pupil what to do rather than what not to do.
Provide a structure for unstructured time e.g. chess club rather than breaktime outside.
Model to the pupil that making mistakes is OK and a part of the learning process.
Use incentives based on pupil's interests e.g. a pause every hour to focus on their interest or obsession, once they have completed their work.
If pupil goes off at a tangent, direct conversation back to the topic in hand; 'Right now we are talking about volcanoes'.
Use immediate and individualised reward systems e.g. collecting a number of stickers.

Strategy sheet: behavioural, emotional and social difficulties (BESD)

Please use the highlighted strategies with . . . (Pupil) in . . . (Form)

Seat pupil by a more settled peer.
If pupil becomes wound up/anxious, allow him/her to remove self to an agreed calm-down area.
Make tasks short, with frequent breaks and opportunities to move around.
Remember that children (and adults) who are stressed find it hard to take in and remember complex information; make instructions short and clear. When pupil is experiencing emotional turbulence or anxiety, provide low-key tasks and increased structure and predictability in the classroom environment.
Set tasks with clear goals, outputs and timescales.
Teach/use clear classroom routines e.g. have all pupils hold an object when it is their turn to talk. Display classroom rules and routines for pupil to refer to. Illustrate them visually – for example, use a traffic-light system to indicate whether pupils can talk or not, or symbols for different noise levels (partner voices, group voices, classroom voice, playground voices).
Expect to teach pupil specific behavioural skills e.g. how to ask for help.
When pupil is misbehaving: <ul><li>Say what you want him or her to do, rather than what you don't – 'N, I want you to keep your hands in your lap' instead of 'N, stop bothering P'.</li><li>Label the behaviour but not the pupil – not 'You big bully' but 'N, bullying is not allowed in our school'.</li><li>Remind pupils of a rule, rather than telling them off – 'N, our rule is we put up our hand to answer', or make a point of praising a pupil who is keeping the rule – 'A, I like the way you put your hand up when you knew the answer'.</li><li>Use the language of choice, reminding pupils of the consequences of the various behavioural choices open to them.</li></ul>
Make an effort to 'catch the pupil being good' and praise them. Aim for a ratio of four positive comments to one negative and teach pupil how to reward themselves: 'You managed to concentrate on your work very well just then; give yourself a pat on the back'.
Devise a private signal system to let the pupil know when they are off-task or behaving inappropriately.
Use a planned reward system for appropriate behaviour.
Enhance access to ICT – use of the internet to research a topic, access to predictive word processing software and onscreen word grids to support writing, opportunities to create presentations.
To help pupil work independently: <ul><li>Actively teach core routines for certain tasks, having pupil practise them with progressively less help until they can quickly tell you and show you what they have to do if you ask them to do that type of task.</li><li>Set independent tasks that have previously been modelled for the whole class.</li><li>Give clear guidelines: 'I expect you to have produced at least three lines by ten past ten; I will be asking you then to share these with your writing partner.'</li><li>Use visual prompts in the form of pictorial task cards.</li><li>Provide support in the form of writing frames, word mats, relevant classroom displays, and prompts such as a card with ideas for 'Five things to do if you are stuck with your work'.</li></ul>

Take steps to build pupil's self-confidence:

- Find out what they know about or are good at, and have them share this with the rest of the class or school.
- Give them responsibilities, for example organising a lunchtime or after-school club, being a playground buddy, helping those who are new to the school.
- Have them keep records of new things they learn and can do.
- Ask them to tutor another pupil with their work.
- Photocopy good pieces of work for them to take home.

Take special steps to build the relationship with the pupil:

- Take extra care to greet the pupil each day and say a word or two individually to them.
- Have lunch with the pupil from time to time. Try to involve them in a lunchtime or after-school club that you run.
- Invite them to help you with daily tasks.
- Listen without giving advice or opinions; show that you understand how the pupil feels... *'That must have made you very angry/upset.'*
- When things go wrong, reject the behaviour, not the pupil ... *'This is not the behaviour I expect to see from someone as kind and helpful as you.'*
- Don't be afraid to tell the pupil you like them and that what happens to them matters to you... *'You really matter to me and it's important to me that you do well this year.'*

Organise time – perhaps during registration – for a teaching assistant to chat with the pupil, giving them a chance to talk about anything that may be troubling them and get themselves ready for learning.

Ask another pupil or a small group to buddy the pupil who is having difficulties, praising them when they achieve easily reachable behavioural targets.

Deploy a teaching assistant to model, coach and reinforce group work skills when the pupil is working collaboratively with other pupils.

Strategy sheet: dyspraxia, motor coordination and associated difficulties*

Please use the highlighted strategies with ... (Pupil) in .... (Form)

Minimise need for extensive handwritten recording – use ICT (predictive word processor, on-screen word banks, graphics packages), bullet points, mind mapping, flow charts, gapped handouts, buddy acting as scribe, photocopied transcripts of notes, pre-prepared Post-its with information the pupil can pick up and place on the page, print-off of IWB page for pupil to annotate
Allow pupil to choose writing tools that are most comfortable for them – pencil, pen, felt pen
Design worksheets so that the layout is uncluttered. Use buff or cream paper, large print (12–14 point) and a clear font such as Arial. Set information out in panels. Signpost sections with key words, symbols and pictures. Put important information in bold or colour.
Check seating – desktop should be at elbow height, pupil should be able to sit right back in their chair with knees bending back at right angles and **feet flat on the floor**. Put box or large book under feet if necessary.
Use aids supplied – portable writing slope, clipboards to attach paper to, non-slip mats, repositional glue sticks used to anchor paper or other materials, ruler and paper backed with Dycem, small tray for equipment, triangular and thick-barrelled pencils/pens /paintbrushes or smooth-flowing rollerball pens, two handled/ loop handled/spring-loaded scissors, handled ruler, transparent pencil case, templates and stencils (e.g. map outlines) for drawing.
Use a reminder handwriting alphabet and numeral formation guide at top of desk.
Use larger-lined book or paper, columns or boxes to place numbers in, squared paper. Attach paper to desk with Blu-Tack.
Provide the pupil with study packs – everything they need for each subject/lesson in a separate folder, plus pack of highlighter pens, Post-it notes, a line tracker for following text, various sized card 'windows' to limit vision to one area of page, sticky labels to use to correct or conceal.
Teach pupil strategies to improve organisation, such as diaries, workplans, checklists of equipment they have to bring to school each day, use of organiser functions on laptop or mobile phone.
Help pupil follow text on board or IWB by writing/highlighting alternate lines in different colours.
Enlarge pages from textbooks, cut out the particular exercise needed and then mount it on a separate page.
If the pupil needs to work through a series of questions, help them keep their place by using a paper clip or blob of Blu-Tack to indicate which question they are on.
Pair pupil with a more coordinated study buddy for practical work.
Provide additional time for practical tasks, changing for PE, putting on coat, etc.
Provide pre-prepared formats (diagrams, charts and graphs) on which pupil can record information.
Teach pupil to talk themselves through visual and spatial tasks – e.g. learn verbal model for letter formation ('b – start at top, down, up, round'), translate maths calculations into verbal problems.
Seat pupil away from distractions with plenty of space each side of them – pupil should have writing arm on the outside edge of shared table. Pupil should be able to see the teacher without turning their body.
Avoid criticism if pupil looks untidy.
Choose resources that don't require manipulation (e.g. number line rather than counters in maths).
Colour code spatially confusable items e.g. × sign in one colour, + sign in another.
Allow ample rest periods as concentration and motor effort is demanding and pupil is easily fatigued.
Write down homework for pupil or give it on a sheet or pre-printed sticky label they can put in their book. Accept homework written down by parents.

* See also speech and language – expression – if speech articulation is a problem

Strategy sheet: dyslexia

Please use the highlighted strategies with … (Pupil) in …. (Form)

Have pupils work in pairs – dyslexic pupil who has good ideas but difficulty with spelling and handwriting with a pupil who is good at writing but not so strong on ideas
Design worksheets so that the layout is uncluttered. Use buff or cream paper, large print (12–14 point) and a clear font such as Arial. Set information out in panels. Signpost sections with key words, symbols and pictures. Put important information in bold or colour.
Have any text that the pupil will struggle with read to them by a 'study buddy' or TA
Avoid asking pupil to copy from board – have them work with a study buddy, or quickly jot things down for them, or use a photocopied transcript
Be aware that the pupil may find it hard to hold questions, information or instructions in their head for long enough to act on them, and: • repeat instructions/questions   • 'chunk' them rather than saying in one long string   • jot them down on a sticky note, or encourage the pupil to do so   • allow time for processing (for example paired discussion with a partner before putting hands up)
Be aware that dyslexic pupils may know something one day and forget it the next, may lose or forget equipment they need, or may forget what they are supposed to be doing in the course of a lesson. Avoid criticism when this happens; instead, talk with them about strategies they can use to help them remember things.
Use ICT supports – laptop, predictive word processing, grids of useful words, sound files attached to information/instructions, sound files of key texts/revision notes for MP3 players, portable electronic phonetic dictionaries, speech-supported texts, spellcheckers, mind mapping software, reading pens, digital audio recorders.
Mark for content rather than presentation. When marking, praise for two correct spellings, target two incorrect spellings and use these errors as teaching points. Suggest a way of avoiding the mistake in future – for example, the similarity of the spelling to other known words, or 'the tricky bit' that has to be learned.
Enable pupil to record their ideas using alternatives to writing: PowerPoint presentations, making posters, oral presentations, dramatic reconstructions, mind maps, matching labels to pictures/diagrams/maps, sorting statements or pictures into categories.
Scaffold writing: • Provide writing frames and templates (e.g. writing up a science experiment) to help structure thinking   • Provide prompt sheets: questions to answer, key words to build each section or paragraph around, sentences or paragraphs to put in correct order, paragraph openings   • Provide clue cards   • Use cloze procedure (where the pupil fills in missing words in text)   • Print off an IWB page used in whole-class session and have pupils add to it/annotate.
Do not expect pupil to easily remember sequences such as days of the week, months of the year, the alphabet, times tables, number facts. Provide aids (for example, a pocket alphabet or calendar, table squares, calculator).
Avoid embarrassing pupil by asking them to read aloud in front of others, unless they volunteer.
Overcome problems in learning by rote by helping pupil recognise patterns, use mnemonics, or use memory strategies that create relationships between items in a list in order to aid recall.
Allow extra time to complete tasks and be aware of the fatigue the pupil may experience because of the amount of effort they have to put in to learning.
Teach pupil strategies to improve organisation, such as diaries, workplans, checklists of equipment they have to bring to school each day, use of organiser functions on mobile phone/laptop.
Provide the pupil with a study pack – spellchecker, highlighter pens, glue sticks, Post-it notes, a line tracker for following text, audio recorder, reading pen, index cards for subject vocabulary or spelling mnemonics, dictionary, sheet of high-frequency words, alphabet strip, memory jogger card for b/d confusion, sticky labels to use to correct or conceal, a tables square, a calendar, a calculator.
Write down homework for pupil, or give it on a pre-printed sticky label or sheet they can stick into their book, or record your instructions on a dictaphone. Allocate a homework buddy they can ring if they have forgotten what to do ('phone a friend').

Strategy sheet: hearing impairment

Please use the highlighted strategies with ... (Pupil) in ... (Form)

Use TA for pre-tutoring – preparing pupil for lesson e.g. explaining new words and concepts.
Seat pupil at front where able to read text, hear and lip-read.
Position sign supporters alongside teacher where pupil can see both.
Ensure light is on teacher's face, i.e. light source behind pupil – don't stand with your back to a window.
Face pupil when speaking to facilitate lip-reading; repeat any instructions that have been given when the pupil could not see the speaker; avoid writing on board or IWB while speaking as you will not be facing pupil.
Don't make the pupil concentrate on lip-reading for too long without a break.
When other pupils contribute, ensure that they speak one at a time. Paraphrase their contributions back to the class.
Speak clearly, naturally and at a normal rate – shouting or exaggerated 'mouthing' distorts normal lip patterns.
Minimise background noise e.g. noisy heater, buzzing light. Make other pupils aware of need for a quiet working environment.
Use short simple instructions. Give one at a time and check for understanding. Repeat instructions first in same words, but then if the pupil does not understand a word use a different one.
Support oral presentations/explanations with charts, diagrams, pictures, real objects or mime. Write topics or headings on the board as you introduce them.
Prepare the pupil before the session/lesson by outlining what it will be about.
Use pupil's name before asking a question or giving an instruction.
Cue pupil in to a change of topic of conversation/presentation – say 'now we are going to talk about ...'.
Question pupil after some other pupils have given examples of what is required.
Accept pupil's spoken utterances but rephrase and give them back in a grammatically correct version.
Be aware that independent writing will reflect the pupil's spoken language levels and will not necessarily be grammatically correct.
Support writing with writing frames and lists of vocabulary to choose from.
Put up a list of key vocabulary for a particular topic or lesson and teach the meaning of each word.
Use a range of ways of recording so that learning is not limited by the pupil's ability to write full English sentences: <ul><li>bullet points and mind maps;</li><li>ordering tasks – for example, ordering cut-out words to make a sentence, or sentences to make a sequence of instructions;</li><li>matching tasks, such as matching labels to pictures/diagrams/maps;</li><li>cloze procedure, where they fill in missing words in text;</li><li>annotating a printout of IWB page;</li><li>PowerPoint presentations;</li><li>making posters, oral presentations, dramatic reconstructions.</li></ul>
Agree private signal that pupil can use to show you when they have not understood.
Try to use video with subtitles; if not available, allow pupil to borrow video material after lesson to go through it again. Don't ask pupil to make notes while watching a video.
Allow extra time to complete tasks and be aware of the fatigue the pupil may experience because of the amount of effort they have to put in to listening.

Strategy sheet: learning difficulties

Please use the highlighted strategies with . . . (Pupil) in . . . (Form)

Use TA for pre-tutoring – preparing pupil for a task so that they come to it already knowing the key vocabulary and concepts.
Link new learning to what pupil already knows – e.g. start lesson with class mind map of what they already know about a subject.
Tell pupils the three key points of the lesson, teach them and recap on them at the end.
Break new learning down into small steps.
Provide multiple examples of new concepts, and take these examples from children's own real-life experience rather than talking in the abstract.
Use visual and kinaesthetic learning – learning from pictures, diagrams, mind maps, using practical equipment, handling objects, moving and doing rather than sitting.
Use scaffolding – having a peer or adult work alongside the pupil at first, then gradually withdraw as confidence grows, or having pupil finish a task that has already been part-done for them.
Use short simple instructions. Give one at a time and check for understanding. Write down and leave up instructions after saying them.
Question pupil after some other pupils have given examples of what is required.
Give pupil time to think, or to talk to a partner before answering a question, or say 'I'm going to come back to you in a minute to ask you xxxx'.
If pupil can't answer a question, scaffold/support till they can rather than saying 'Can anyone help x?'; echo back the pupil's answers in expanded form.
Buddy the pupil with a more able peer.
Have any text that the pupil will struggle with read to them by a 'study buddy' or TA.
Put up a list of key vocabulary for a particular topic or lesson and teach the meaning of each word.
To help pupil extract the salient points from information that they are given, use highlighter pens or provide cards telling them what they have to look out for on a visit, in a text or from sources such as film.
Make learning strategies explicit by 'thinking aloud' yourself.
Help pupil develop and generalise effective learning strategies – when successful, ask them to identify what they did to solve the problem/find the information.
Model to the pupil that making mistakes is OK and a part of the learning process.
Agree a private signal that the pupil can use to show you when they have not understood.
Pair a higher-attaining group with a lower-attaining one and provide a range of collaborative activities so that pupils can help one another.
Prepare pupils for writing – have them work in a group with you or a TA to rehearse orally what they want to say, then plan the writing together.
Enable pupil to record their ideas using alternatives to writing: PowerPoint presentations, making posters, oral presentations, dramatic reconstructions, mind maps, matching labels to pictures/diagrams/maps, sorting statements or pictures into categories.
Use software that supports writing, with onscreen word grids from which they can choose the words they need.
Scaffold writing: ● Provide writing frames and templates (e.g. writing up a science experiment) to help structure thinking. ● Supply prompt sheets: questions to answer, key words to build each section or paragraph around, sentences or paragraphs to put in correct order, paragraph openings. ● Provide clue cards. ● Use cloze procedure (where the pupil fills in missing words in text). ● Print off an IWB page used in whole-class session and have pupils add to it/annotate.
Give homework instructions on a sheet and make time to explain them. Allocate a homework buddy to ring if they need help ('phone a friend').

Strategy sheet: speech, language and communication needs

Please use the highlighted strategies with … (Pupil) in …. (Form)

Use TA for pre-tutoring – preparing pupil for a task so that they come to it already knowing the key vocabulary and concepts.
Begin work on a new topic with pupil's existing knowledge and experiences – make a mind map or other visual representation of what they already know.
When you start a new topic, develop a class chart of the vocabulary that pupils will find useful or need to learn. Teach each word by helping children build a web of associations – what it sounds like, what it means, how it fits in a sentence.
Use cued listening – give pupil a small number of questions that they will have to answer after listening to teacher presentation or video input.
Use pupil's name before asking a question or giving an instruction.
Give directions before an activity, not during it.
Keep verbal instructions simple, and in the order you want them carried out. Be aware of how many 'information-carrying' words you are using : 'Get your maths book from the pile on **my desk**; on a **clean page**, write the **date** and then **copy down** the **calculations on the board**' has more information-carrying words than many adults will be able to remember.
Give pupil time (at least 10 seconds) to respond and then, if necessary, repeat what you said. Use the same words unless you think the vocabulary was too difficult to understand.
Check for understanding – ask the pupil to tell you what they have to do.
Agree a private signal pupil can use to show you they have not understood, or teach them to say 'Sorry, I didn't understand that – can you say it again, please?' Praise them for asking for clarification.
Support your oral presentations/explanations with pictures, real objects or mime. Use visuals (real objects, photographs, symbols) appropriate to pupil's developmental level rather than chronological age. Use visual timetables.
Display classroom rules and routines, illustrated by pictures, for pupil to refer to. Illustrate them visually – for example, use a traffic light system to indicate whether pupils can talk or not, or symbols for different noise levels (partner voices, group voices, classroom voice, playground voices).
Use symbols to support spoken language and text (www.widgit.com).
Use visual summaries of discussions – mind maps, flow charts, diagrams, comic strip format, graphic organisers (www.graphic.org)
Cue pupil in to a change of topic of conversation/presentation: say 'Now we are going to talk about …'
Question pupil after some other pupils have given examples of what is required.
Give pupil time to think, or to talk to a partner before answering a question, or say 'I'm going to come back to you in a minute to ask you xxxx. But first I'm going to ask y a question'.
If pupil can't answer a question, scaffold/support till they can rather than saying 'Can anyone help x?'
Use a hierarchy of questions – start with an open question ('What do you think might happen next?'), then if support is needed frame the question as alternatives ('Do you think x or y?')
Use question prompt card to help pupils know how to respond e.g. Where? question requires a place.
Pair pupil with a study buddy to repeat instructions and demonstrate tasks.
Accept pupil's spoken utterances but rephrase and give them back in a grammatically correct and expanded version
Support oral work with talk frames/key phrases ('First … next … finally', 'I think … but on the other hand').
Provide topic-related role-play opportunities and model the language to be used in role-play.

Talk aloud about what you are doing using statements which give children examples of the language they might use.
Support writing with writing frames and lists of vocabulary to choose from.
Use a range of ways of recording so that learning is not limited by the pupil's ability to write full English sentences: • bullet points and mind maps; • ordering tasks – for example, ordering cut-out words to make a sentence, or sentences to make a sequence of instructions; • matching tasks, such as matching labels to pictures/diagrams/maps; • cloze procedure, where they fill in missing words in text; • annotating a print-off of IWB page. • PowerPoint presentations • making posters, oral presentations, dramatic reconstructions
Provide the pupil with a study pack – glossaries of key subject vocabulary, highlighter pens, glue stick, Post-it notes, index cards to make their own mind maps/cartoon strips/key word lists, templates for writing up science experiments, etc
Allow extra time to complete tasks and be aware of the fatigue the pupil may experience because of the amount of effort they have to put in to learning
Write down homework for pupil, or give it on a pre-printed sticky label or sheet they can stick into their book, or record your instructions on a dictaphone. Allocate a homework buddy they can ring if they have forgotten what to do ('phone a friend')

Strategy sheet: visual impairment

Please use the highlighted strategies with . . . (Pupil) in . . . (Form)

Use TA for pre-tutoring – preparing pupil for lesson e.g. explaining concepts that rely on vision for understanding.
Don't ask pupil if they can see what is on board/IWB etc. (they may not know) – check by using symbols that pupil knows then use same-size font/background/colour as the symbols you have checked.
Avoid pupil having to look directly into a light source – do not sit or stand with the light behind you.
Use clear, well-spaced print that is suitably contrasted with the background according to individual pupil's needs (for x, y colour on z background). Use non-glossy, non-reflective paper. Use photocopies of masters not of faint blurred versions.
Give verbal information to replace/supplement information from pictures, questions, facial expression.
Use tactile experience to replace/supplement visual input (for example, if class is watching sugar cubes dissolve in a beaker, pupil can put their hand in beaker and feel it dissolve).
Ensure pupil has an individual copy of print material being read, in the appropriate format (e.g. large print, Braille). This applies to information on classroom walls too (posters, key vocabulary lists).
Say pupil's name before asking a question or giving an instruction and indicate who is talking in a class discussion.
Provide pupil with own copy of materials to be written on board or IWB; read aloud what you or other pupils are writing up.
Use larger-lined paper, columns or boxes to place numbers in, squared paper. Have pupil use dark pen instead of pencil.
When alerting pupils to an action, artefact, illustration or example don't just point – describe what you want the pupils to take notice of and if necessary describe what it is.
Ensure pupil uses aids supplied – such as CCTV, hand-held and portable video magnifiers, book stands, speech output software, digital accessible information system.
Ensure pupil has access to the most appropriate medium for recording work (heavily lined paper, laptop, Braille machine, tape recorder, headphones, digital accessible information system). Access to power supply or space for Braille machine may be required.
Ensure pupil has all the curriculum materials and equipment required to hand and that the materials are organised and contained consistently and securely (use Dycem non-slip mat, a high-sided tray or container with compartments).
Raise position of text (e.g. use sloping desk, reading stands).
Minimise need for extensive handwritten recording – use ICT (predictive word processor, onscreen word banks, graphics packages), bullet points, mind mapping, flow charts, gapped handouts, buddy acting as scribe, photocopied transcripts of notes, printout of IWB page for pupil to annotate.
Use tactile indicators – Blu-Tack, paper clips – to help pupil find information, locate where they need to be on page, keep track of which question they are on in a series.
Allow extra time to complete tasks and be aware of the fatigue the pupil may experience because of the amount of effort they have to put into learning.
Record your homework instructions on a dictaphone. Allocate a homework buddy they can ring if they have forgotten what to do ('phone a friend').

Provision map (primary)

PROVISION	YR	Y1	Y2	Y3	Y4	Y5	Y6
Language intervention							
Literacy intervention							
Maths intervention							
Coordination programme							
EAL provision							
1–1 SEAL work (counselling, solution-focused work, etc.)							
Small group SEAL work							
In-class support for individuals							
Attendance and extra-curricular provision							
Gifted and talented provision							
Other							

Provision map (secondary)

PROVISION	Y7	Y8	Y9	Y10	Y11
Targeted (Wave 2) literacy intervention					
Targeted (Wave 2) maths intervention					
Targeted (Wave 2) oral language interventions					
Further SEN (Wave 3) literacy intervention					
Further SEN (Wave 3) mathematics intervention					
EAL provision					
1–1 mentoring for aspirations/engagement with learning					
SEAL small group work					
1–1 SEAL work (counselling, solution-focused, etc.)					
In-class support for individuals					
Out of school/extra-curricular provision					
Gifted and talented provision					
Other					

Intervention plan: nurture group

Name of provision	**NURTURE GROUP**
Aims of the programme	To develop the skills young children need in order to learn: the ability to settle, listen, concentrate, share and make friends.
Description of programme	Small class of up to 12 children taught by a teacher and a TA. Children register with their mainstream class and spend some time there each week, but spend most of the day in the nurture group room. This is designed to replicate a nurturing home, with areas themed around home, kitchen, work and play.
Target group	Children who are unable to respond in a mainstream class, are seriously disruptive or withdrawn, and failing to learn because their basic emotional and social needs have not been met in their early years. Usually Reception age.
Entry level	Scores on Boxall Profile that indicate developmental levels well below those expected of competently functioning children, or behaviours which are preventing the child making progress both academically and socially.
Exit level	Teacher judgement based on changes to Boxall Profile or use of Nurture Group Reintegration Readiness Scale (Doyle, 2001) – numerical score 218 (70%) or above.
Length of intervention	Two to five terms.
Frequency	Daily.
Delivered by	Teacher and TA or nursery nurse.
Suggested start date	Any time.
Groupings	Group of up to 12.
Assessment method	Boxall Profile.
Monitoring arrangements	HT/Deputy HT observation using checklist of criteria for effective nurture groups from Nurture Group Network.

Task	Date/Information	Checklist tick when completed
Identify children to be assessed on Boxall Profile	Names:	
Set a date for assessment	Date:	
Select children for the group	Names:	
Set a date for a parent meeting	Date:	
Set a date for the intervention programme to begin	Date:	
Set a date for HT/Deputy HT observation	Date:	
Set a date for post-programme assessments	Date:	
Set dates for 3- and 6-month follow-up assessments	Date:	
Complete evaluation and disseminate outcomes to SLT	Date:	

Intervention plan: SEAL focus group

Name of provision	**SEAL FOCUS GROUP – MANAGING STRONG FEELINGS**
Aims of the programme	To accelerate pupil progress towards SEAL learning outcomes. 'I understand why feelings sometimes "take over" or get out of control and know what makes me angry or upset', 'I have a range of strategies for managing impulses and strong emotions so they do not lead me to behave in ways that would have negative consequences for me or for other people.'
Description of programme	6, 2-hour small group sessions in school followed by 1 day off-site team challenge activities.
Target group	Year 8 pupils who have difficulty in managing strong feelings.
Entry level	Low scores on SEAL pupil and adult self-rating scale (managing feelings).
Exit level	
Length of intervention	7 weeks.
Frequency	Weekly.
Delivered by	LSU teacher and learning mentor (LM).
Suggested start date	Spring term.
Groupings	Maximum 8 with a balance of pupils – some impulsive, some easily upset, no more than 4 who are often angry.
Assessment method	Pupils who might benefit from the scheme are identified using self and tutor referral. Pupil, parent and form teacher rating scales are then used to select final group. The same rating scales are repeated at the end of the intervention. Evaluation is via changes to rating scales and reductions in number of times per month pupil is placed in detention or referred to HoY.

Task	Date/Information	Checklist tick when completed
Identify pupils who might benefit	Names:	
Set a date for pupil meetings (to secure sign-up and complete self-rating scales)	Date:	
Set a date for parent meetings (to include use of rating scales)	Date:	
Set a date for tutor completion of ratings scales	Date:	
Select pupils for the group	Names:	
Fix a timetable for the sessions each week	Times:	
Fix dates for initial planning (half day) and post-session reviews/forward planning for the teacher and LM	Dates:	
Decide where the sessions will take place	Location:	
Set a date for the intervention programme to begin	Date:	
Set a date for INCO to monitor	Date:	
Set a date for end of intervention post-programme assessments	Date:	
Set dates for 3- and 6-month follow-up assessments	Dates:	
Complete evaluation and disseminate outcomes to SLT	Date:	

Intervention plan: Talking Partners

Name of provision	**TALKING PARTNERS**
Aims of the programme	To improve speaking and listening skills across the curriculum.
Description of programme	The programme provides structured activities which encourage and support pupils' developing oral language skills in a variety of situations. Activities particularly support achievement of NLS objectives.
Target group	End of FS to Year 3.
Entry level	Teacher assessment based upon child's oracy across the curriculum.
Exit level	
Length of intervention	10 weeks.
Frequency	3 × 20 mins weekly.
Delivered by	TA, who has been trained to deliver the programme.
Suggested start date	Flexible.
Groupings	Maximum 3.
Assessment method	Renfrew Language Scales pre- and post-intervention (grammar and information). Observation sheet. Measure against speaking and listening curricular target. Child summary sheets.
Monitoring arrangements	INCO to observe TA twice during the 10-week programme

Task	Date/Information	Checklist tick when completed
Identify children to be screened	Names:	
Set a date for screening	Date:	
Select children for the group	Names:	
Fix a timetable for the sessions each week	Times:	
Allocate half a day of preparation time for the TA	Date:	
Decide where the sessions will take place	Location:	
Fix a time for the weekly teacher/ TA review session	Time:	
Set a date for the intervention programme to begin	Date:	
Set a date for the parent meeting	Date:	
Set a date for the progress checks during the programme	Date:	
Set dates for INCO to observe session	Date:	
Set a date for post-programme assessments	Date:	
Complete evaluation and disseminate outcomes to SLT	Date:	

Intervention plan: Reading Recovery

Name of provision	**READING RECOVERY**
Aims of the programme	To generate accelerated learning back to the appropriate NLS Framework for teaching objectives.
Description of programme	Reading Recovery is a Wave 3 intervention programme for children who have made very little progress in reading and writing during their first year in school. It involves a daily 1-to-1 lesson with a highly trained teacher.
Target group	Year 1/Year 2.
Entry level	Lowest-attaining pupils.
Exit level	Age-appropriate National Curriculum levels in reading and writing.
Length of intervention	12 to 20 weeks.
Frequency	30 mins daily.
Delivered by	Teacher with Reading Recovery teaching qualification.
Suggested start date	After the child has been in school for 3 terms.
Groupings	1.
Assessment method	Book band level/running record. Writing sample. BAS reading test. Reading Recovery Observation Survey.
Monitoring arrangements	Reading Recovery teacher to be observed teaching by LA Teacher Leader.

Task	Date/Information	Checklist tick when completed
Identify children to be screened	Names:	
Set a date for screening	Date:	
Select children to take part	Names:	
Fix a timetable for the sessions each week	Times:	
Decide where the sessions will take place	Location:	
Fix date for LA Teacher Leader to monitor teaching	Date:	
Set a date for the intervention programme to begin	Date:	
Set times for liaison with class teacher		
Set dates for post-programme assessments	Date:	
Set dates for 3- and 6-month follow-up assessments	Date:	
Complete evaluation and disseminate outcomes to SLT	Date:	

Intervention plan: Further Literacy Support

Name of provision	**FURTHER LITERACY SUPPORT (FLS)**
Aims of the programme	To generate accelerated learning back to the appropriate NLS Framework teaching objectives.
Description of programme	3 modules each lasting 4 weeks. Overall focus is on consolidating objectives from Year 4 and Year 5, terms 1 and 2. The main emphasis is on writing. Pupils use a workbook which is supplemented by optional homework. These sessions are additional to the daily literacy hour.
Target group	Year 5.
Entry level	3c.
Exit level	3a.
Length of intervention	12 weeks.
Frequency	30 mins per session.
Delivered by	TA, who has been trained to deliver the programme, delivers 3 sessions per week. Teacher delivers guided reading and guided writing.
Suggested start date	Spring term.
Groupings	Maximum 6.
Monitoring arrangements	Literacy coordinator to observe one session.
Assessment method	4 screenings. Book band level/running record. Writing sample. Flow chart – entry and exit. Progress checks.

Task	Date/Information	Checklist tick when completed
Identify children to be screened	Names:	
Set a date for screening	Date:	
Select children for the group	Names:	
Fix a timetable for the sessions each week	Times:	
Allocate half a day of preparation time for the TA	Date:	
Decide where the sessions will take place	Location:	
Fix a time for the weekly teacher/TA review session	Time:	
Set a date for the parent meeting	Date:	
Set a date for the intervention programme to begin	Date:	
Set a date for the progress checks during the programme	Date:	
Set a date for SENCO to observe session	Date:	
Set a date for post-programme assessments	Date:	
Complete evaluation and disseminate outcomes to SLT	Date:	

Intervention plan: Catch Up Literacy

Name of provision	**CATCH UP LITERACY**
Aims of the programme	To address the problem of underachievement rooted in literacy difficulties.
Description of programme	Catch Up Literacy is a one-to-one, book-based intervention for struggling readers. It uses Catch Up Literacy assessments for learning to determine what the learner can do and where their needs lie, and to set Catch Up Literacy targets. These help to inform individualised, one-to-one sessions. The intervention is centred on two, highly-structured 15-minute sessions per week, delivered by a TA.
Target Group	Learners who are struggling readers rather than beginner readers.
Entry level	P level 7 or above
Exit level	National Curriculum level 4
Length of intervention	An average of 6–12 months (depending on need)
Frequency	2 × 15 minutes a week
Delivered by	TA who has completed Open College Network accredited/Ofqual recognised training.
Suggested start date	Flexible
Groupings	1–1
Assessment method	Catch Up Literacy assessments for learning Standardised tests Tracking through Catch Up Literacy levels and/or National Curriculum levels.
Monitoring arrangements	Catch Up Coordinator undertakes 'Delivering Catch Up Literacy' and 'Managing Catch Up Literacy' training and uses the Catch Up Coordinator Action Plan to support/monitor/observe TA.

Task	Date/Information	Checklist tick when completed
Select children to take part	Names:	
Catch Up Literacy-trained TA assesses children using Catch Up Literacy assessments for learning	Date:	
Fix a timetable for the sessions each week	Times:	
Decide where the sessions will take place	Location:	
TA/Catch Up Coordinator implement Action Plan	Date:	
Set a date for the intervention to begin	Date:	
Set a date for parent meetings	Date:	
Set times for liaison with class teacher		
Set a date for post-intervention assessments	Date:	
Set dates for 3- and 6-month follow-up assessments	Date:	
Complete evaluation and disseminate outcomes to SLT	Date:	

Intervention plan: Numbers Count

Name of provision	**NUMBERS COUNT**
Aims of the programme	To enable children to reach age-related expectations in numeracy.
Description of programme	Numbers Count is a Wave 3 intervention for children with very significant mathematical difficulties.
Target group	Aimed mainly at Year 2 children but also used in Y1 and 3
Entry level	P6-L1C
Exit level	Age appropriate NC levels
Length of intervention	Generally 12 weeks
Frequency	30 mins 3 to 5 times a week – minimum 40 lessons.
Delivered by	Teacher with Numbers Count qualification.
Suggested start date	Flexible
Groupings	1–1, pairs or threes
Assessment method	Sandwell Numeracy Test NC sublevel teacher assessment
Monitoring arrangements	Numbers Count teacher to be observed teaching by Every Child Counts Teacher Leader.

Task	Date/Information	Checklist tick when completed
Select children to take part	Names:	
NC teacher assesses children using Sandwell test	Date:	
Fix a timetable for the sessions each week	Times:	
Decide where the sessions will take place	Location:	
Fix a date when Teacher Leader will monitor teaching	Date:	
Set a date for the intervention programme to begin	Date:	
Set a date for the initial parent meeting	Date:	
Set times for liaison with class teacher	Date:	
Set dates for session observation by TA(s), class teacher	Dates:	
Set a date for post-programme assessments	Date:	
Set dates for 3- and 6-month follow-up assessments	Date:	
Complete evaluation and disseminate outcomes to SLT	Date:	

Intervention plan: 1stClass@Number

Name of provision	1STCLASS@NUMBER
Aims of the programme	To enable children to reach age-related expectations in numeracy.
Description of programme	1stClass@Number is an intervention programme for children who have fallen behind their peers in numeracy.
Target group	Children at L1C – usually Year 2 children
Entry level	L1C
Exit level	L2C
Length of intervention	8 weeks
Frequency	3 × 30 minutes a week
Delivered by	Trained TA
Suggested start date	Flexible
Groupings	Up to 4 children in a group
Assessment method	Sandwell Numeracy Test NC sublevel teacher assessment
Monitoring arrangements	TA to be observed teaching by SENCO or (where available) Numbers Count teacher

Task	Date/Information	Checklist tick when completed
Select children to take part	Names:	
SENCO or NC teacher assesses children using Sandwell test	Date:	
Fix a timetable for the sessions each week	Times:	
Decide where the sessions will take place	Location:	
Fix a date when SENCO or Numbers Count teacher will monitor teaching	Date:	
Set a date for the intervention programme to begin	Date:	
Set a date for parent meetings	Date:	
Set times for liaison with class teacher	Date:	
Set a date for post-programme assessments	Date:	
Set dates for 3- and 6-month follow-up assessments	Date:	
Complete evaluation and disseminate outcomes to SLT	Date:	

Intervention plan: Wave 3 Maths

Name of provision	**SUPPORTING CHILDREN WITH GAPS IN THEIR MATHEMATICAL UNDERSTANDING (WAVE 3 MATHS)**
Aims of the programme	To increase children's rates of progress in mathematics by using targeted approaches to tackle fundamental errors and misconceptions.
Description of programme	The materials focus on number and calculation, tackling areas such as understanding the structure of number and operations between numbers. Problem-solving is integrated and exemplified in the materials, and opportunities are provided for children to develop mathematical vocabulary.
Target group	Aimed mainly at Key Stage 2 children who, for any reason, demonstrate fundamental errors and misconceptions that are preventing them making progress. Can also be used in secondary schools.
Entry level	Class/subject teacher assessment that identifies significant errors and misconceptions.
Exit level	Class/subject teacher assessment showing child no longer exhibits the error/misconception.
Length of intervention	Flexible
Frequency	Flexible – short teaching sessions several times a week.
Delivered by	Ideally a teacher delivers the first teaching activity to tackle the error or misconception. This is then followed up with 'spotlight' sessions with a TA trained to deliver the programme.
Suggested start date	Flexible
Groupings	1–1
Assessment method	Tracking sheets, supplied in the pack NC sublevel teacher assessment
Monitoring arrangements	SENCO to observe TA once during the intervention

Task	Date/Information	Checklist tick when completed
Select children to take part	Names:	
Class/subject teacher assesses children using Tracking Charts	Date:	
Fix a timetable for the sessions each week	Times:	
Allocate half a day of preparation time for the TA	Date:	
Decide where the sessions will take place	Location:	
Fix a date when SENCO will monitor teaching	Date:	
Fix a time for the weekly teacher/TA review session	Time:	
Set a date for the intervention programme to begin	Date:	
Set a date for the parent meeting	Date:	
Set a date for post-programme assessments	Date:	
Set dates for 3- and 6-month follow-up assessments	Date:	
Complete evaluation and disseminate outcomes to SLT	Date:	

Intervention plan: Catch Up Numeracy

Name of provision	**CATCH UP NUMERACY**
Aims of the programme	To address the problem of underachievement rooted in numeracy difficulties.
Description of programme	Catch Up Numeracy is a 1–1 intervention for learners who struggle with numeracy. It uses Catch Up Numeracy assessments for learning, based on components of numeracy, to create a personalised profile which forms the basis for individualised, one-to-one sessions. The intervention is centred on two, highly-structured fifteen-minute sessions per week, delivered by a TA.
Target group	Learners who are struggling with numeracy rather than learners who are beginning numeracy.
Entry level	P level 7 and above
Exit level	National Curriculum level 4
Length of intervention	An average of 6–12 months (depending on need)
Frequency	2 × 15 minutes a week
Delivered by	TA who has completed Open College Network accredited/Ofqual recognised training
Suggested start date	Flexible
Groupings	One
Assessment method	Catch Up Numeracy assessments for learning Standardised tests Tracking through Catch Up Numeracy levels and/or National Curriculum levels
Monitoring arrangements	Catch Up Coordinator undertakes 'Delivering Catch Up Numeracy' and 'Managing Catch Up Numeracy' training and uses Catch Up Coordinator Action Plan to support/monitor/observe TA.

Task	Date/Information	Checklist tick when completed
Select children to take part	Names:	
Catch Up Numeracy-trained TA assesses children using Catch Up Numeracy assessments for learning	Date:	
Fix a timetable for the sessions each week	Times:	
Decide where the sessions will take place	Location:	
TA/Catch Up Coordinator implement Action Plan	Date:	
Set a date for the intervention to begin	Date:	
Set a date for parent meetings	Date:	
Set times for liaison with class teacher		
Set a date for post-intervention assessments	Date:	
Set dates for 3- and 6-month follow-up assessments	Date:	
Complete evaluation and disseminate outcomes to SLT	Date:	

Intervention plan: Learning Challenge

Name of provision	**LEARNING CHALLENGE**
Aims of the programme	To help pupils improve their organisation of themselves and of their learning, so that they will be better equipped to take advantage of what is offered to them in lessons.
Description of programme	A series of seven challenge activities covering a range of organisational skills.
Target group	KS3 Pupils who are disorganised in their preparation for schoolwork or homework, or who have poorly developed learning strategies.
Entry level	Attainment in one or more of the core subjects that is up to two years below age-related expectations .
Exit level	
Length of intervention	Flexible
Frequency	Flexible
Delivered by	Volunteer coaches – TAs, parent volunteers, governors, form tutors, learning mentors, librarians, or other students.
Suggested start date	Flexible
Groupings	1–1
Assessment method	A target group of pupils who will benefit from the scheme is identified using the diagnostic tools provided in the materials. The teacher who is organising the scheme analyses the pupils' difficulties in organising their learning by means of an interview and information from subject teachers and form tutors, and sets pupil targets. The teacher organiser re-assesses pupils at the end of the intervention against the targets set.
Monitoring arrangements	Organising teacher will observe all coaches at least once.

Task	Date/ Information	Checklist tick when completed
Identify which pupils will be supported through the Learning Challenge	Names:	
Decide the extent and duration of support for each pupil		
Allocate pupils to coaches;	Name: Coach:	
Fix a timetable for the sessions each week	Times:	
Decide where the sessions will take place	Location:	
Fix dates to monitor sessions	Dates:	
Fix times for support meetings coaches/organising teacher	Time:	
Set a date for the intervention programme to begin	Date:	
Set a date for the parent meeting	Date:	
Set dates for observation of coaching	Dates:	
Set a date for post-programme assessments	Date:	
Complete evaluation and disseminate outcomes to SLT	Date:	

Record of intervention programme

WEEK COMMENCED											
Names	**Pre-intervention assessment outcomes**	**Wk 1**	**Wk 2**	**Wk 3**	**Wk 4**	**Wk 5**	**Wk 6**	**Wk 7**	**Wk 8**	**Wk 9**	**Wk 10**	**Post-intervention assessment outcomes**
Sessions run											
Weekly meeting with teacher											
Evaluation											

Notes:
Write in all dates in advance where possible.
Tick in the weekly box if the child attended the session.
Continue on further sheet where programmes last longer than 10 weeks.
If assessments are on another sheet, write 'see attached sheet' and staple to the record sheets.

Monitoring the quality of intervention sessions

QUALITY FEATURES	✓	EVIDENCE
The right pupils have been targeted.		
The location is appropriate.		
The frequency of the intervention is as specified.		
The session length is as specified.		
The session content matches that specified in the programme.		
Resources have been pre-prepared and are well managed.		
The adult and the pupils know what the learning objectives are.		
The adult has sufficient subject knowledge to promote learning.		
The session is planned and adjusted on the basis of assessment and pupils are helped to identify their own learning targets and to assess their own progress.		
Key instructions and learning points are given concisely and clearly and repeated as necessary.		
Behaviour is well managed and the adult promotes interaction between the pupils in the group.		
The adult promotes pupils' independence as learners, helping them recognise what strategies they are using successfully and apply them in other situations.		
The adult creates a secure and supportive learning environment where there is safety to have a go and make mistakes.		
The adult challenges pupils and expects the most from them.		
Teaching styles and approaches are active, lively and multisensory; the session is well paced.		
Class or subject teacher and additional adult plan and review the intervention jointly.		
There are opportunities for pupils to apply their learning and have it reinforced in class/across the school.		
Parental involvement is secured as specified in the programme.		

Actions:

References

Achievement for All (2012) *Achievement for All Anthology Pilot 2009–2011*. Newbury: Achievement for All.

Audit Commission (2002) *Special Educational needs: a mainstream issue?* London: Audit Commission.

Beard, R., Pell, G., Shorrocks-Taylor, D. and Swinnerton, B., with Sawyer, V., Willcocks, J. and Yeomans, D. (2005) *Follow-up Study of the National Evaluation of the National Literacy Strategy Further Literacy Support Programme*. Reading: Centre for British Teachers.

BECTA (2010) *I'm stuck, can you help me? A report into parents' involvement in school work at home*. Coventry: BECTA.

Black, P., Harrison, C., Lee, C., Marshall, B. and Wiliam, D. (2003) *Assessment for Learning: Putting It into Practice*. Maidenhead: Open University Press.

Blatchford, P., Russell, A. and Webster, R. (2012) *Reassessing the Impact of Teaching Assistants: How research challenges practice and policy*. Abingdon: Routledge.

Brooks, G. (1996) *Family Literacy Works*. London: NFER/BSA.

Brooks, G. (1998) *Family Numeracy Adds Up*. London: NFER/BSA.

Brooks, G. and Pahl, K. (2008) *Effective and inclusive practices in early literacy, language and numeracy: a review of programmes and practice in the UK and internationally*. London: CfBT Education Trust.

Casey, J. (2007) *GCSEs: what can a parent do? 101 tips to ensure success*. Bristol: Futurelink Publishing.

Centre for Studies in Inclusive Education (2002) *Index for Inclusion*. Bristol: CSIE.

Chapman, C., Ainscow, M., Miles, S. and West, M. (2011). *Leadership that promotes the achievement of students with special educational needs and disabilities*, Nottingham: National College for School Leadership.

Clarke, S. (2001) *Unlocking Formative Assessment*. London: Hodder and Stoughton.

Cochrane, S. (2006) *Putting the Pieces Together: A guide to provision management*. London: London Regional Partnership.

Cole, B. (2005) Mission impossible? Special educational needs, inclusion and the re-conceptualisation of the role of the SENCO in England and Wales. *European Journal of Special Needs Education*, 20 (3): 287–307.

DCSF (2007a) *Social and Emotional Aspects of Learning for Secondary Schools*. London: DCSF.

Desforges, C. and Abouchaar, A. (2003) *The Impact of Parental Involvement, Parental Support and Family Education on Pupil Achievement and Adjustment: a review of the literature*. London: DfES.

Desforges, C. (2007) *Children in the Secondary School Age Range with Moderate Special Educational Needs (MLD): A research review.* London: Esmée Fairbairn Foundation.

DfE (2011) *Special Educational Needs in England, January 2011.* London: DfE.

DfE (2011b) *Support and Aspiration: A new approach to special educational needs and disability.* London: DfE.

DfE (2012a) *Support and Aspiration: A new approach to special educational needs and disability. Progress and next steps.* London: DfE.

DfE (2012b) *Government Proposes Biggest Reforms to Special Educational Needs in 30 years*, Press Notice. London: DfE.

DfES (2001a) *SEN Toolkit.* London: DfES.

DfES (2001b) *Special Educational Needs Code of Practice.* London: DfES.

DfES (2003) *Models and Images.* London: DfES.

DfES (2004a) *Assessment for Learning.* London: DfES.

DfES (2004b) *Excellence and Enjoyment: Learning and teaching in the primary years.* London: DfES.

DfES (2004c) *Learning and Teaching for Children with Special Educational Needs in the Primary Years.* London: DfES.

DfES (2004d) *Removing Barriers to Achievement: The government's strategy for SEN.* London: DfES.

DfES (2004e) *Strengthening Teaching and Learning through the Use of Curricular Targets.* London: DfES.

DfES (2004f) *The Intensifying Support Programme.* London: DfES.

DfES (2005a) *Excellence and Enjoyment: Social and emotional aspects of learning.* London: DfES.

DfES (2005b) *Higher Standards, Better Schools for All.* London: DfES.

DfES (2005c) *Leading on Inclusion.* London: DfES.

DfES (2005d) *Maximising Progress: Ensuring the attainment of pupils with SEN.* London: DfES.

DfES (2005e) *Supporting Children with Gaps in their Mathematical Understanding.* London: DfES.

DfES (2005f) *The Effective Management of Teaching Assistants to Improve Standards in Literacy and Mathematics.* London: DfES.

DfES (2006a) *Effective Leadership: Ensuring the progress of pupils with SEN and/or disabilities.* London: DfES.

DfES (2006b) *Excellence and Enjoyment: Social and emotional aspects of learning: Family SEAL.* London: DfES.

DfES (2006c) *Excellence and Enjoyment: Social and emotional aspects of learning: small group activities.* London: DfES.

DfES (2006d) *Leading on Intervention.* London: DfES.

DfES (2006e) *Secondary Intervention: Progression maps.* London: DfES.

DfES (2006f) *Strengthening Teaching and Learning through the Use of Curricular Targets: the Intensifying Support Programme professional development meetings* (PDMs). London: DfES.

DfES (2006g) *2020 Vision. Report of the Teaching and Learning Review Group.* London: DfES.

DfES (2007) *Making Good Progress*. London: DfES.

DoH (2010) *Person Centred Planning: Advice for using person-centred thinking, planning and reviews in schools and transition*. London: Department of Health.

Doyle, R. (2001) Using a readiness scale for reintegrating pupils with social, emotional and behavioural difficulties from a Nurture Group into their mainstream classroom – a pilot study. *British Journal of Special Education, 28* (3): 126–32.

Easton, C., Gee, G., Durbin, B., and Teeman, D. (2011). *Early Intervention, Using the CAF Process, and its Cost-effectiveness: Findings from LARC3*. Slough: NFER.

Ellis, S., Tod, J., Graham-Matheson, L. (2012) *Special Educational Needs – Reflection, Renewal and Reality*. Birmingham: NASUWT.

Everard, B. and Morris, G. (1990) *Effective School Management*. London: PCP.

Every Child a Chance Trust (2009) *The Long Term Costs of Literacy Difficulties (2nd edition)* London: Every Child a Chance Trust.

Feiler, A. (2003) A home visiting project for Reception children predicted to experience literacy difficulties. *British Journal of Special Education, 30* (3).

Flouri, E. and Buchanan, A. (2002) What predicts good relationships with parents in adolescence and partners in adult life. *Journal of Family Psychology, 16,* 186–98.

Freeman, J. (2010) *Gifted Lives*. London: Routledge.

Fullan, M. (2001) *The New Meaning of Educational Change,* 3rd edn. Columbia: Teachers College Press.

Furlong, M., McGilloway, S., Bywater, T., Hitchings, J., Smith, S.M. and Donnelly, M. (2012) Behavioural and cognitive-behavioural group-based parenting programmes for early-onset conduct problems in children aged 3 to 12 years. *The Cochrane Library, 2012,* Issue 2.

Gerber, S., Finn, J., Achilles, C. and Boyd-Zaharias, J. (2001) Teacher aides and students' academic achievement, *Educational Evaluation and Policy Analysis, 23* (2): 123–43.

Giangreco, M., Cloninger, C. and Iverson, V. (1993) *Choosing Options and Accommodations for Children (COACH): A guide to planning inclusive education*. Baltimore: Paul H Brookes.

Giangreco, M., Edelman, S., Luisellu, T. and Macfarland, S. (1997) Helping or hovering? Effects of instructional assistant proximity on students with disabilities, *Exceptional Children, 64,* 7–180.

Goepel, J. (2009) Constructing the Individual Education Plan: confusion or collaboration? *Support for Learning, 24* (3): 126–32.

Goodall, J. and Vorhaus, J. (2011) *Review of Best Practice in Parental Engagement*. London: DfE.

Gross, J. (1994) Asperger Syndrome: a label worth having? *Educational Psychology in Practice, 10* (2).

Gross, J. (1996). The weight of the evidence. *Support for Learning, 11* (1): 3–8.

Gross, J. (2000) Paper promises? Making the Code work for you. *Support for Learning, 15* (3): 126–33.

Gross, J. (2002) *Special Educational Needs in the Primary School: A practical guide,* 3rd edn. Buckingham: Open University Press.

Gross, J. and White, A. (2003) *Special Educational Needs and School Improvement*. London: David Fulton.

House of Commons Education and Skills Select Committee (2006) *Special Educational Needs: Third Report of Session 2005–6.* London: HMSO.

Howes, A. (2003) Teaching reforms and the impact of paid adult support on participation in learning in mainstream schools, *Support for Learning,* 18 (4): 147–53.

Huberman, M. (1983) Recipes for busy kitchens: A situational analysis of routine knowledge use in schools. *Knowledge,* 4 (4): 478–510.

Humphreys, N. and Squires, G. (2011) *Achievement for All National Evaluation: Final Report.* London, DfE.

Independent Review Unit (2006) *IRU Statement for 2006.* London: DfES.

Independent Review Unit (2007) *IRU Statement on SEN and Disability – meeting need, minimising bureaucracy.* London: DfES.

Klein, R. (2000) *Defying Disaffection.* London: Trentham Books.

Knoster, T. (1991) Presentation at TASH conference, Washington D.C. (adapted by Knoster from Enterprise Group, Ltd.).

Lamb, B. (2009) *Lamb Inquiry: Special educational needs and parental confidence.* London: DCSF.

Lexmond, J., Bazalgette, L. and Margo, J. (2011) *The Home Front.* London: Demos.

Lindsay, G., Davies, H., Band, S., Cullen, M., Cullen, C., Strand, S., Hasluck, C., Evans, R. and Stewart-Brown, S. (2008) *Parenting Early Intervention Pathfinder Evaluation.* London: DCSF.

Lindsay, G., Cullen, M., Cullen, S., Dockrell, J., Strand, S., Arweck, E., Hegarty, S. and Goodlad, S. (2010) *Evaluation of impact of DfE investment in initiatives designed to improve teacher workforce skills in relation to SEN and disabilities.* London: DfE.

Lingard, T. (2001) Does the Code of Practice help secondary school SENCOs to improve learning? *British Journal of Special Education,* 28 (4): 187–90.

Moyles, J. and Suschitzky, W. (1997) *Jills of all Trades: Classroom assistants in KS1 classes.* London: University of Leicester/ATL.

Murray, P. and Sanderson, H. (2007) *Developing Person-centred Approaches in Schools.* Stockport: HSA Press.

National Institute for Health and Clinical Excellence (2006) *Parent-Training Education Programmes in the Management of Children with Conduct Disorders.* NICE technology appraisal guidance: 102.

Norwich, B. and Kelly, N. (2004) *A Study of Promising Practices of Pupil Participation in SEN Procedures in South-West Mainstream Schools.* Exeter: University of Exeter School of Lifelong Learning.

NUT (2004) *Special Educational Needs Co-ordinators and the Revised Code of Practice: An NUT Survey.* London: National Union of Teachers.

Office of the Children's Commissioner (2012) *They Never Give Up on You: School Exclusions Enquiry.* London: Office of the Children's Commissioner.

Ofsted (1999) *The SEN Code of Practice: Three years on.* London: Ofsted.

Ofsted (2004) *Special Educational Needs and Disability: Towards inclusive schools.* London: Ofsted.

Ofsted (2006) *Inclusion: Does it matter where pupils are taught?* London: Ofsted.

Ofsted (2010) *The Special Educational Needs and Disability Review.* London: Ofsted.

Ofsted (2011) *The Annual Report of Her Majesty's Chief Inspector of Education, Children's Services and Skills (Maintained Schools)* London: Ofsted.

Ofsted (2012) *Subsidiary Guidance: Supporting the inspection of maintained schools and academies from January 2012.* London: Ofsted.

Papps, I. and Dyson, A. (2004) *The costs and benefits of earlier identification and effective intervention.* London: DfES.

Pinkus, S. (2005) Bridging the gap between policy and practice: adopting a strategic vision for partnership working in special education. *British Journal of Special Education,* 32 (4): 184–7.

Pinney, A. (2004) *Reducing Reliance on Statements: An investigation into local authority practice and outcomes.* London: DfES.

Scott, S., Spender, Q., Doolan, M., Jacobs, B. and Aspland, H. (2001) Multicentre controlled trial of parenting groups for childhood antisocial behaviour in clinical practice, *British Medical Journal,* 323: 1–7.

Sylva, K., Melhuish, E., Sammons, P., Siraj-Blatchford, I., Taggart, B. and Elliot, K. (2003) *The Effective Provision of Pre-School Education (EPPE) Project: Findings from the Pre-school Period.* London: Institute of Education, University of London.

Tymms, P. and Merrell, C. (2006) Screening and interventions for inattentive, hyperactive and impulsive children. *European Journal of Special Needs Education,* 21 (3): 321–37.

Wedell, K. (2002) What is additional and different about IEPs? *British Journal of Special Education,* 29 (4): 204.

Index

Figures are indicated by **bold** page numbers, tables by *italics*.